THE ARMY of
DR. MOREAU

ISBN: 978-1-63140-239-5

18 17 16 15 1 2 3 4

IDW®

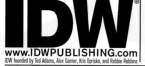

www.IDWPUBLISHING.com

IDW founded by Ted Adams, Alex Garner, Kris Oprisko, and Robbie Robbins

Ted Adams, CEO & Publisher
Greg Goldstein, President & COO
Robbie Robbins, EVP/Sr. Graphic Artist
Chris Ryall, Chief Creative Officer/Editor-in-Chief
Matthew Ruzicka, CPA, Chief Financial Officer
Alan Payne, VP of Sales
Dirk Wood, VP of Marketing
Lorelei Bunjes, VP of Digital Services
Jeff Webber, VP of Digital Publishing & Business Development

Facebook: **facebook.com/idwpublishing**
Twitter: **@idwpublishing**
YouTube: **youtube.com/idwpublishing**
Instagram: **instagram.com/idwpublishing**
deviantART: **idwpublishing.deviantart.com**
Pinterest: **pinterest.com/idwpublishing/idw-staff-faves**

Originally published digitally by Monkeybrain Comics as THE ARMY OF DR. MOREAU issues #1–6.

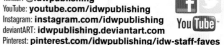

DAVID F. WALKER writer

Thanks to Carl and Sara for turning the words into pictures and giving them color. Allison and Chris, and everyone who is part of the greatness that is Monkeybrain. Much love and respect to my mom, who bought me my first comic book, and my first paperback copy of The Island of Dr. Moreau.

CARL SCIACCHITANO artist

To my parents, brother, and Galen, without whose unwavering support this book—and my career—would not have been possible.

SARA MACHAJEWSKI colorist

To Gen, for all of her understanding and support to help make this happen.

WALKER & SCIACCHITANO book design

STEVE WILLHITE prentiss journal illustrations

CHAPTER ONE

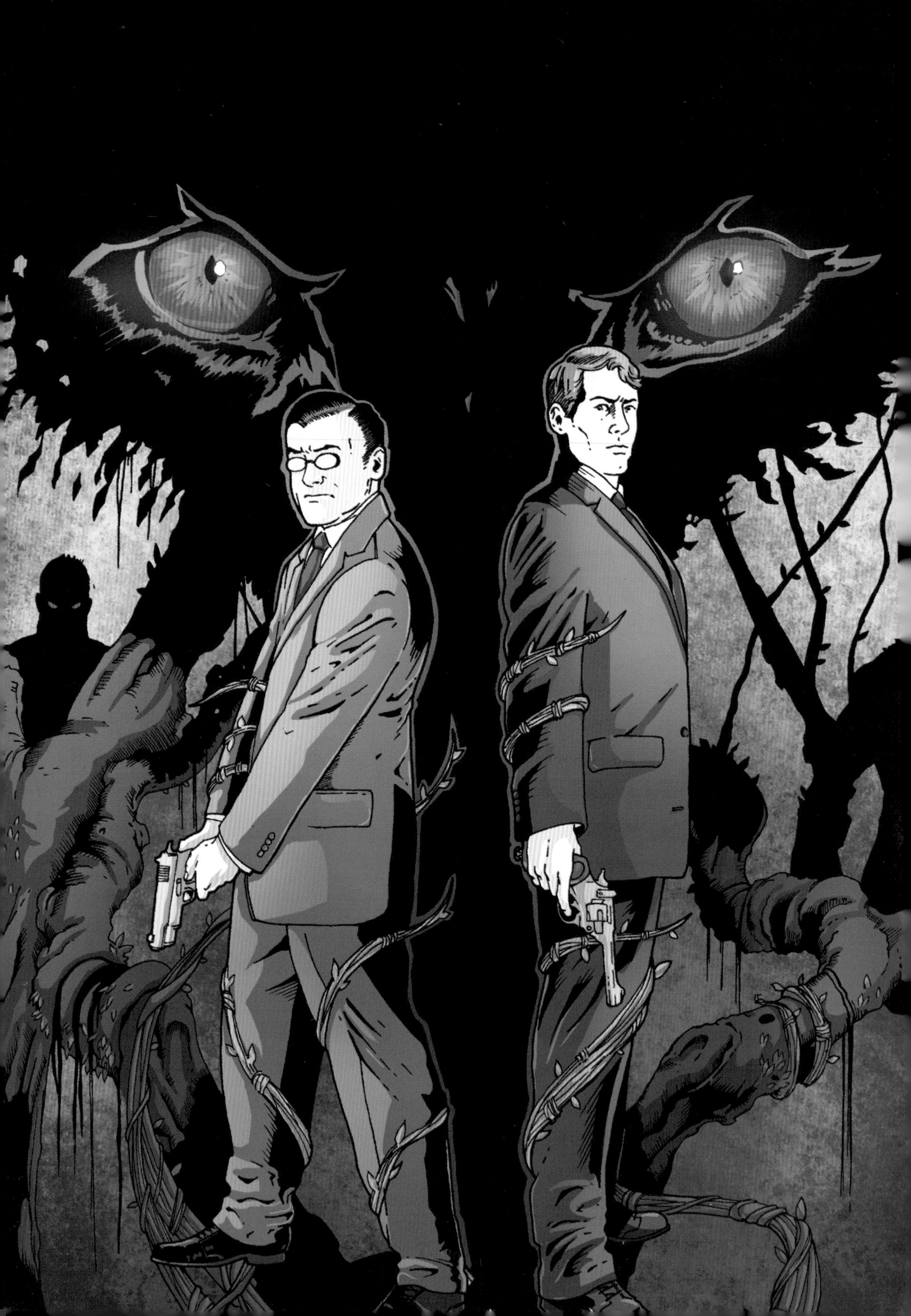

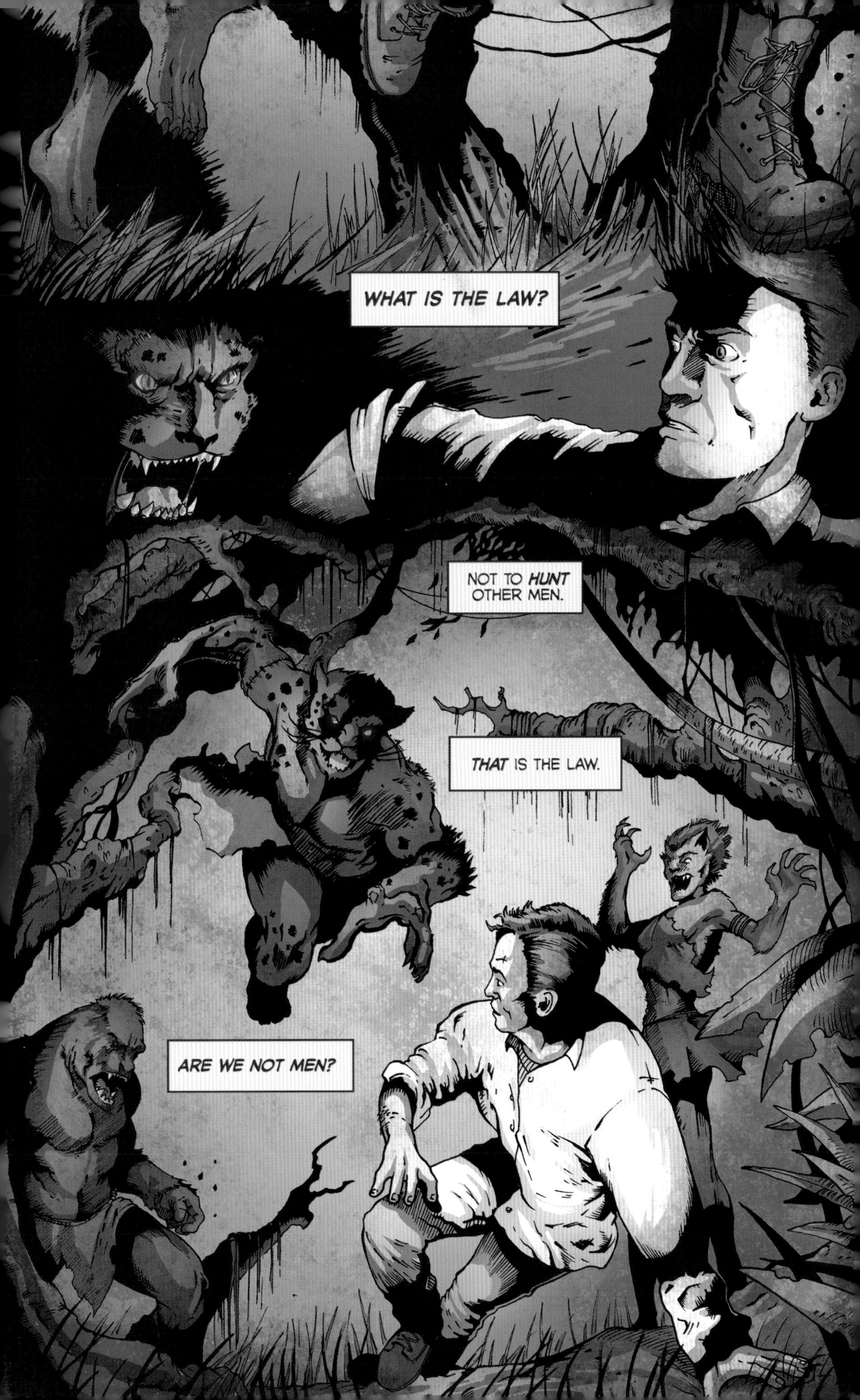
WHAT IS THE LAW?
NOT TO *HUNT* OTHER MEN.
THAT IS THE LAW.
ARE WE NOT MEN?

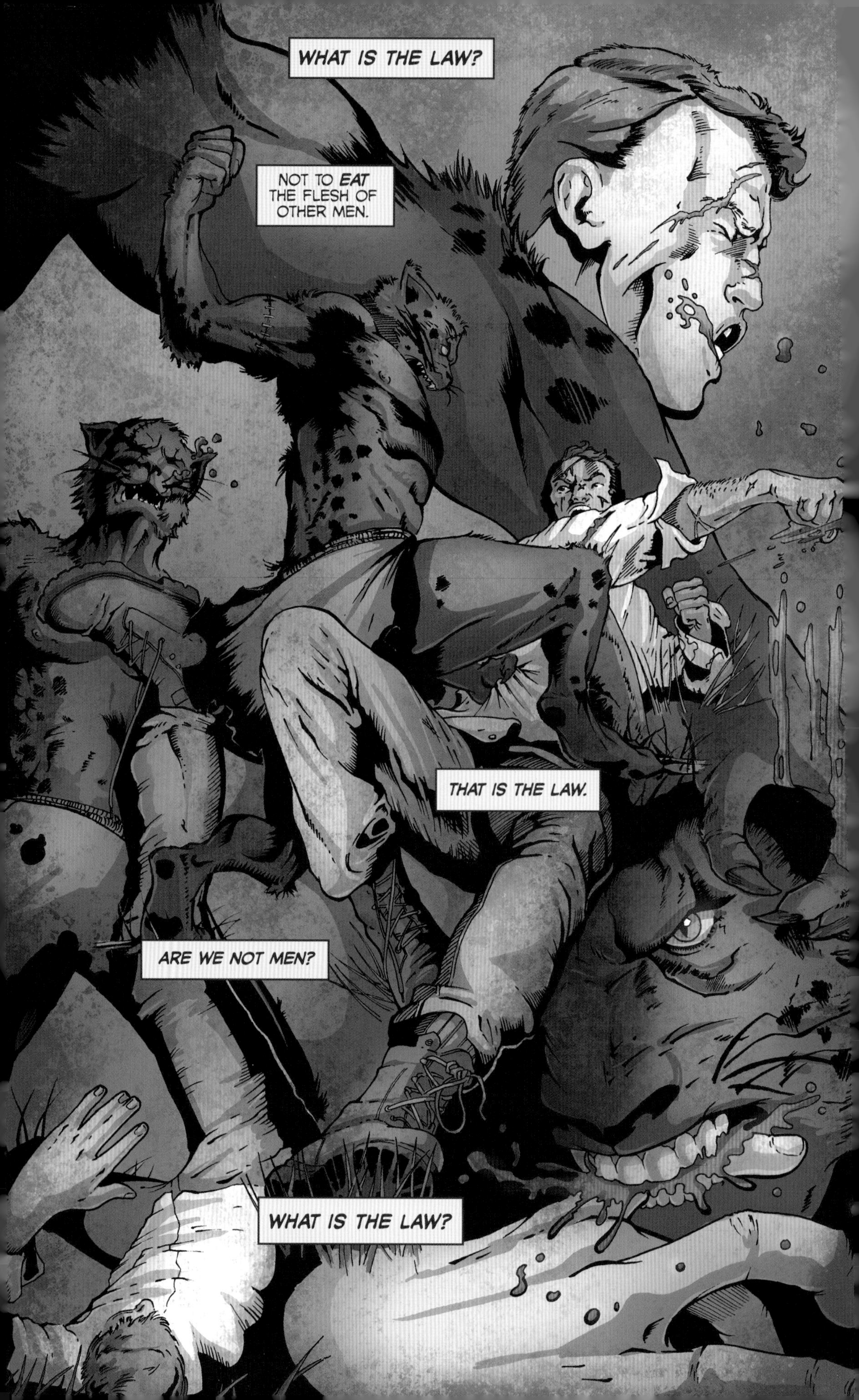
WHAT IS THE LAW?
NOT TO EAT THE FLESH OF OTHER MEN.
THAT IS THE LAW.
ARE WE NOT MEN?
WHAT IS THE LAW?

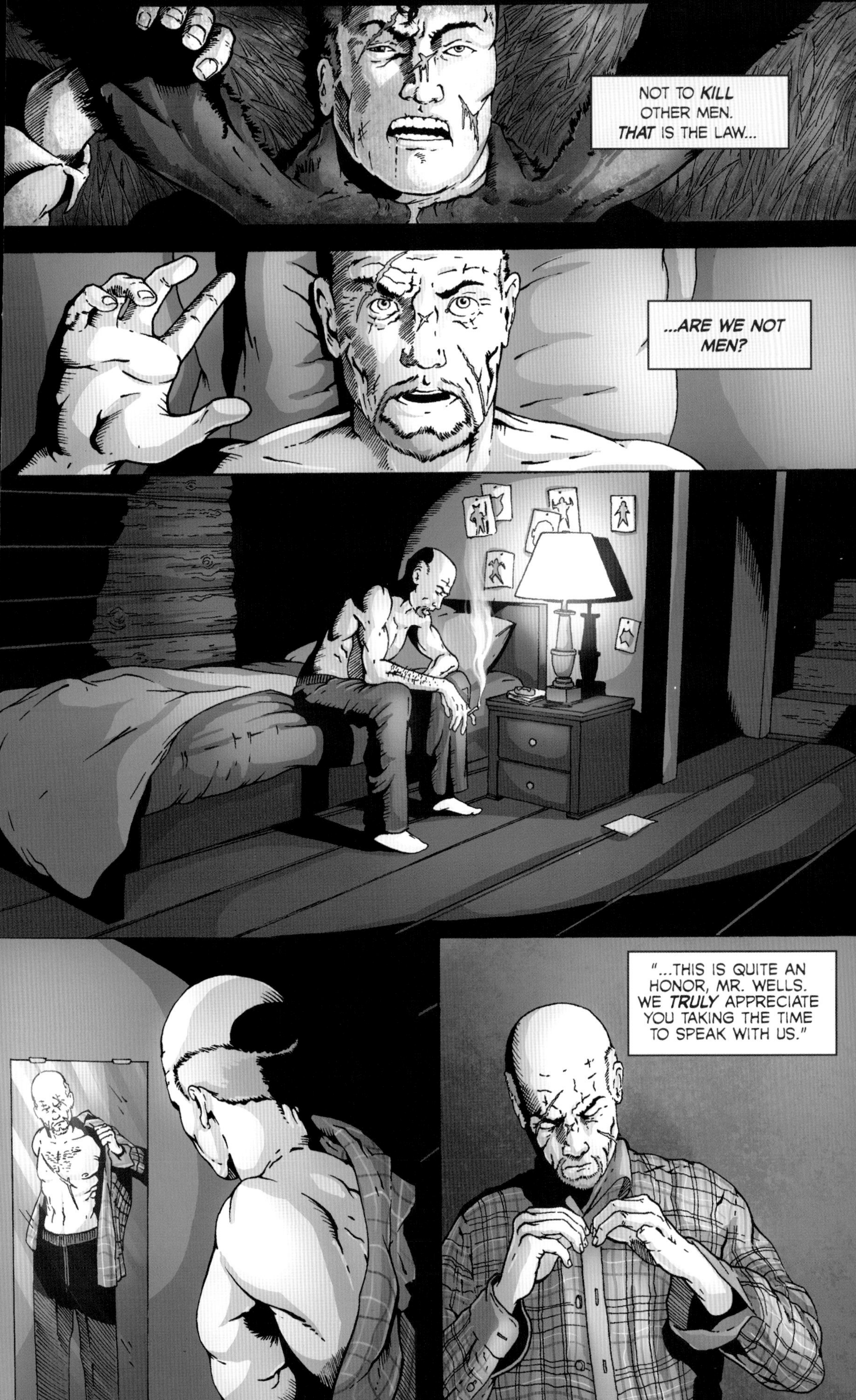
NOT TO KILL OTHER MEN. THAT IS THE LAW...
...ARE WE NOT MEN?
"...THIS IS QUITE AN HONOR, MR. WELLS. WE TRULY APPRECIATE YOU TAKING THE TIME TO SPEAK WITH US."

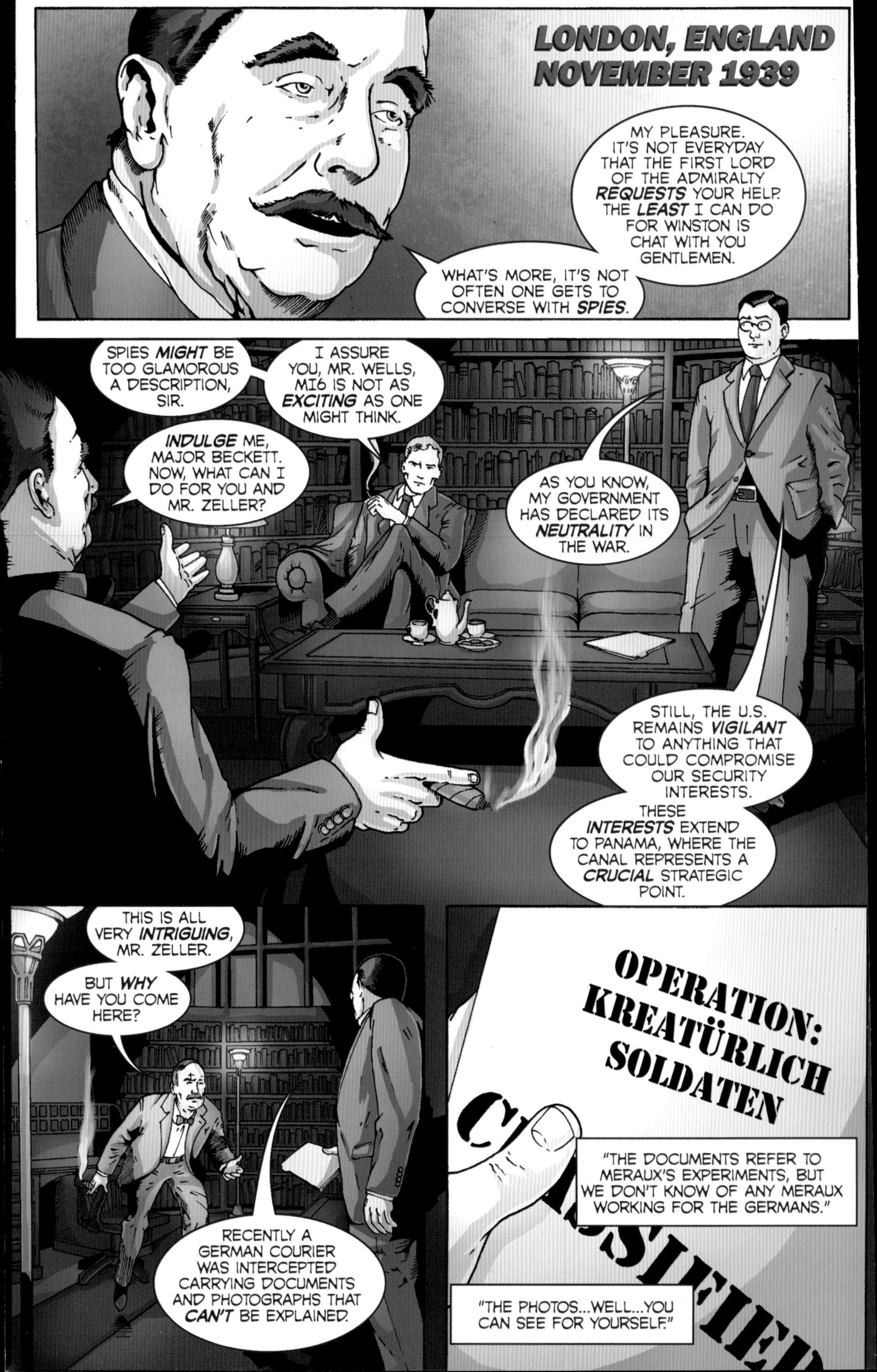
LONDON, ENGLAND
NOVEMBER 1939
MY PLEASURE. IT'S NOT EVERYDAY THAT THE FIRST LORD OF THE ADMIRALTY REQUESTS YOUR HELP. THE LEAST I CAN DO FOR WINSTON IS CHAT WITH YOU GENTLEMEN.
WHAT'S MORE, IT'S NOT OFTEN ONE GETS TO CONVERSE WITH SPIES.
SPIES MIGHT BE TOO GLAMOROUS A DESCRIPTION, SIR.
I ASSURE YOU, MR. WELLS, MI6 IS NOT AS EXCITING AS ONE MIGHT THINK.
INDULGE ME, MAJOR BECKETT. NOW, WHAT CAN I DO FOR YOU AND MR. ZELLER?
AS YOU KNOW, MY GOVERNMENT HAS DECLARED ITS NEUTRALITY IN THE WAR.
STILL, THE U.S. REMAINS VIGILANT TO ANYTHING THAT COULD COMPROMISE OUR SECURITY INTERESTS.
THESE INTERESTS EXTEND TO PANAMA, WHERE THE CANAL REPRESENTS A CRUCIAL STRATEGIC POINT.
THIS IS ALL VERY INTRIGUING, MR. ZELLER.
BUT WHY HAVE YOU COME HERE?
RECENTLY A GERMAN COURIER WAS INTERCEPTED CARRYING DOCUMENTS AND PHOTOGRAPHS THAT CAN'T BE EXPLAINED.
OPERATION: KREATÜRLICH SOLDATEN
"THE DOCUMENTS REFER TO MERAUX'S EXPERIMENTS, BUT WE DON'T KNOW OF ANY MERAUX WORKING FOR THE GERMANS."
"THE PHOTOS...WELL...YOU CAN SEE FOR YOURSELF."

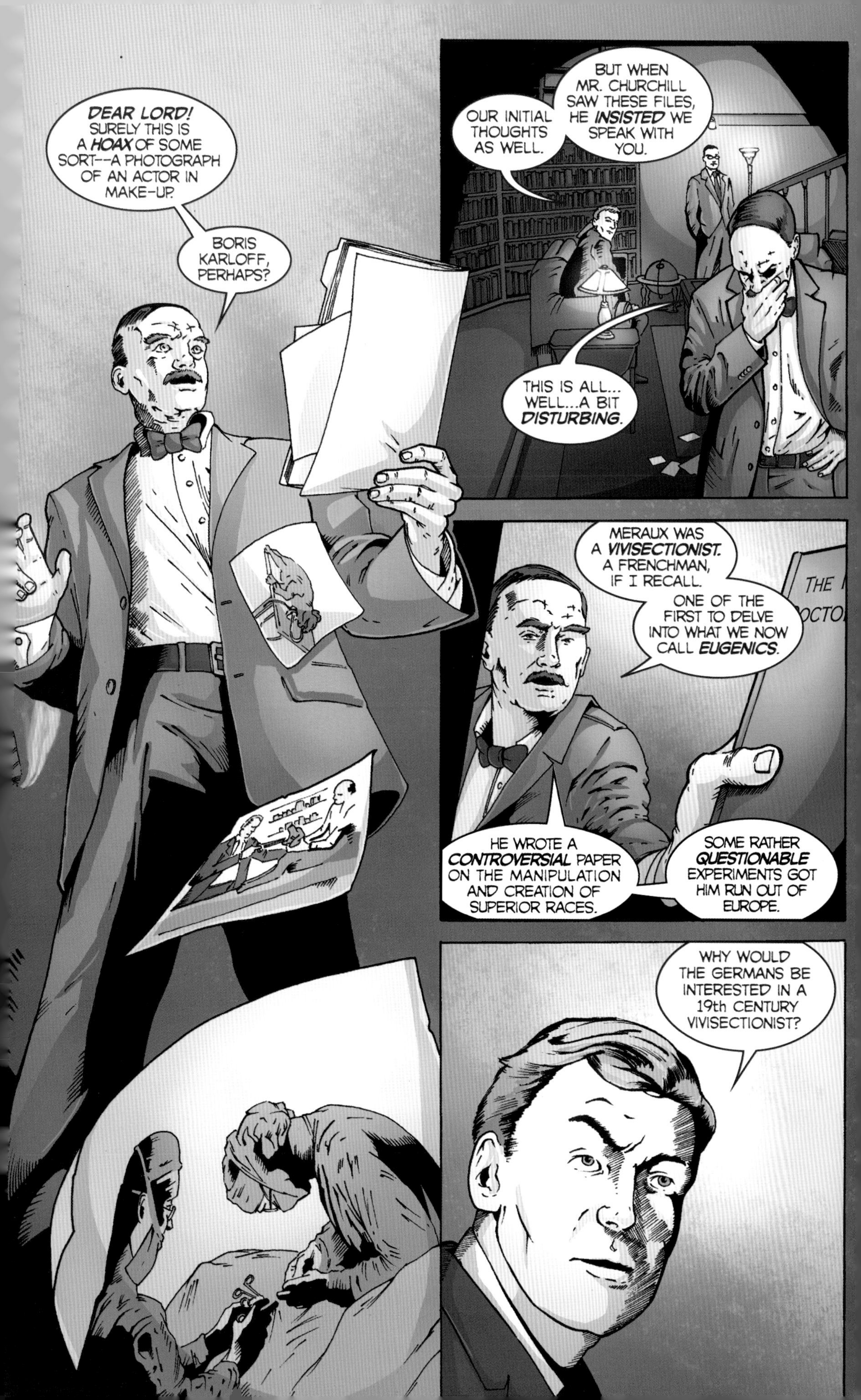
DEAR LORD! SURELY THIS IS A HOAX OF SOME SORT--A PHOTOGRAPH OF AN ACTOR IN MAKE-UP.
BORIS KARLOFF, PERHAPS?
OUR INITIAL THOUGHTS AS WELL.
BUT WHEN MR. CHURCHILL SAW THESE FILES, HE INSISTED WE SPEAK WITH YOU.
THIS IS ALL... WELL...A BIT DISTURBING.
MERAUX WAS A VIVISECTIONIST. A FRENCHMAN, IF I RECALL.
ONE OF THE FIRST TO DELVE INTO WHAT WE NOW CALL EUGENICS.
HE WROTE A CONTROVERSIAL PAPER ON THE MANIPULATION AND CREATION OF SUPERIOR RACES.
SOME RATHER QUESTIONABLE EXPERIMENTS GOT HIM RUN OUT OF EUROPE.
WHY WOULD THE GERMANS BE INTERESTED IN A 19th CENTURY VIVISECTIONIST?

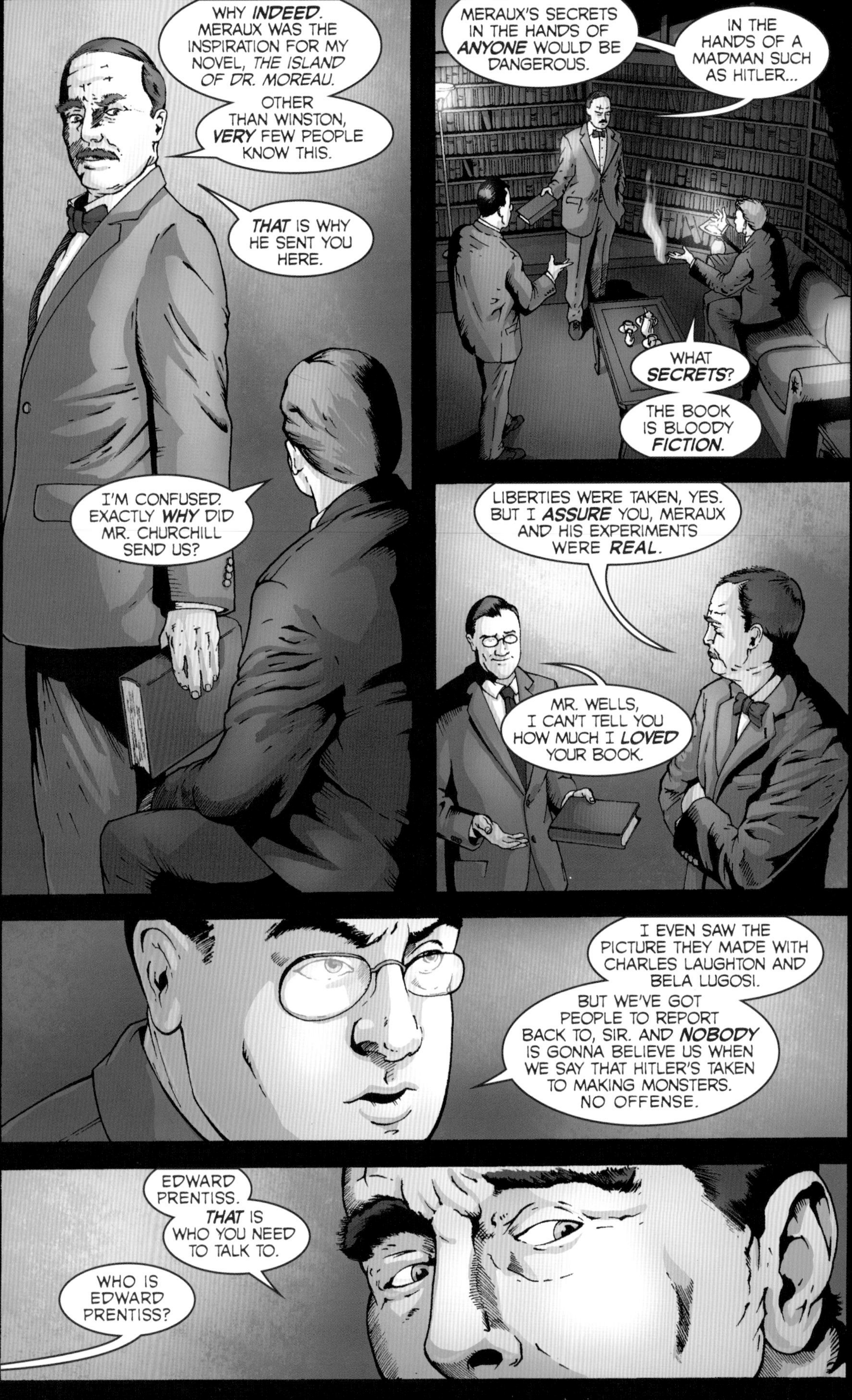
WHY INDEED. MERAUX WAS THE INSPIRATION FOR MY NOVEL, THE ISLAND OF DR. MOREAU.
OTHER THAN WINSTON, VERY FEW PEOPLE KNOW THIS.
THAT IS WHY HE SENT YOU HERE.
I'M CONFUSED. EXACTLY WHY DID MR. CHURCHILL SEND US?
MERAUX'S SECRETS IN THE HANDS OF ANYONE WOULD BE DANGEROUS.
IN THE HANDS OF A MADMAN SUCH AS HITLER...
WHAT SECRETS?
THE BOOK IS BLOODY FICTION.
LIBERTIES WERE TAKEN, YES. BUT I ASSURE YOU, MERAUX AND HIS EXPERIMENTS WERE REAL.
MR. WELLS, I CAN'T TELL YOU HOW MUCH I LOVED YOUR BOOK.
I EVEN SAW THE PICTURE THEY MADE WITH CHARLES LAUGHTON AND BELA LUGOSI.
BUT WE'VE GOT PEOPLE TO REPORT BACK TO, SIR. AND NOBODY IS GONNA BELIEVE US WHEN WE SAY THAT HITLER'S TAKEN TO MAKING MONSTERS. NO OFFENSE.
EDWARD PRENTISS. THAT IS WHO YOU NEED TO TALK TO.
WHO IS EDWARD PRENTISS?

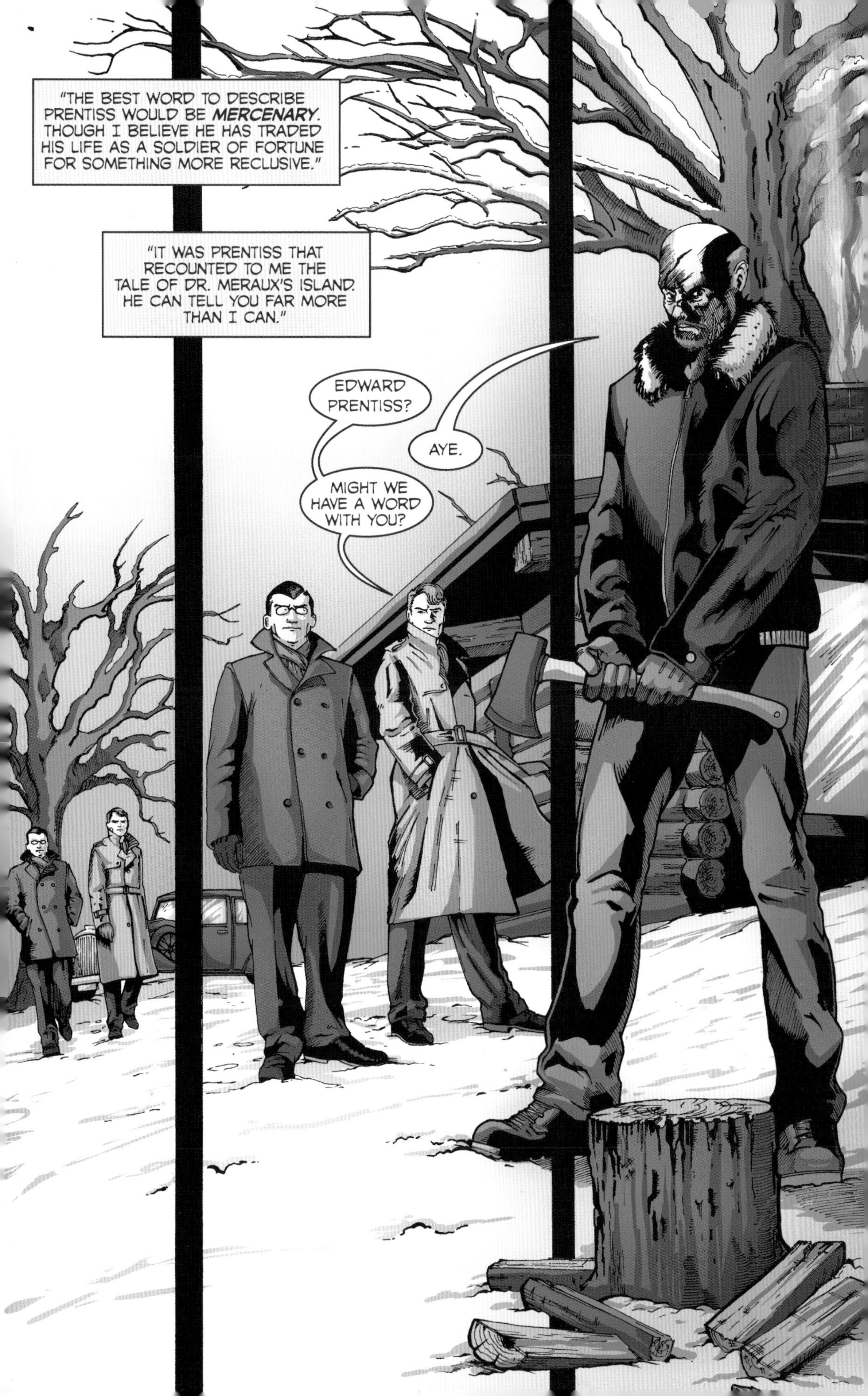
"THE BEST WORD TO DESCRIBE PRENTISS WOULD BE **MERCENARY**. THOUGH I BELIEVE HE HAS TRADED HIS LIFE AS A SOLDIER OF FORTUNE FOR SOMETHING MORE RECLUSIVE."
"IT WAS PRENTISS THAT RECOUNTED TO ME THE TALE OF DR. MERAUX'S ISLAND. HE CAN TELL YOU FAR MORE THAN I CAN."
EDWARD PRENTISS?
AYE.
MIGHT WE HAVE A WORD WITH YOU?

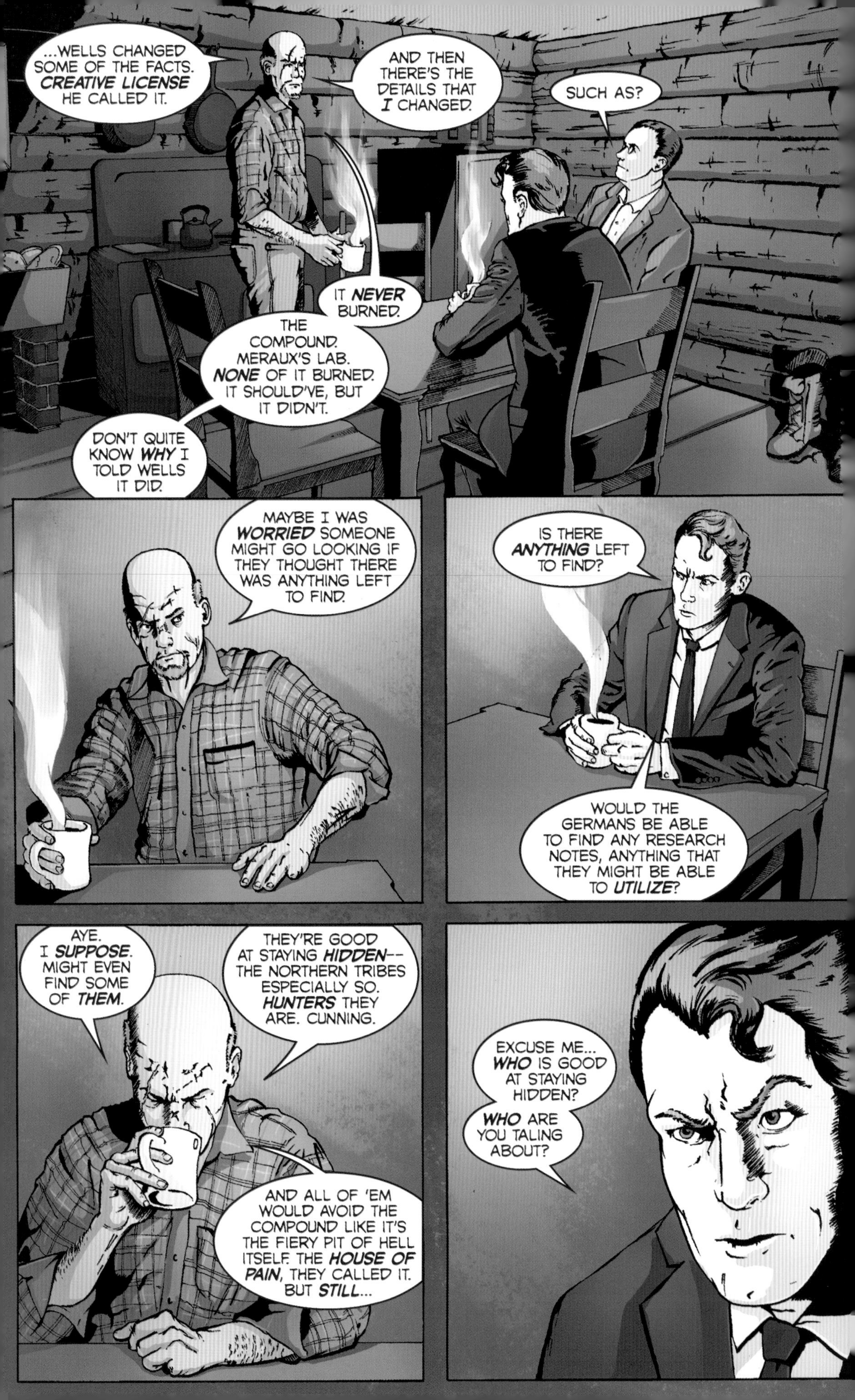
...WELLS CHANGED SOME OF THE FACTS. CREATIVE LICENSE HE CALLED IT.
AND THEN THERE'S THE DETAILS THAT I CHANGED.
SUCH AS?
IT NEVER BURNED.
THE COMPOUND. MERAUX'S LAB. NONE OF IT BURNED. IT SHOULD'VE, BUT IT DIDN'T.
DON'T QUITE KNOW WHY I TOLD WELLS IT DID.
MAYBE I WAS WORRIED SOMEONE MIGHT GO LOOKING IF THEY THOUGHT THERE WAS ANYTHING LEFT TO FIND.
IS THERE ANYTHING LEFT TO FIND?
WOULD THE GERMANS BE ABLE TO FIND ANY RESEARCH NOTES, ANYTHING THAT THEY MIGHT BE ABLE TO UTILIZE?
AYE. I SUPPOSE. MIGHT EVEN FIND SOME OF THEM.
THEY'RE GOOD AT STAYING HIDDEN-- THE NORTHERN TRIBES ESPECIALLY SO. HUNTERS THEY ARE. CUNNING.
AND ALL OF 'EM WOULD AVOID THE COMPOUND LIKE IT'S THE FIERY PIT OF HELL ITSELF. THE HOUSE OF PAIN, THEY CALLED IT. BUT STILL...
EXCUSE ME... WHO IS GOOD AT STAYING HIDDEN?
WHO ARE YOU TALING ABOUT?

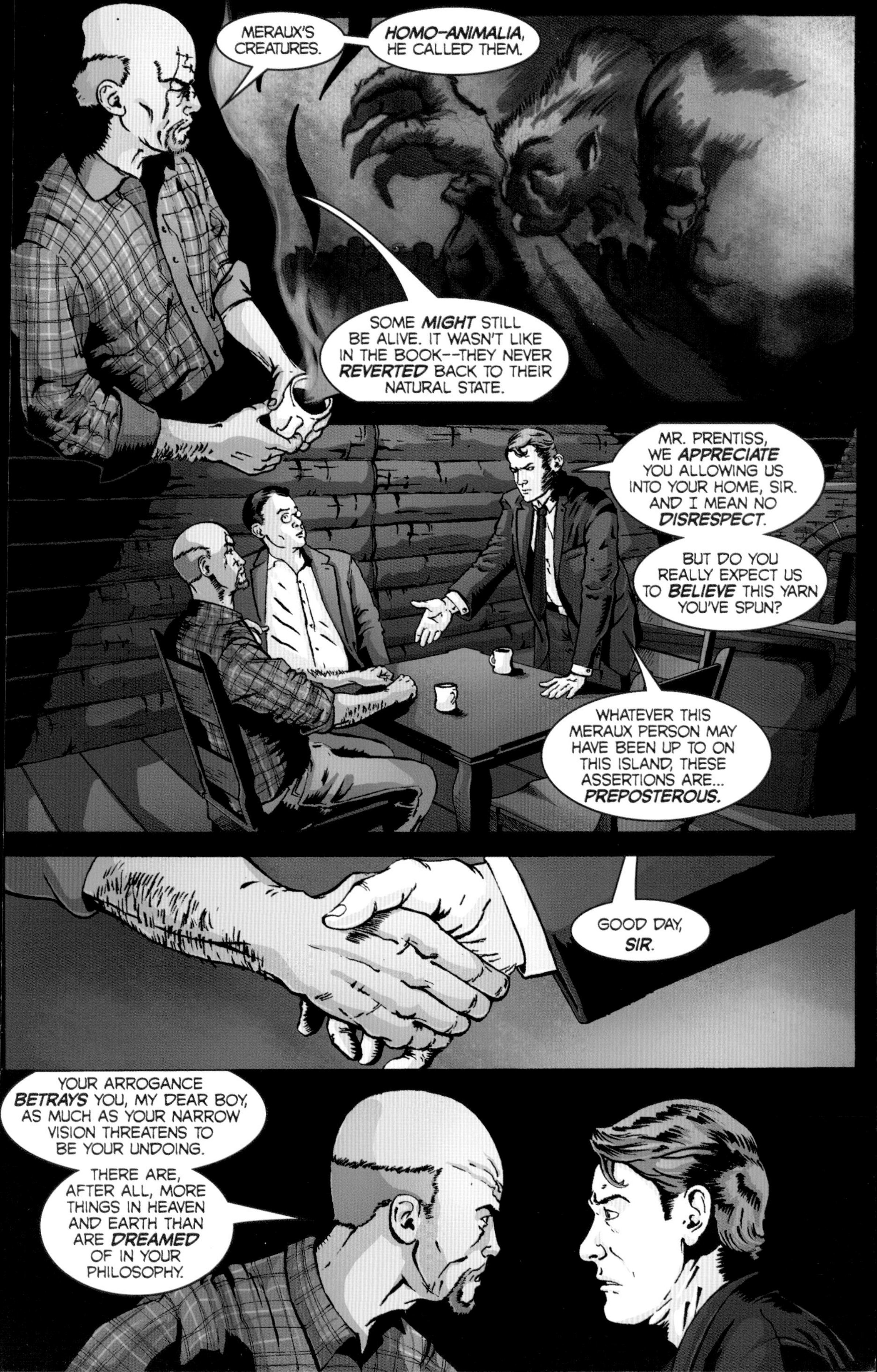
MERAUX'S CREATURES.
HOMO-ANIMALIA, HE CALLED THEM.
SOME MIGHT STILL BE ALIVE. IT WASN'T LIKE IN THE BOOK--THEY NEVER REVERTED BACK TO THEIR NATURAL STATE.
MR. PRENTISS, WE APPRECIATE YOU ALLOWING US INTO YOUR HOME, SIR. AND I MEAN NO DISRESPECT.
BUT DO YOU REALLY EXPECT US TO BELIEVE THIS YARN YOU'VE SPUN?
WHATEVER THIS MERAUX PERSON MAY HAVE BEEN UP TO ON THIS ISLAND, THESE ASSERTIONS ARE... PREPOSTEROUS.
GOOD DAY, SIR.
YOUR ARROGANCE BETRAYS YOU, MY DEAR BOY, AS MUCH AS YOUR NARROW VISION THREATENS TO BE YOUR UNDOING.
THERE ARE, AFTER ALL, MORE THINGS IN HEAVEN AND EARTH THAN ARE DREAMED OF IN YOUR PHILOSOPHY.

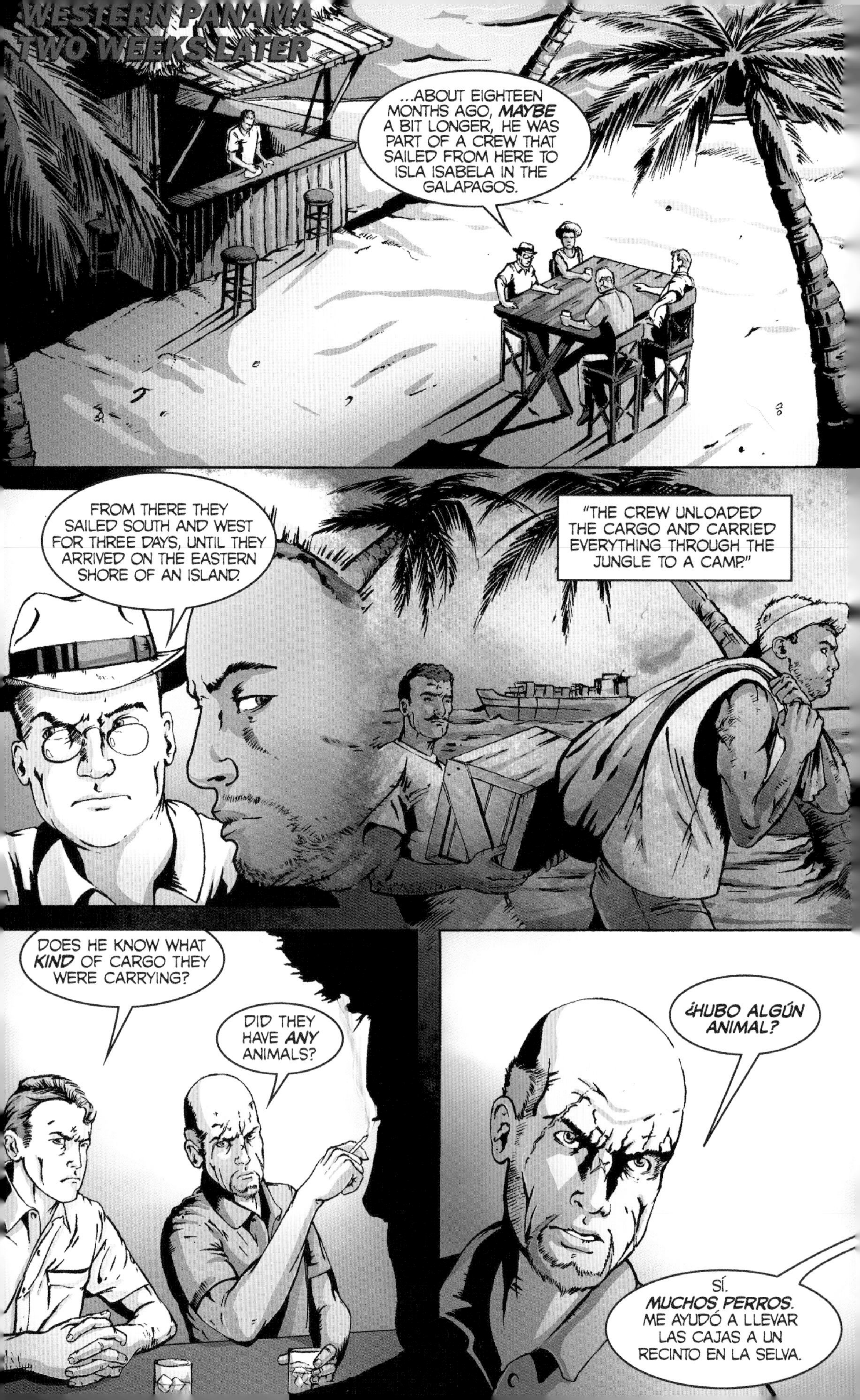

WESTERN PANAMA TWO WEEKS LATER
...ABOUT EIGHTEEN MONTHS AGO, MAYBE A BIT LONGER, HE WAS PART OF A CREW THAT SAILED FROM HERE TO ISLA ISABELA IN THE GALAPAGOS.
FROM THERE THEY SAILED SOUTH AND WEST FOR THREE DAYS, UNTIL THEY ARRIVED ON THE EASTERN SHORE OF AN ISLAND.
"THE CREW UNLOADED THE CARGO AND CARRIED EVERYTHING THROUGH THE JUNGLE TO A CAMP."
DOES HE KNOW WHAT KIND OF CARGO THEY WERE CARRYING?
DID THEY HAVE ANY ANIMALS?
¿HUBO ALGÚN ANIMAL?
SÍ. MUCHOS PERROS. ME AYUDÓ A LLEVAR LAS CAJAS A UN RECINTO EN LA SELVA.

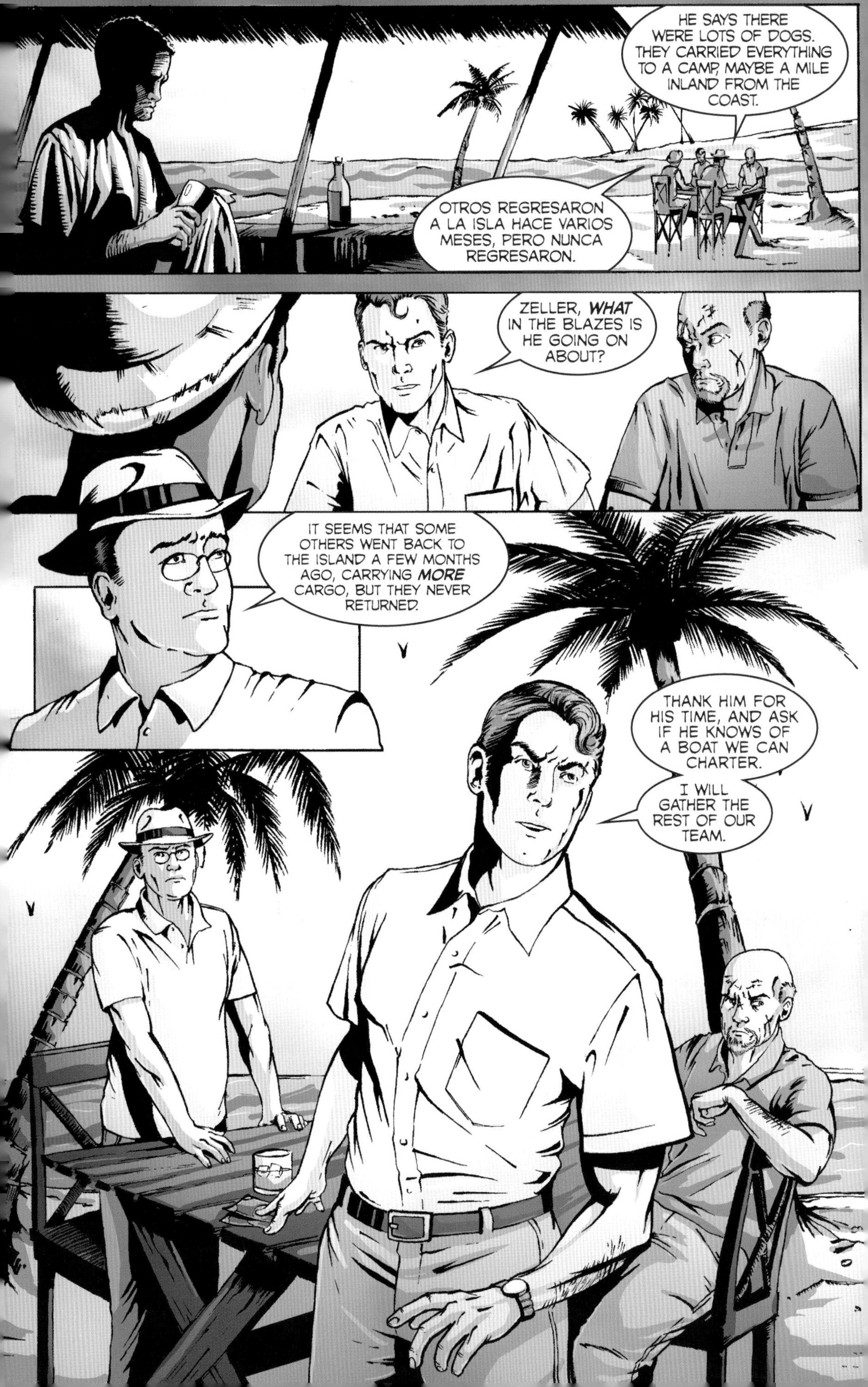
HE SAYS THERE WERE LOTS OF DOGS. THEY CARRIED EVERYTHING TO A CAMP, MAYBE A MILE INLAND FROM THE COAST.
OTROS REGRESARON A LA ISLA HACE VARIOS MESES, PERO NUNCA REGRESARON.
ZELLER, WHAT IN THE BLAZES IS HE GOING ON ABOUT?
IT SEEMS THAT SOME OTHERS WENT BACK TO THE ISLAND A FEW MONTHS AGO, CARRYING MORE CARGO, BUT THEY NEVER RETURNED.
THANK HIM FOR HIS TIME, AND ASK IF HE KNOWS OF A BOAT WE CAN CHARTER.
I WILL GATHER THE REST OF OUR TEAM.

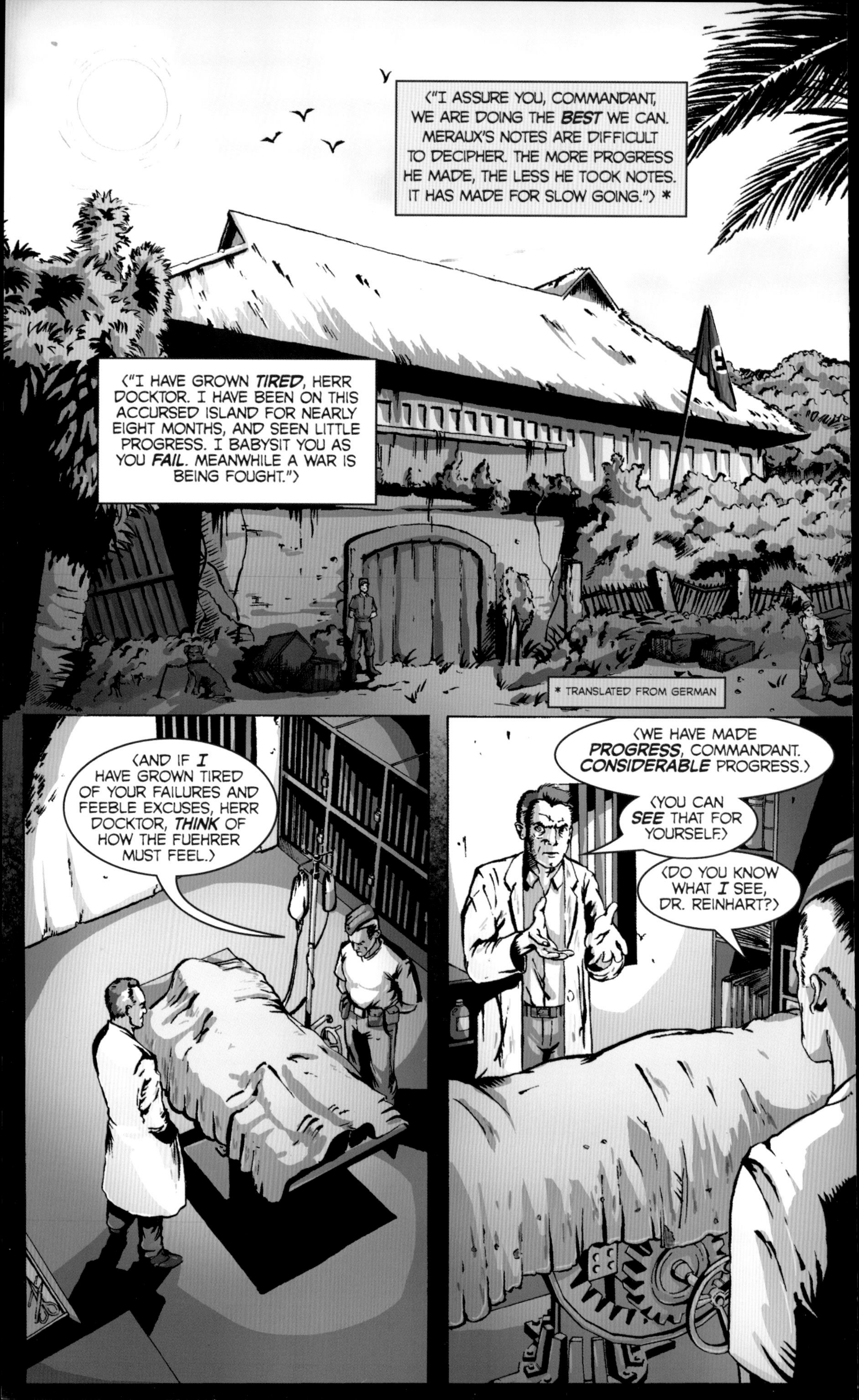

<("I ASSURE YOU, COMMANDANT, WE ARE DOING THE **BEST** WE CAN. MERAUX'S NOTES ARE DIFFICULT TO DECIPHER. THE MORE PROGRESS HE MADE, THE LESS HE TOOK NOTES. IT HAS MADE FOR SLOW GOING.") *
<("I HAVE GROWN **TIRED**, HERR DOCKTOR. I HAVE BEEN ON THIS ACCURSED ISLAND FOR NEARLY EIGHT MONTHS, AND SEEN LITTLE PROGRESS. I BABYSIT YOU AS YOU **FAIL**. MEANWHILE A WAR IS BEING FOUGHT.")
* TRANSLATED FROM GERMAN
<AND IF **I** HAVE GROWN TIRED OF YOUR FAILURES AND FEEBLE EXCUSES, HERR DOCKTOR, **THINK** OF HOW THE FUEHRER MUST FEEL.>
<WE HAVE MADE **PROGRESS**, COMMANDANT. **CONSIDERABLE** PROGRESS.>
<YOU CAN **SEE** THAT FOR YOURSELF.>
<DO YOU KNOW WHAT **I** SEE, DR. REINHART?>

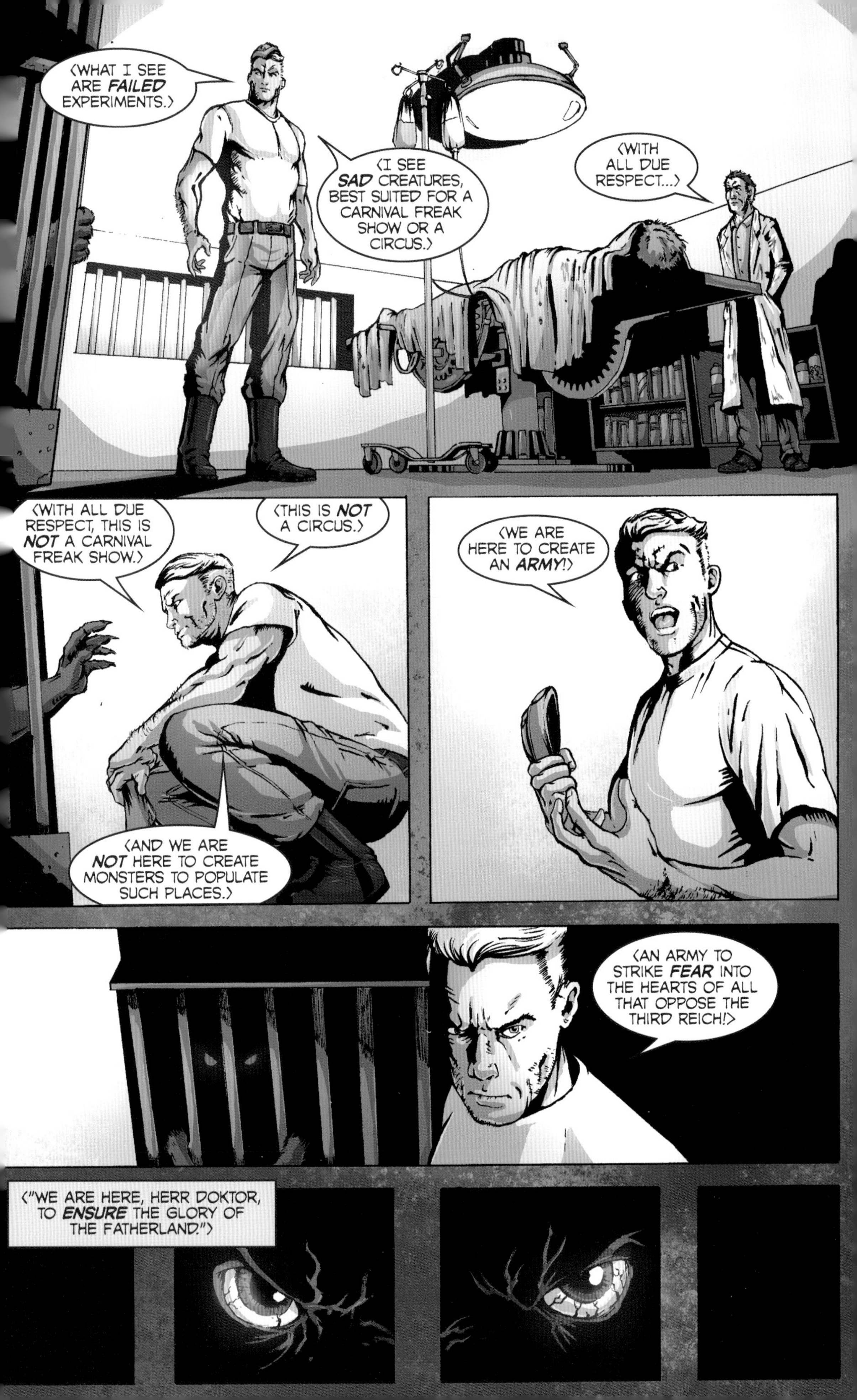

(WHAT I SEE ARE FAILED EXPERIMENTS.)
(I SEE SAD CREATURES, BEST SUITED FOR A CARNIVAL FREAK SHOW OR A CIRCUS.)
(WITH ALL DUE RESPECT...)
(WITH ALL DUE RESPECT, THIS IS NOT A CARNIVAL FREAK SHOW.)
(THIS IS NOT A CIRCUS.)
(AND WE ARE NOT HERE TO CREATE MONSTERS TO POPULATE SUCH PLACES.)
(WE ARE HERE TO CREATE AN ARMY!)
(AN ARMY TO STRIKE FEAR INTO THE HEARTS OF ALL THAT OPPOSE THE THIRD REICH!)
("WE ARE HERE, HERR DOKTOR, TO ENSURE THE GLORY OF THE FATHERLAND.")

TOP SECRET

THIS IS A COVER SHEET

BASIC SECURITY REQUIREMENTS ARE CONTAINED IN AR 380-5

THE UNAUTHORIZED DISCLOSURE OF THE INFORMATION CONTAINED IN THE ATTACHED DOCUMENT(S) COULD RESULT IN EXCEPTIONALLY GRAVE DANGER TO THE UNITED STATES

RESPONSIBILITY OF PERSONS HANDLING THE ATTACHED DOCUMENT(S)

1. Enter on DA Form 969 your name and the date you had access to the document(s).
2. Exercise the necessary safeguards to prevent unauthorized disclosure by never leaving the document(s) unattended except when properly secured in a locked safe.
3. Transfer the document(s) only to persons who need to know and who possess the required security clearance.
4. Obtain a receipt whenever relinquishing control of the document(s).

STORAGE

Store as prescribed in AR 380-5.

REPRODUCTION

TOP SECRET material may be copied, extracted, or reproduced only when the classifying authority has authorized such actions.

DISPOSITION

This cover sheet should be removed when document(s) are filed in a permanent file, declassified, destroyed, or mailed.

(This cover sheet is unclassified when separated from classified documents)

TOP SECRET

DA LABEL 24 1 FEB 59 PREVIOUS EDITIONS OF THIS LABEL ARE OBSOLETE AGL (1) 4-59-40M-71603

Prentiss, E. - Journal

Prentiss, E. - Journal

TOP SECRET

August ? 1894

It is as if I have found myself trapped within a nightmare. By my own reckoning, I have been here for two weeks, though I cannot be certain of the date.

After considerable inquiry on my part, Meraux has divulged to me truth of these monstrous apparitions that have revealed themselves to me. He calls these apparitions "homo-animalia" -- though I would just as soon call them monsters. These misshapen brutes are the result of endless toil in the chamber of horrors Meraux calls his laboratory. I have heard emitting from this laboratory screams of such anguish and despair, and on several occasion I have heard him refer to this place by the more fitting name, the House of Pain.

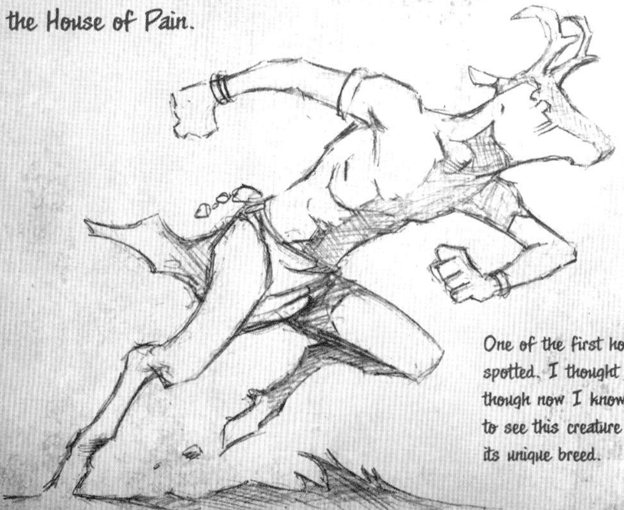

One of the first homo-animalia that I spotted. I thought it a hallucination, though now I know the truth. I have yet to see this creature again, or any quite of its unique breed.

TOP SECRET

Prentiss, E. - Journal

Meraux often refers to these homo-animalia as his "children." To be sure, he is a cruel father, prone to disciplinary measures most extreme in nature. His ~~creatures~~ children cower in fear at the thought of his lash, reciting some odd scripture I have yet to fully discern.

It is often difficult to understand what these beasts are saying, though they do, in fact, speak. It is, however, as if they are speaking a foreign tongue. I have been able to comprehend their repeated inquiry, "What is the law?" It is their gruff, beastly responses--grunts and growls, mostly-- that I have yet to comprehend. Montague has informed me the responses are Meraux's Laws of Man -- the rules by which he seems to lord over these creatures.

I must take care to learn these laws, if for no other reason than to better understand how a madman such as Meraux lords over such monstrosities as his ~~creations~~ children.

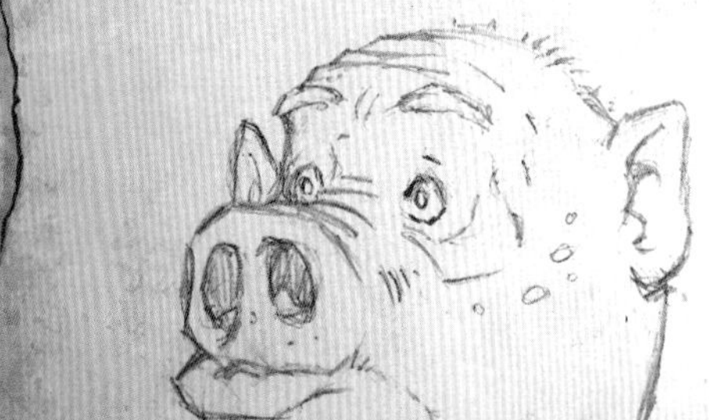

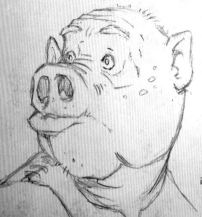

Some type of pig creature. There are many of this particular type, both "male" and "female."

Why pigs? Perhaps they make for easier experimentation?

They are quite docile, and surprisingly intelligent.

TOP SECRET

Prentiss, E. - Journal

TOP SECRET

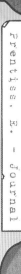

The Sayer of the Law --

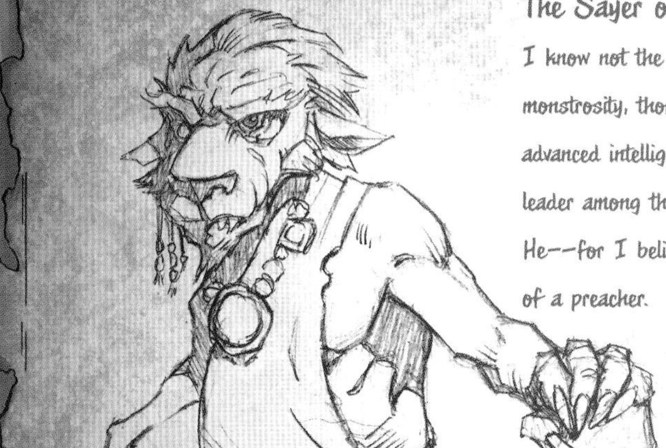

I know not the origins of this particular monstrosity, though he appears to be of advanced intelligence. He is something of a leader among these homo-animalia.

He--for I believe it is a HE--is something of a preacher.

As of yet, I have not learned all of the Laws of Man, though my understanding of the laws, and the animalistic grunts that pass for language has improved.

1. Not to shed blood of other men.
2. Not to eat the flesh of other men.
3. Not to hunt other men.
4. Not to walk on all fours (?)

TOP SECRET

CHAPTER TWO

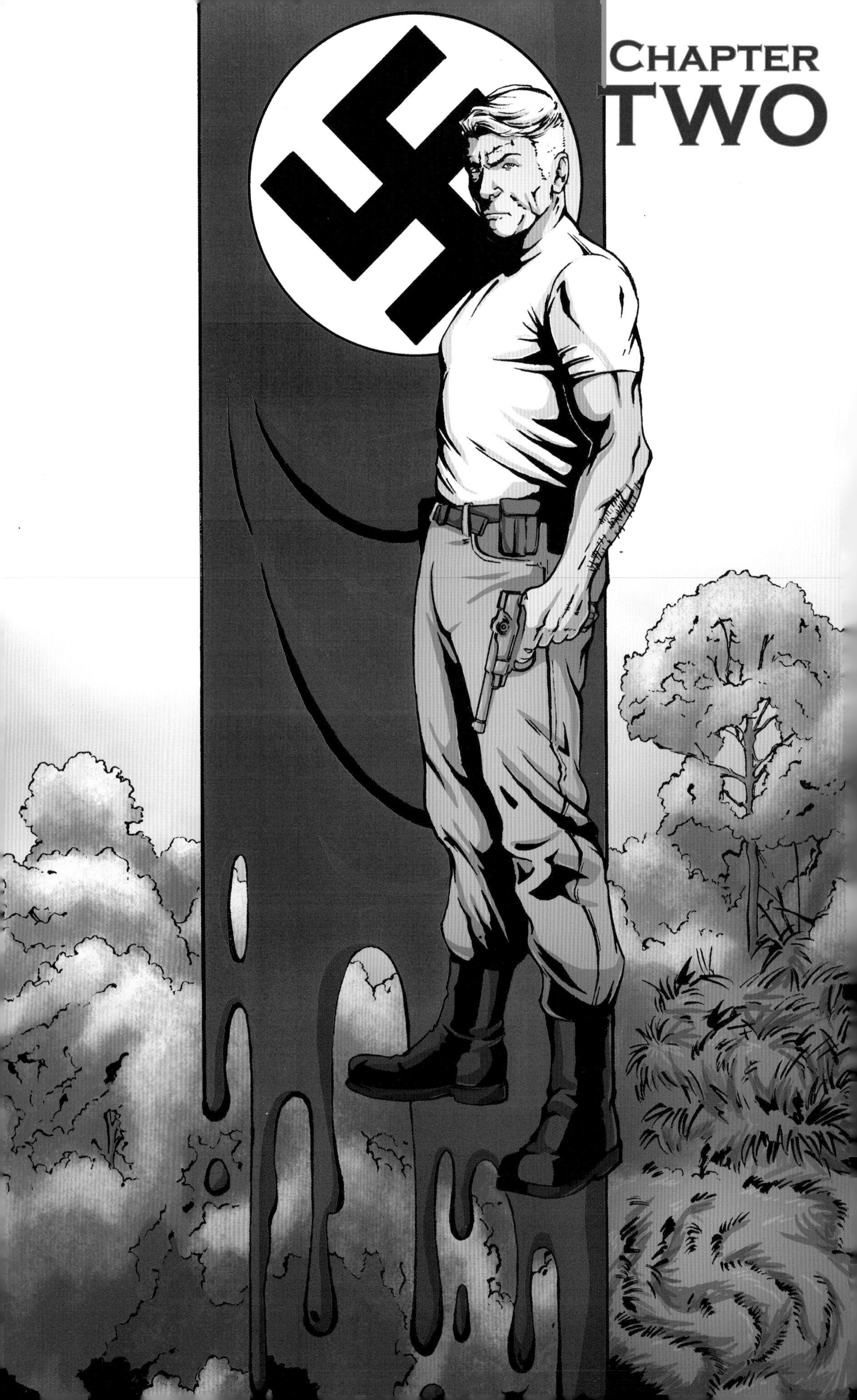

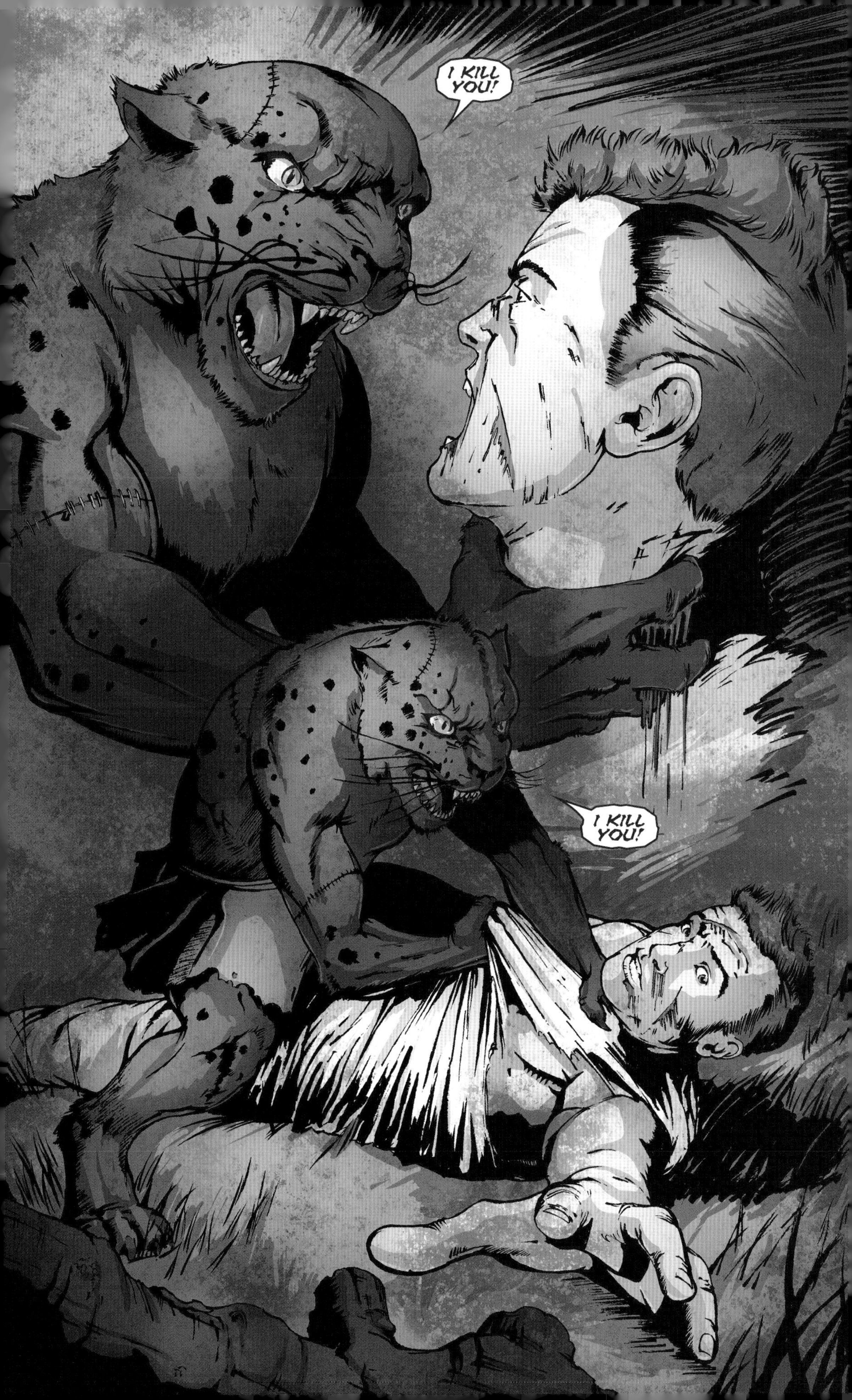
I KILL YOU!
I KILL YOU!

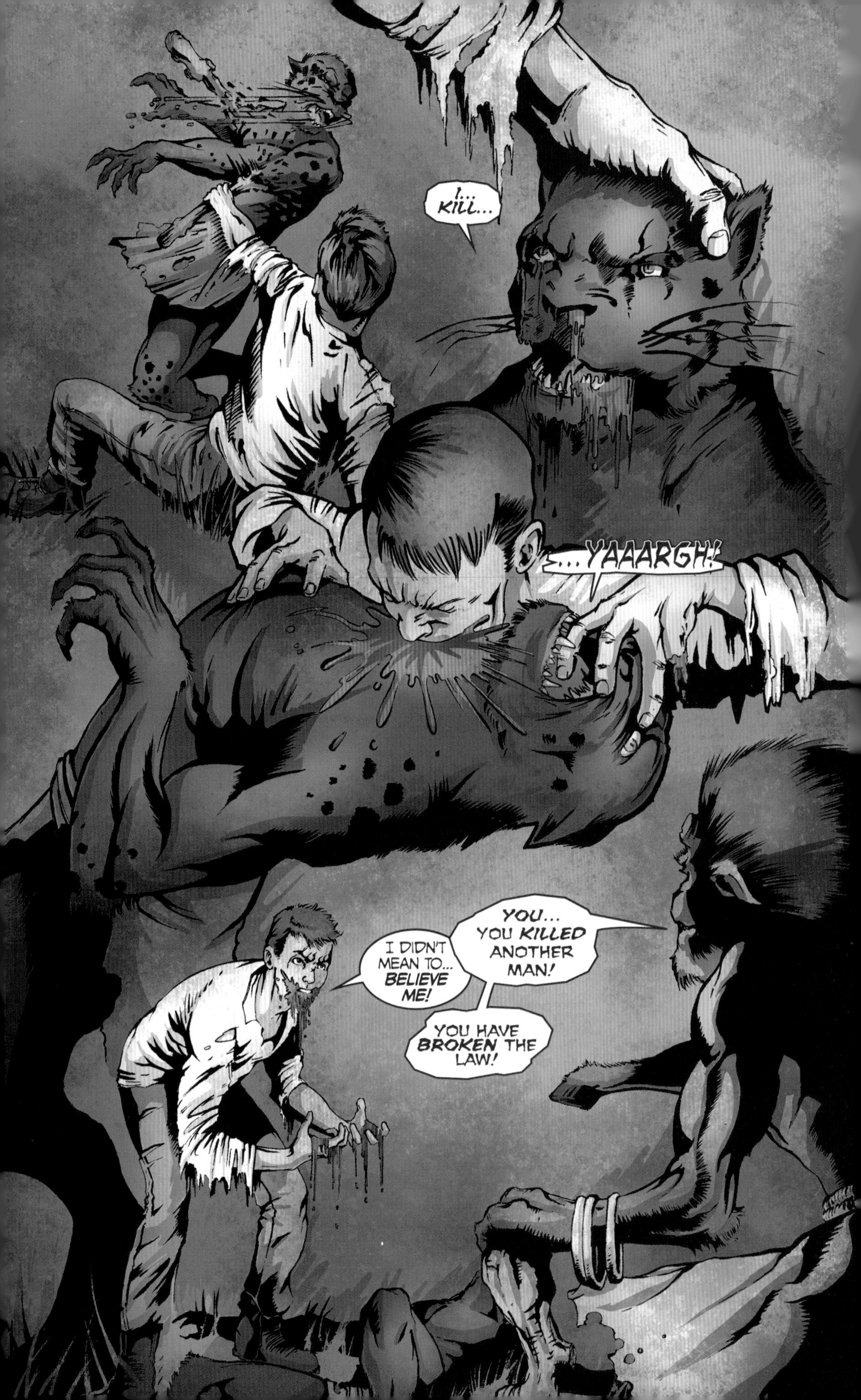
I... KILL...
...YAAARGH!
YOU... YOU KILLED ANOTHER MAN!
I DIDN'T MEAN TO... BELIEVE ME!
YOU HAVE BROKEN THE LAW!

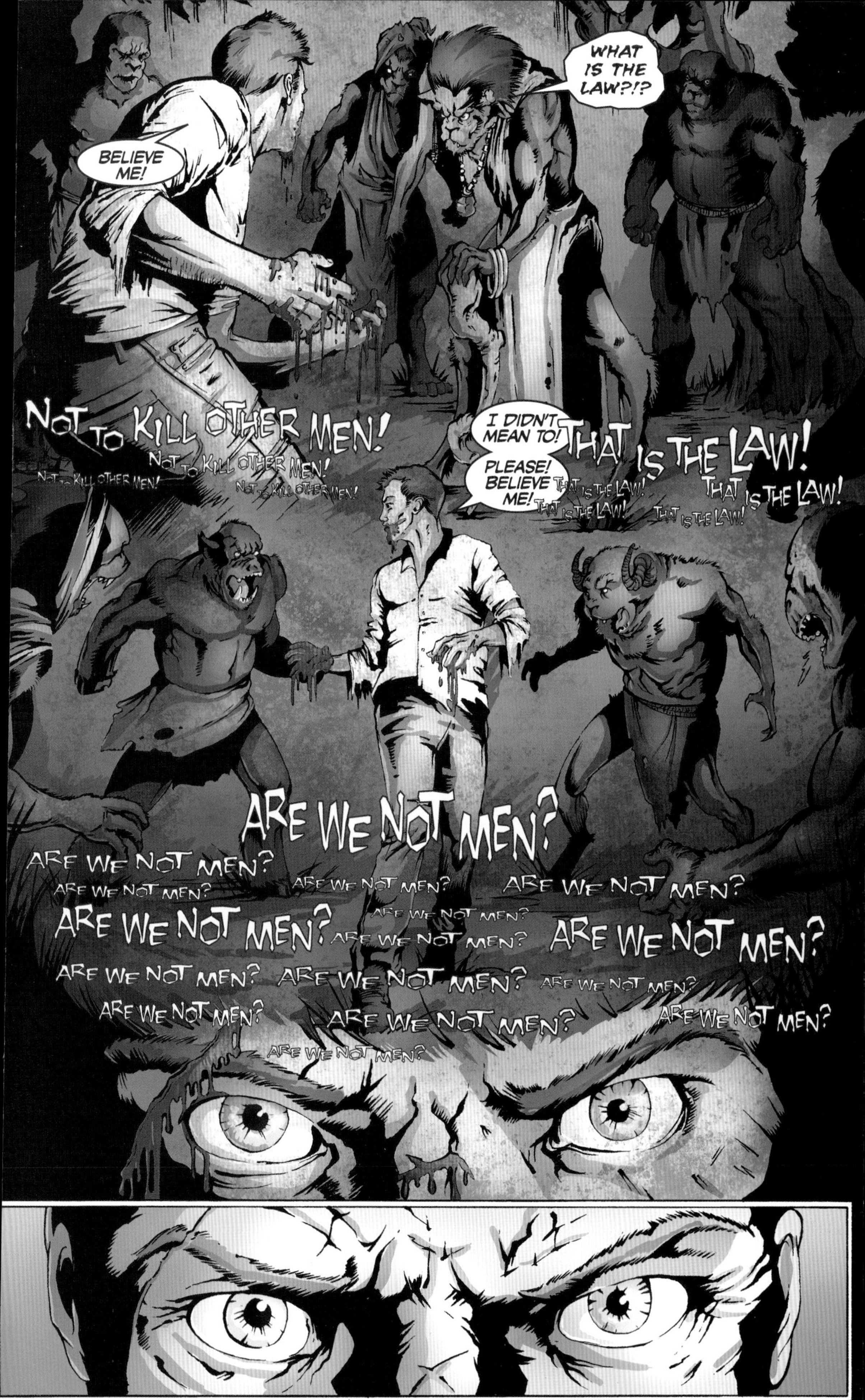
WHAT IS THE LAW?!?
BELIEVE ME!
NOT TO KILL OTHER MEN!
NOT TO KILL OTHER MEN!
NOT TO KILL OTHER MEN!
NOT TO KILL OTHER MEN!
I DIDN'T MEAN TO!
PLEASE! BELIEVE ME!
THAT IS THE LAW!
THAT IS THE LAW!
THAT IS THE LAW!
THAT IS THE LAW!
THAT IS THE LAW!
THAT IS THE LAW!
ARE WE NOT MEN?
ARE WE NOT MEN?
ARE WE NOT MEN?
ARE WE NOT MEN?
ARE WE NOT MEN?
ARE WE NOT MEN?
ARE WE NOT MEN?
ARE WE NOT MEN?
ARE WE NOT MEN?
ARE WE NOT MEN?
ARE WE NOT MEN?
ARE WE NOT MEN?
ARE WE NOT MEN?
ARE WE NOT MEN?
ARE WE NOT MEN?
ARE WE NOT MEN?

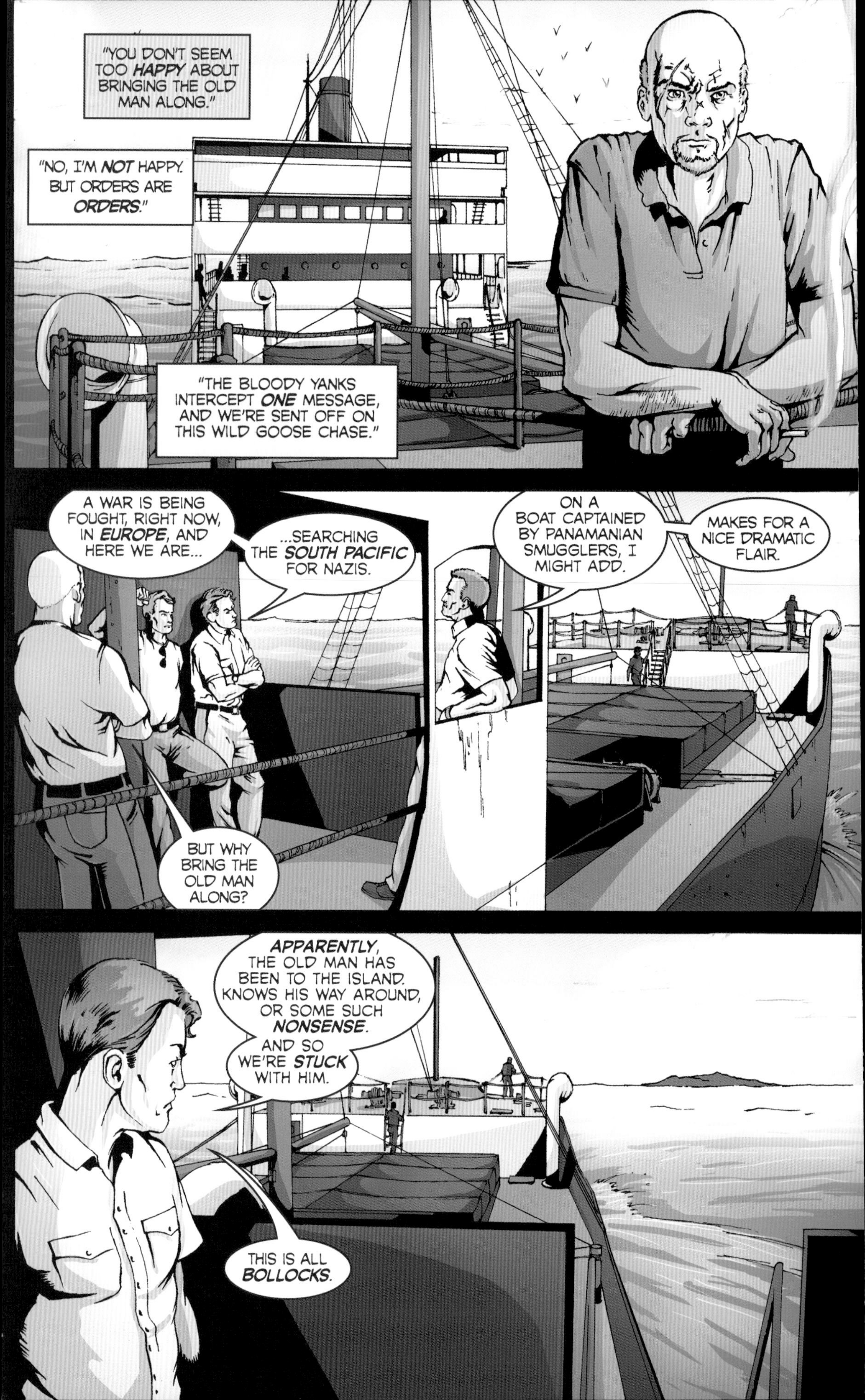
"YOU DON'T SEEM TOO HAPPY ABOUT BRINGING THE OLD MAN ALONG."
"NO, I'M NOT HAPPY. BUT ORDERS ARE ORDERS."
"THE BLOODY YANKS INTERCEPT ONE MESSAGE, AND WE'RE SENT OFF ON THIS WILD GOOSE CHASE."
A WAR IS BEING FOUGHT, RIGHT NOW, IN EUROPE, AND HERE WE ARE...
...SEARCHING THE SOUTH PACIFIC FOR NAZIS.
BUT WHY BRING THE OLD MAN ALONG?
ON A BOAT CAPTAINED BY PANAMANIAN SMUGGLERS, I MIGHT ADD.
MAKES FOR A NICE DRAMATIC FLAIR.
APPARENTLY, THE OLD MAN HAS BEEN TO THE ISLAND. KNOWS HIS WAY AROUND, OR SOME SUCH NONSENSE.
AND SO WE'RE STUCK WITH HIM.
THIS IS ALL BOLLOCKS.

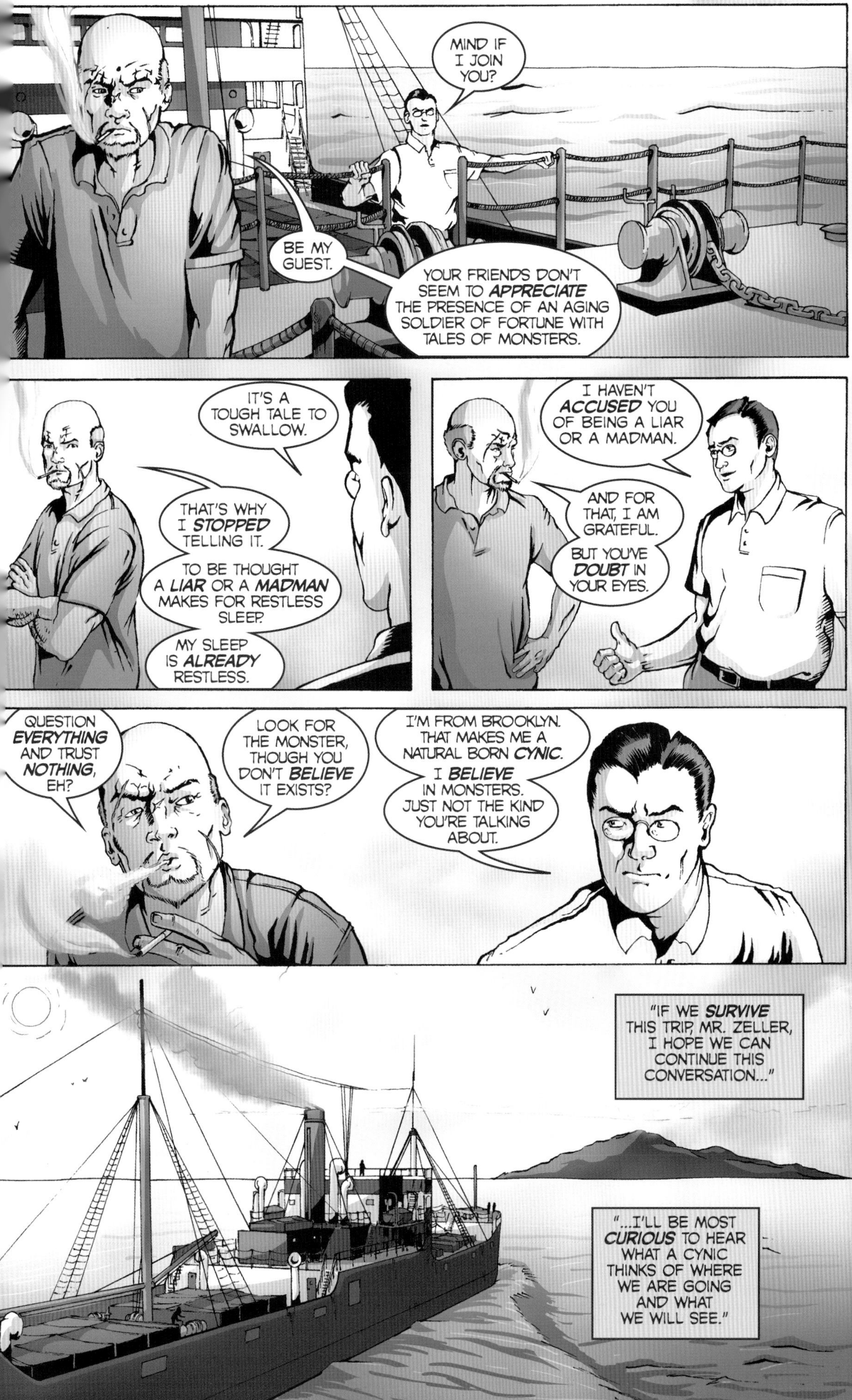
MIND IF I JOIN YOU?
BE MY GUEST.
YOUR FRIENDS DON'T SEEM TO APPRECIATE THE PRESENCE OF AN AGING SOLDIER OF FORTUNE WITH TALES OF MONSTERS.
IT'S A TOUGH TALE TO SWALLOW.
THAT'S WHY I STOPPED TELLING IT.
TO BE THOUGHT A LIAR OR A MADMAN MAKES FOR RESTLESS SLEEP.
MY SLEEP IS ALREADY RESTLESS.
I HAVEN'T ACCUSED YOU OF BEING A LIAR OR A MADMAN.
AND FOR THAT, I AM GRATEFUL.
BUT YOU'VE DOUBT IN YOUR EYES.
QUESTION EVERYTHING AND TRUST NOTHING, EH?
LOOK FOR THE MONSTER, THOUGH YOU DON'T BELIEVE IT EXISTS?
I'M FROM BROOKLYN. THAT MAKES ME A NATURAL BORN CYNIC.
I BELIEVE IN MONSTERS. JUST NOT THE KIND YOU'RE TALKING ABOUT.
"IF WE SURVIVE THIS TRIP, MR. ZELLER, I HOPE WE CAN CONTINUE THIS CONVERSATION..."
"...I'LL BE MOST CURIOUS TO HEAR WHAT A CYNIC THINKS OF WHERE WE ARE GOING AND WHAT WE WILL SEE."

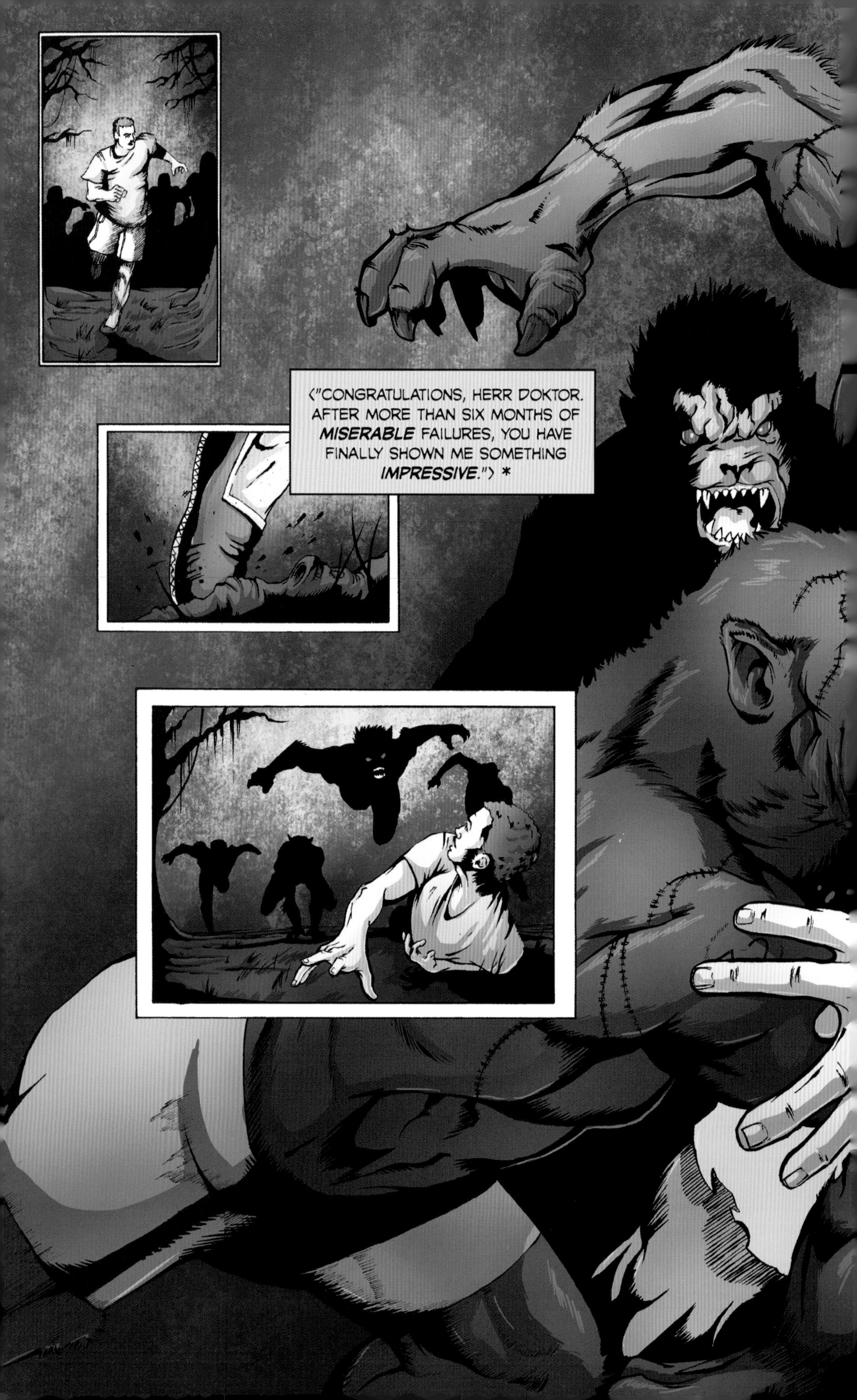
<"CONGRATULATIONS, HERR DOKTOR. AFTER MORE THAN SIX MONTHS OF *MISERABLE* FAILURES, YOU HAVE FINALLY SHOWN ME SOMETHING *IMPRESSIVE*."> *

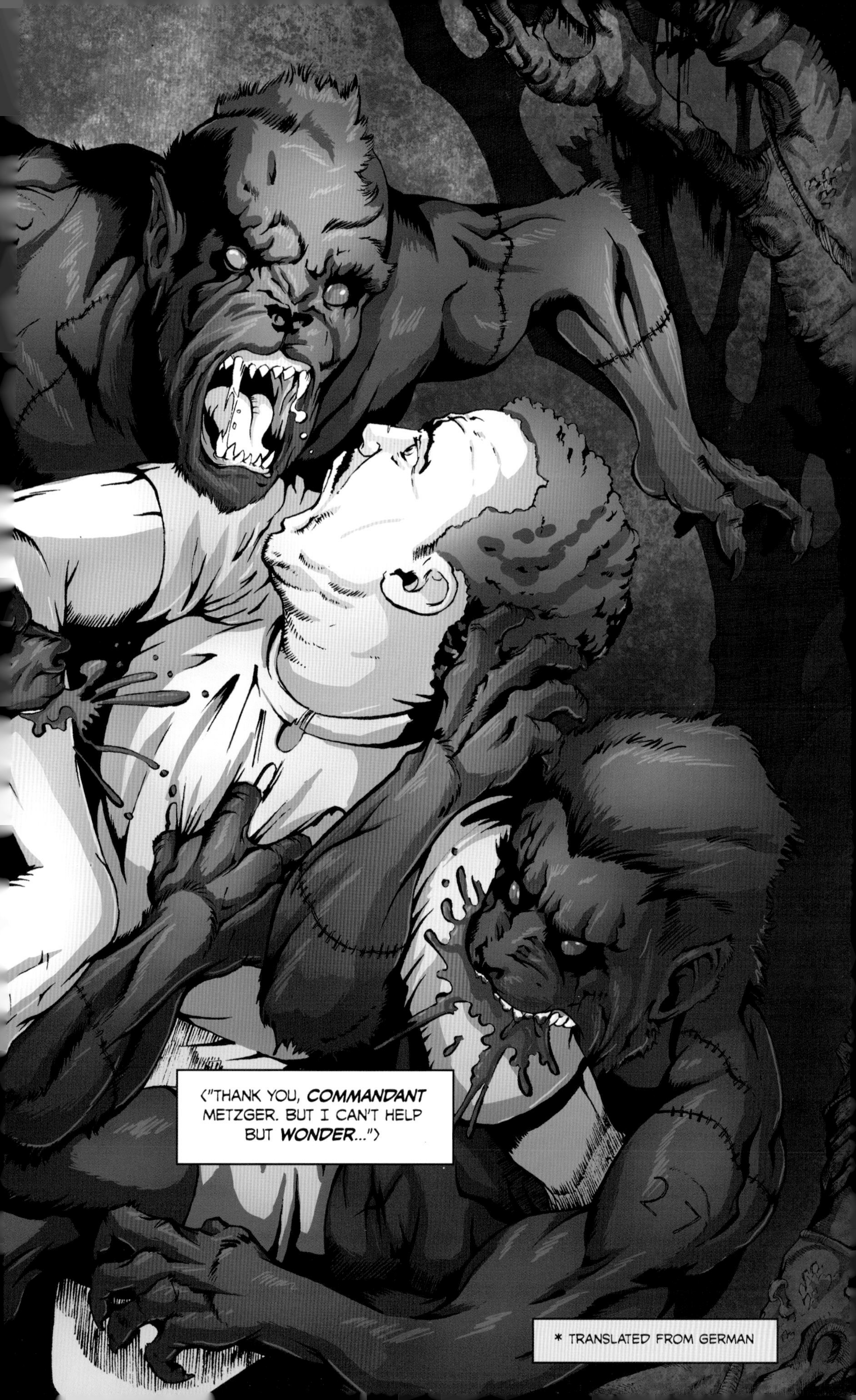

<"THANK YOU, COMMANDANT METZGER. BUT I CAN'T HELP BUT WONDER...">
* TRANSLATED FROM GERMAN

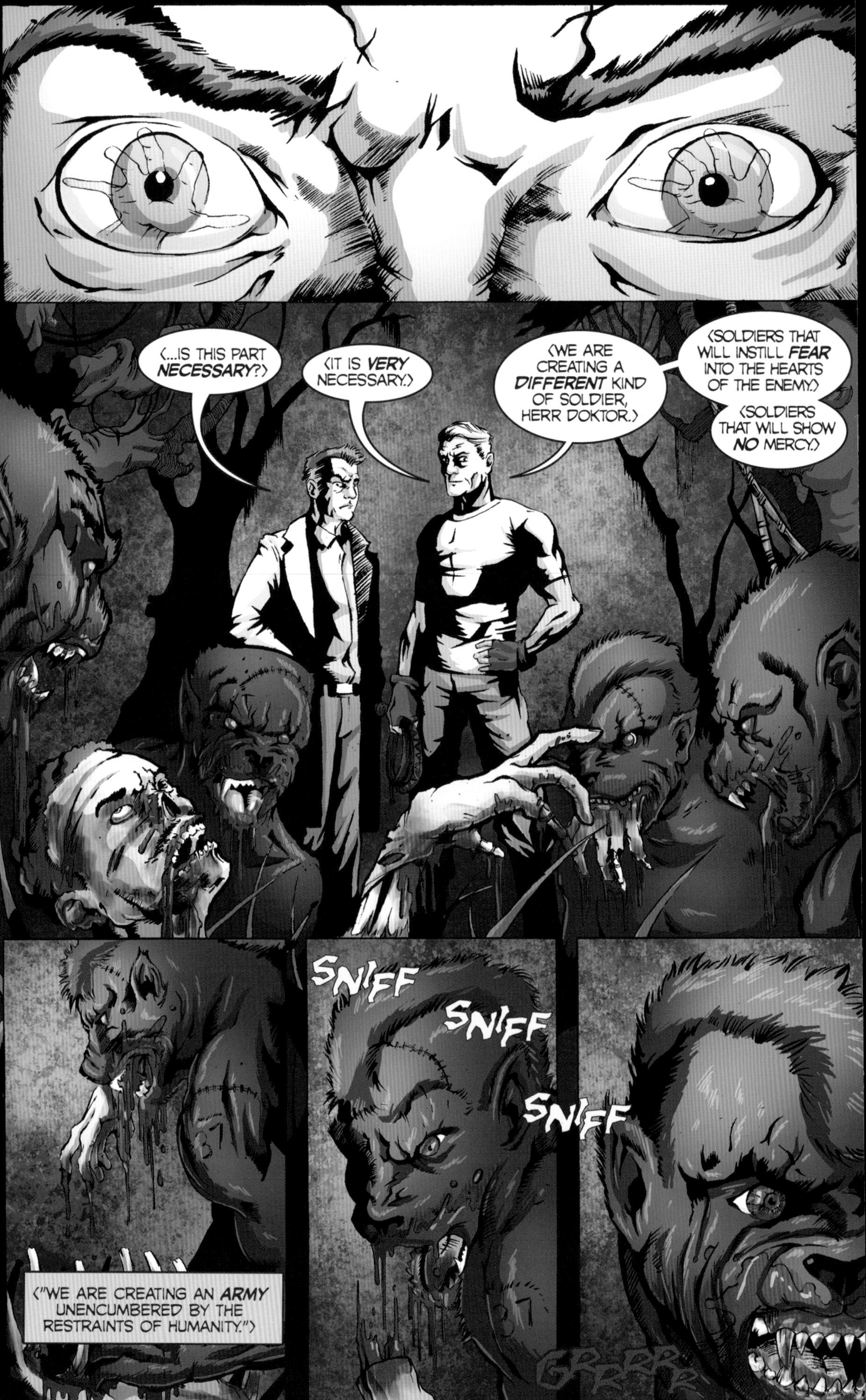
‹...IS THIS PART **NECESSARY**?›
‹IT IS **VERY** NECESSARY.›
‹WE ARE CREATING A **DIFFERENT** KIND OF SOLDIER, HERR DOKTOR.›
‹SOLDIERS THAT WILL INSTILL **FEAR** INTO THE HEARTS OF THE ENEMY.›
‹SOLDIERS THAT WILL SHOW **NO** MERCY.›
‹"WE ARE CREATING AN **ARMY** UNENCUMBERED BY THE RESTRAINTS OF HUMANITY."›
SNIFF
SNIFF
SNIFF

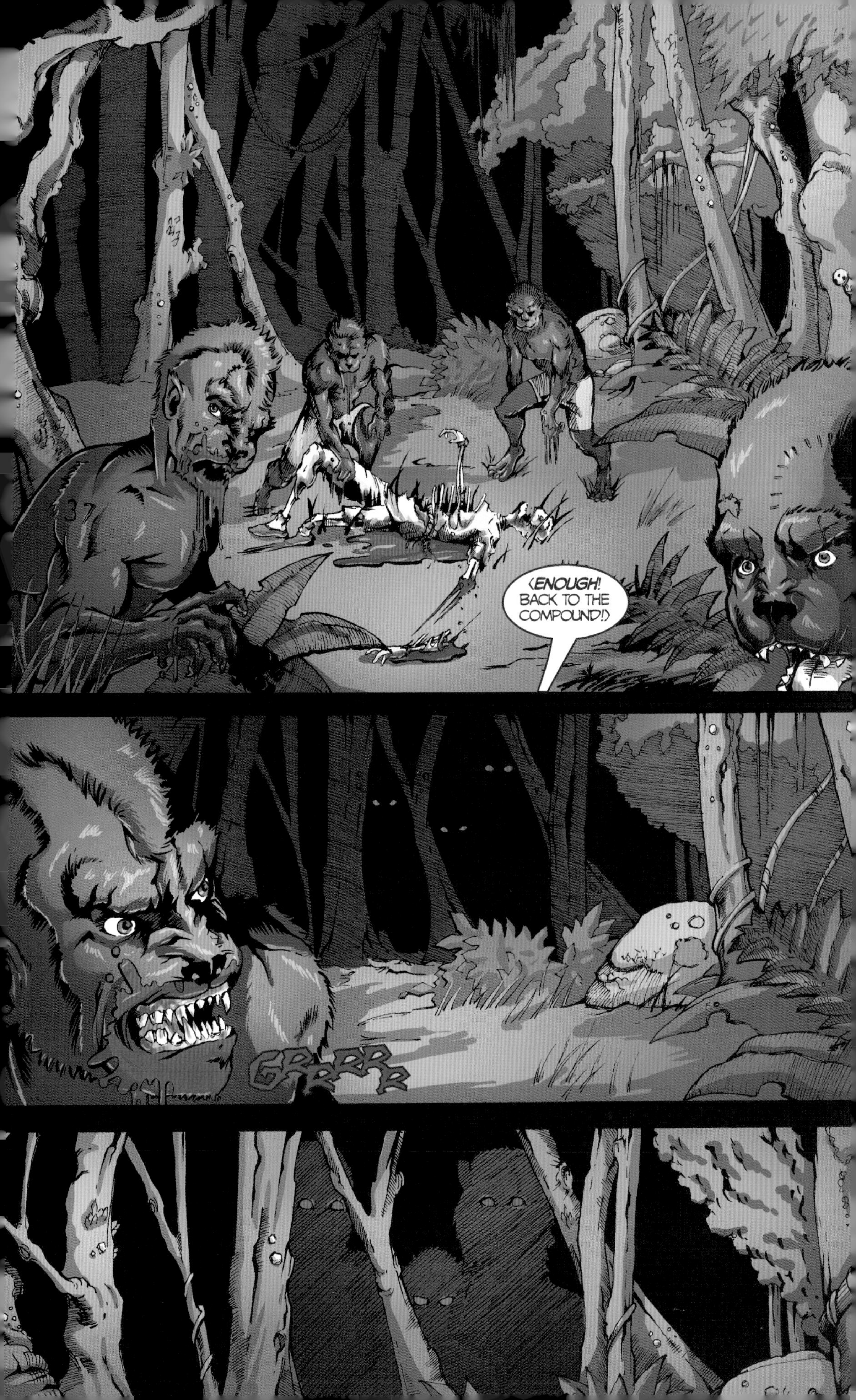
‹ENOUGH! BACK TO THE COMPOUND!›
GRRRRR

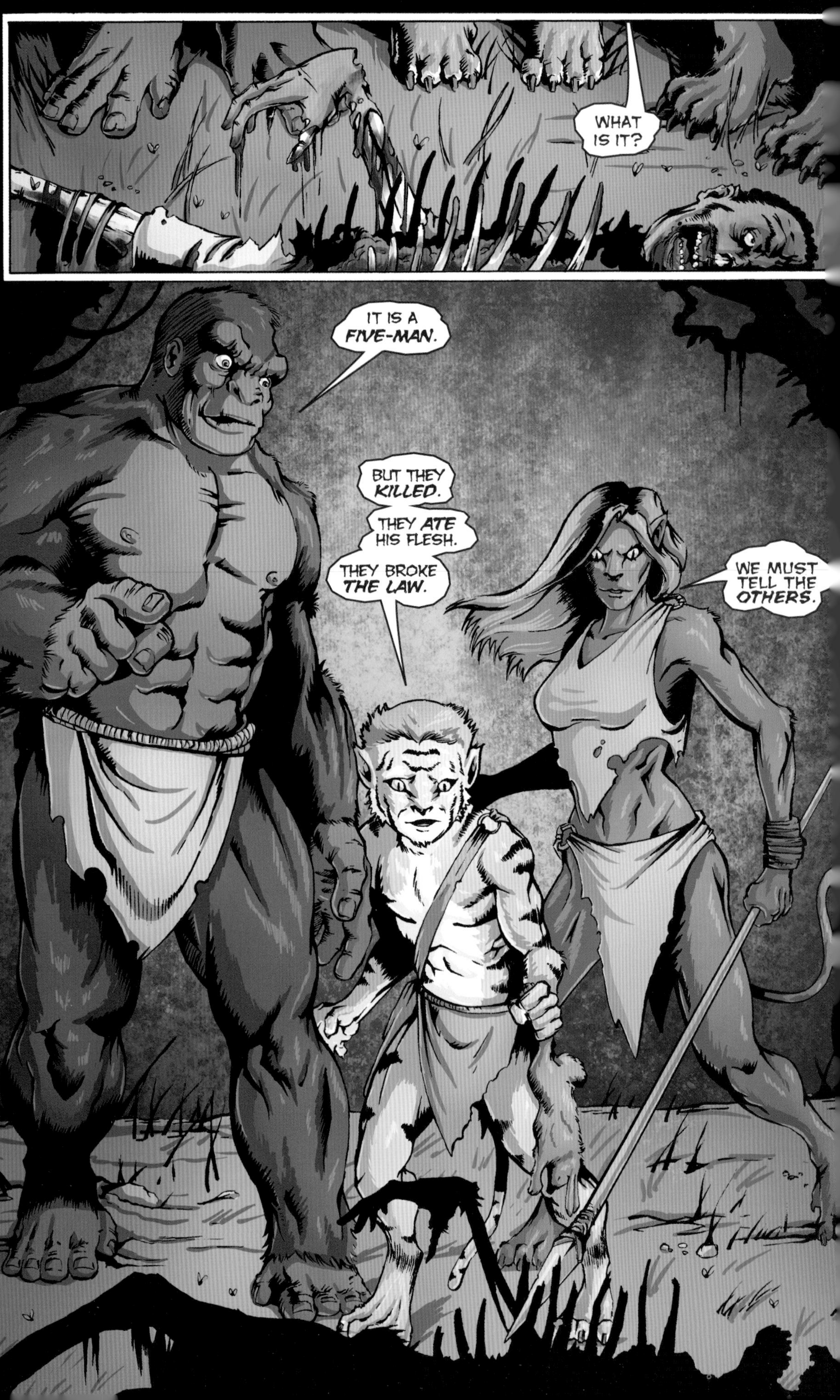
WHAT IS IT?
IT IS A *FIVE-MAN*.
BUT THEY *KILLED*.
THEY *ATE* HIS FLESH.
THEY BROKE *THE LAW*.
WE MUST TELL THE *OTHERS*.

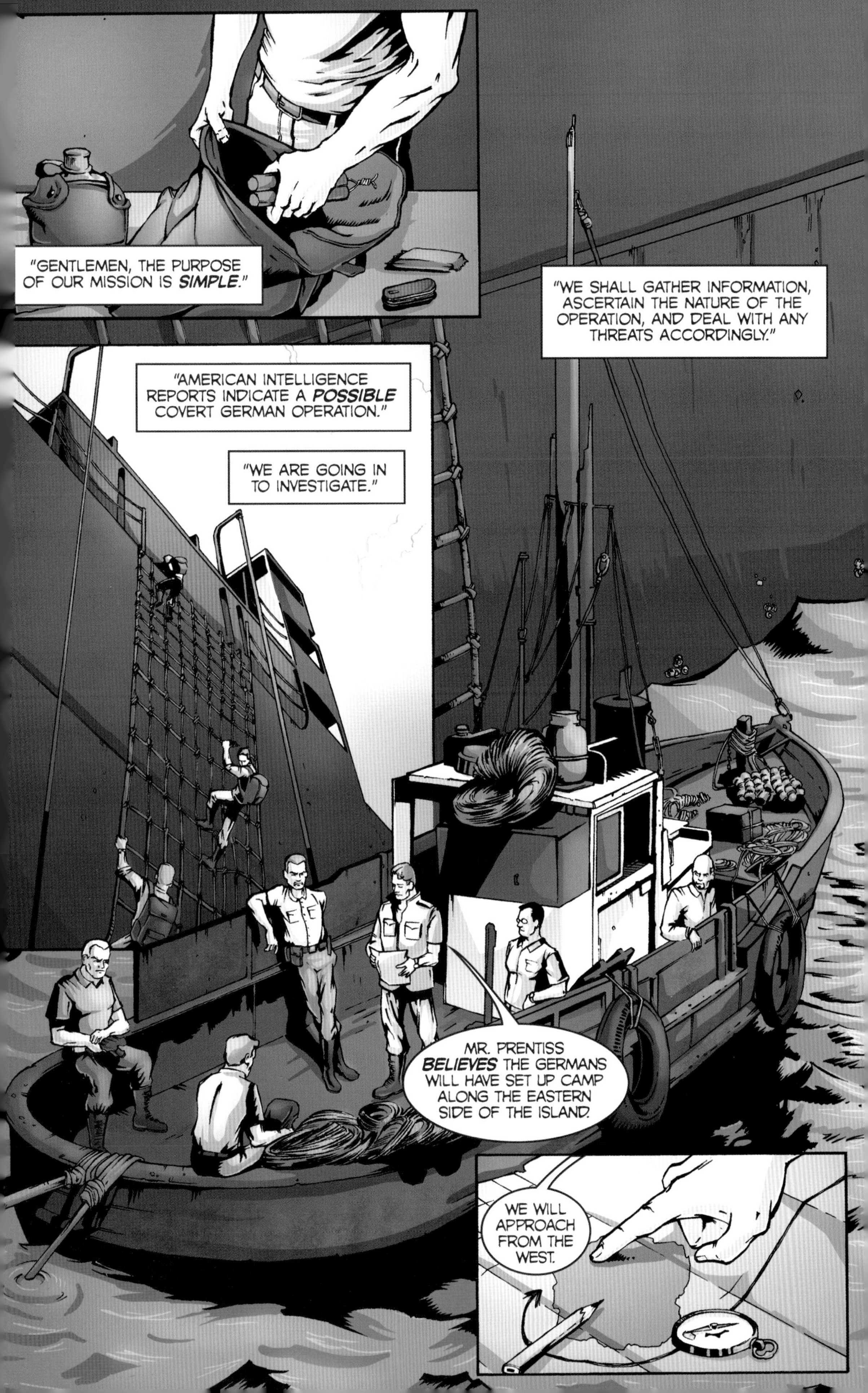
"GENTLEMEN, THE PURPOSE OF OUR MISSION IS *SIMPLE*."
"AMERICAN INTELLIGENCE REPORTS INDICATE A *POSSIBLE* COVERT GERMAN OPERATION."
"WE ARE GOING IN TO INVESTIGATE."
"WE SHALL GATHER INFORMATION, ASCERTAIN THE NATURE OF THE OPERATION, AND DEAL WITH ANY THREATS ACCORDINGLY."
MR. PRENTISS **BELIEVES** THE GERMANS WILL HAVE SET UP CAMP ALONG THE EASTERN SIDE OF THE ISLAND.
WE WILL APPROACH FROM THE WEST.

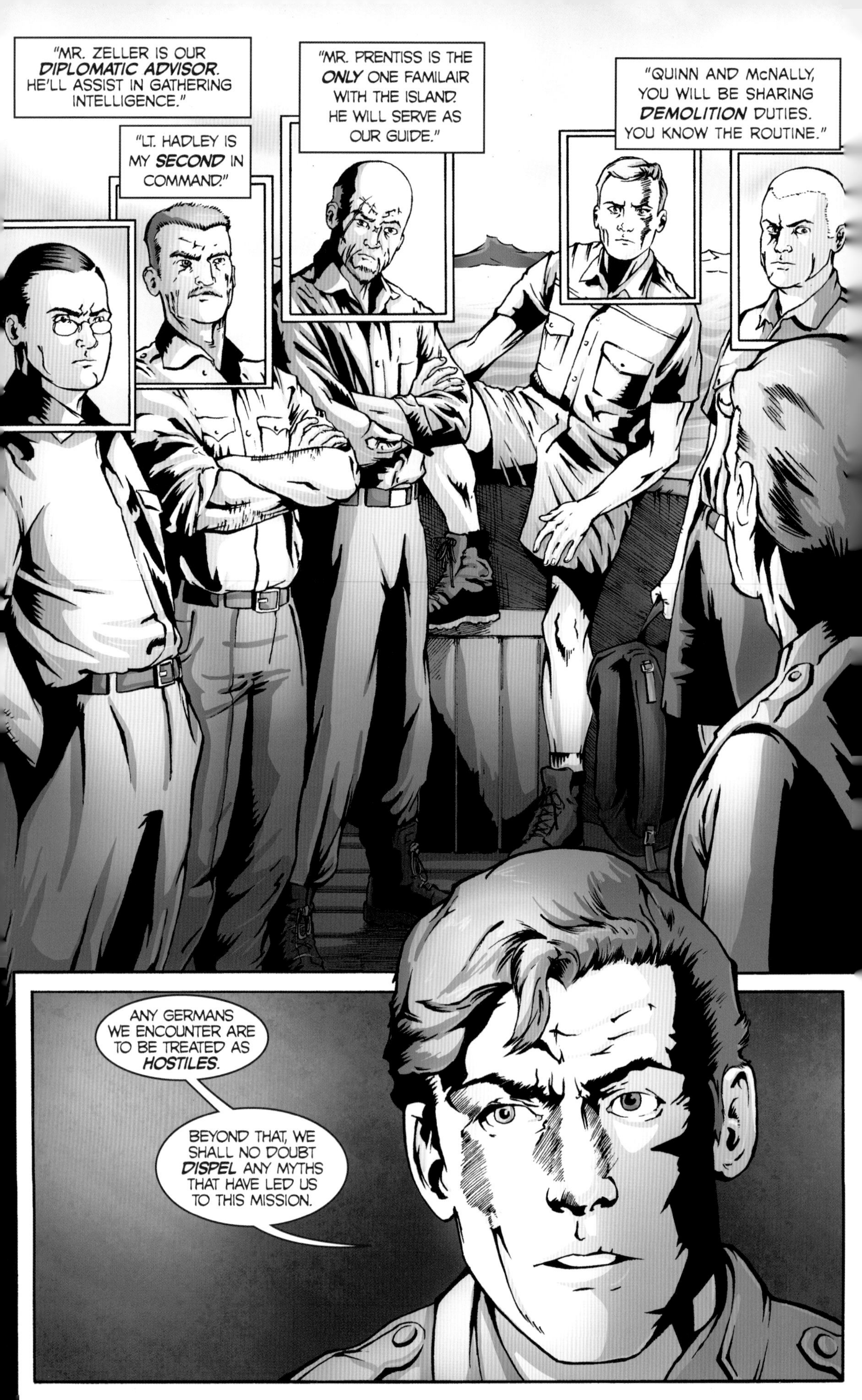
"MR. ZELLER IS OUR DIPLOMATIC ADVISOR. HE'LL ASSIST IN GATHERING INTELLIGENCE."
"LT. HADLEY IS MY SECOND IN COMMAND."
"MR. PRENTISS IS THE ONLY ONE FAMILAIR WITH THE ISLAND. HE WILL SERVE AS OUR GUIDE."
"QUINN AND McNALLY, YOU WILL BE SHARING DEMOLITION DUTIES. YOU KNOW THE ROUTINE."
ANY GERMANS WE ENCOUNTER ARE TO BE TREATED AS HOSTILES.
BEYOND THAT, WE SHALL NO DOUBT DISPEL ANY MYTHS THAT HAVE LED US TO THIS MISSION.

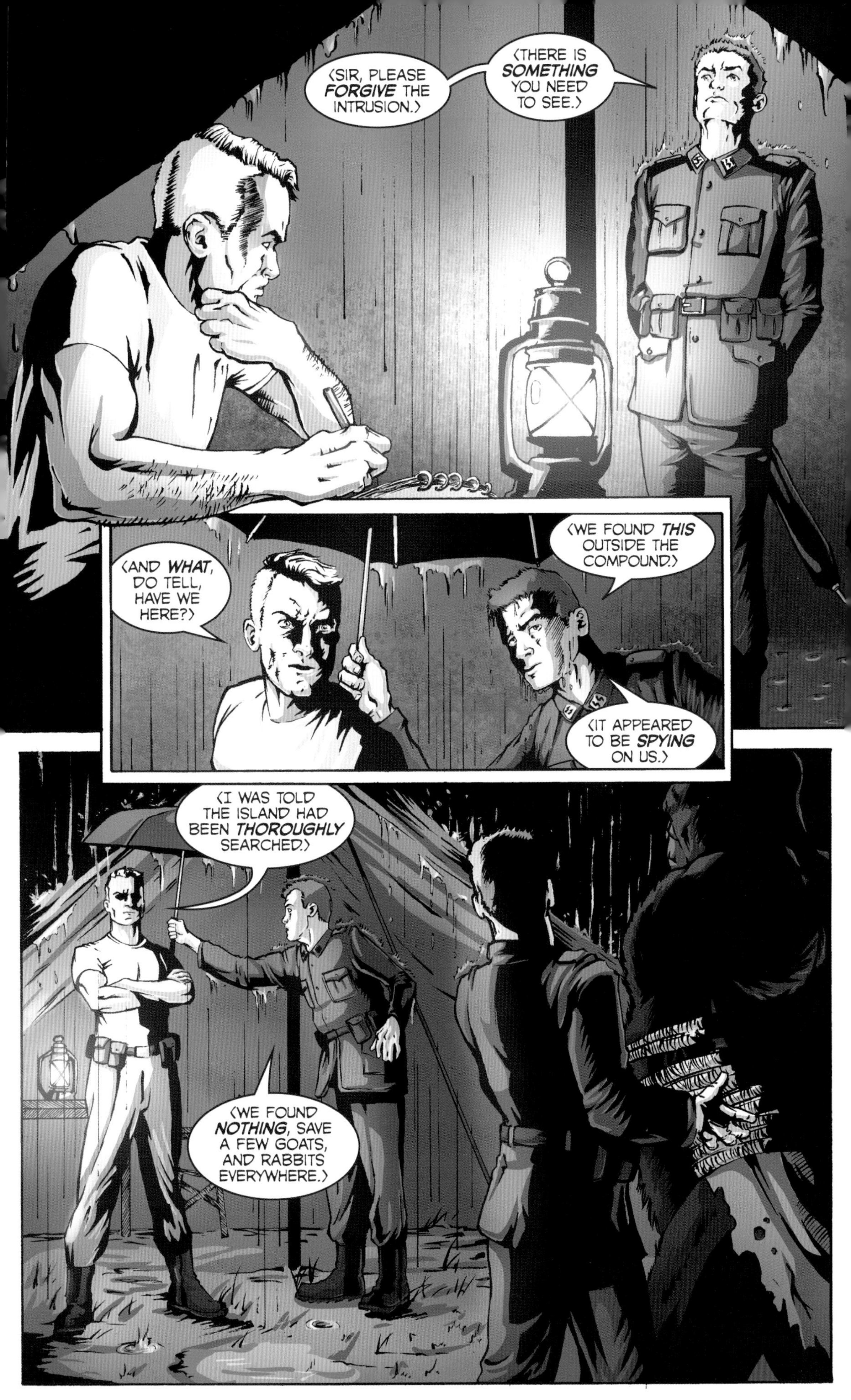
‹SIR, PLEASE *FORGIVE* THE INTRUSION.›
‹THERE IS *SOMETHING* YOU NEED TO SEE.›
‹AND *WHAT*, DO TELL, HAVE WE HERE?›
‹WE FOUND *THIS* OUTSIDE THE COMPOUND.›
‹IT APPEARED TO BE *SPYING* ON US.›
‹I WAS TOLD THE ISLAND HAD BEEN *THOROUGHLY* SEARCHED.›
‹WE FOUND *NOTHING*, SAVE A FEW GOATS, AND RABBITS EVERYWHERE.›

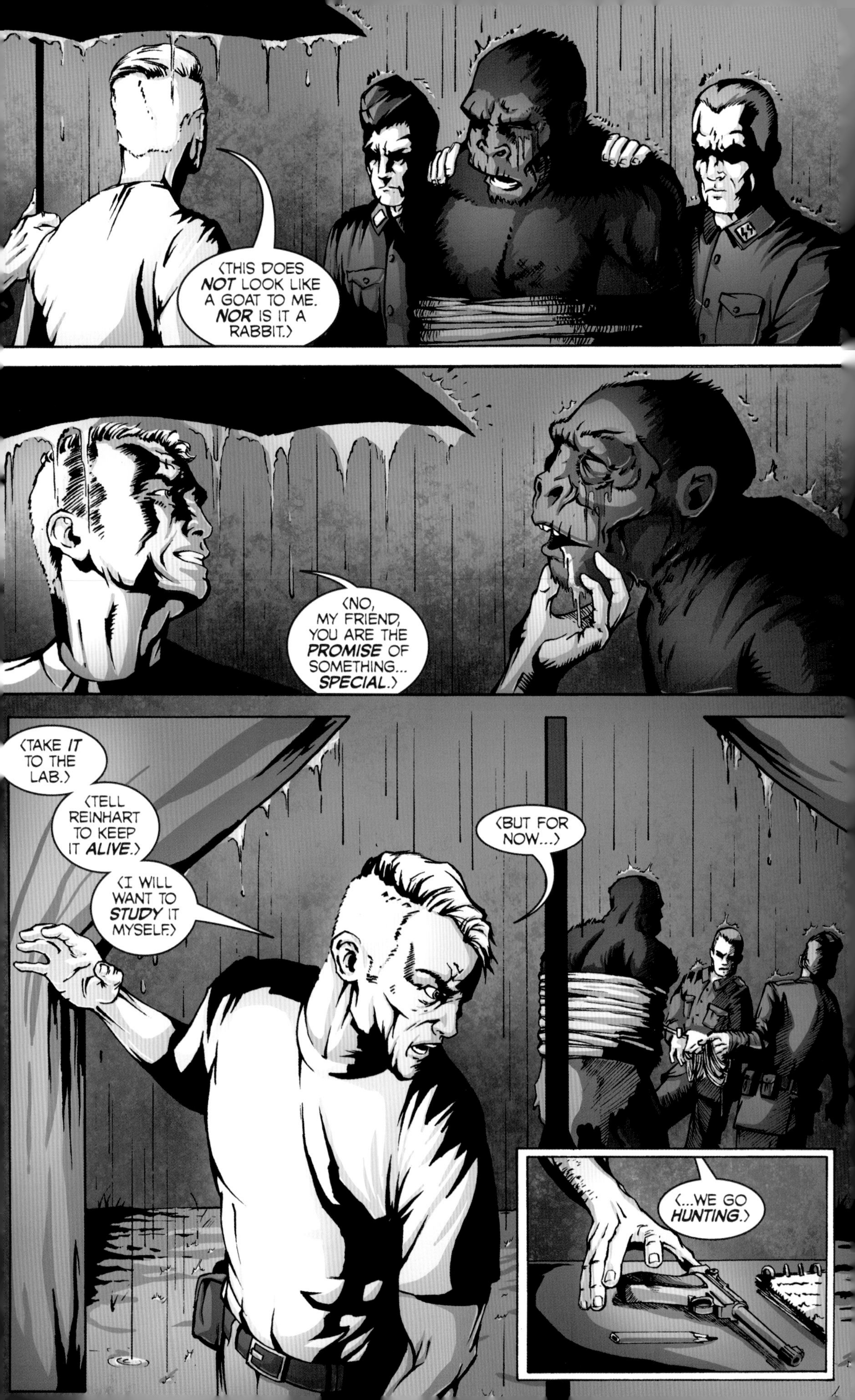

‹THIS DOES NOT LOOK LIKE A GOAT TO ME. NOR IS IT A RABBIT.›
‹NO, MY FRIEND, YOU ARE THE PROMISE OF SOMETHING... SPECIAL.›
‹TAKE IT TO THE LAB.›
‹TELL REINHART TO KEEP IT ALIVE.›
‹I WILL WANT TO STUDY IT MYSELF.›
‹BUT FOR NOW...›
‹...WE GO HUNTING.›

TOP SECRET

THIS IS A COVER SHEET

*BASIC SECURITY REQUIREMENTS ARE CONTAINED
IN AR 380-5*

THE UNAUTHORIZED DISCLOSURE OF THE INFORMATION CONTAINED
IN THE ATTACHED DOCUMENT(S) COULD RESULT IN EXCEPTION-
ALLY GRAVE DANGER TO THE UNITED STATES

RESPONSIBILITY OF PERSONS HANDLING THE ATTACHED DOCUMENT(S)

1. Enter on DA Form 969 your name and the date you had access to the document(s).
2. Exercise the necessary safeguards to prevent unauthorized disclosure by never leaving the document(s) unattended except when properly secured in a locked safe.
3. Transfer the document(s) only to persons who need to know and who possess the required security clearance.
4. Obtain a receipt whenever relinquishing control of the document(s).

STORAGE

Store as prescribed in AR 380-5.

REPRODUCTION

TOP SECRET material may be copied, extracted, or reproduced only when the classifying authority has authorized such actions.

DISPOSITION

This cover sheet should be removed when document(s) are filed in a permanent file, declassified, destroyed, or mailed.

(This cover sheet is unclassified when separated from classified documents)

TOP SECRET

DA LABEL 24
1 FEB 59   PREVIOUS EDITIONS OF THIS LABEL ARE OBSOLETE   AGL (1) 4-59-40M-71603

Zeller, A. - Correspondence

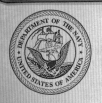

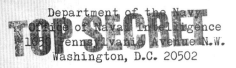

Department of the Navy
Office of Naval Intelligence
1650 Pennsylvania Avenue N.W.
Washington, D.C. 20502

TOP SECRET

TOP SECRET Oct. 2, 1939

From: Lt. Zeller, Naval Intelligence
To: Col. Eaton, Army Intelligence

Subject: Intercepted German Correspondence

Col. Eaton,

I have gone over the hand-written note you asked me to translate. As you know, the paper had been soaked in blood (I assume as a result from the struggle involved in its interception), and the hand writing itself was difficult to decipher. I had an especially difficult time making sense of the term "Kreatürlich Soldaten," which translates in English to "Creature Soldiers" or "Creaturely Soldiers." Here is the translation of the German communiqué recently intercepted in Panama:

"Although Dr. Reinhart and his colleagues have found many of Meraux's original notes, their inability to recreate his work has grown tedious. It has taken close to six months for Reinhart to achieve a level of failure with the Creature Soldiers that almost qualifies as success. Until recently, the attempts to duplicate Meraux's experiments have been pathetic at best. To date, more than two dozen test subjects have been operated on, resulting in ghastly monstrosities, many of which needed to be destroyed. The more recent test subjects show the most promise, though I remain skeptical of this program. If we are to succeed, we will need more specimens and more supplies."

Sincerely,

TOP SECRET

CHAPTER THREE

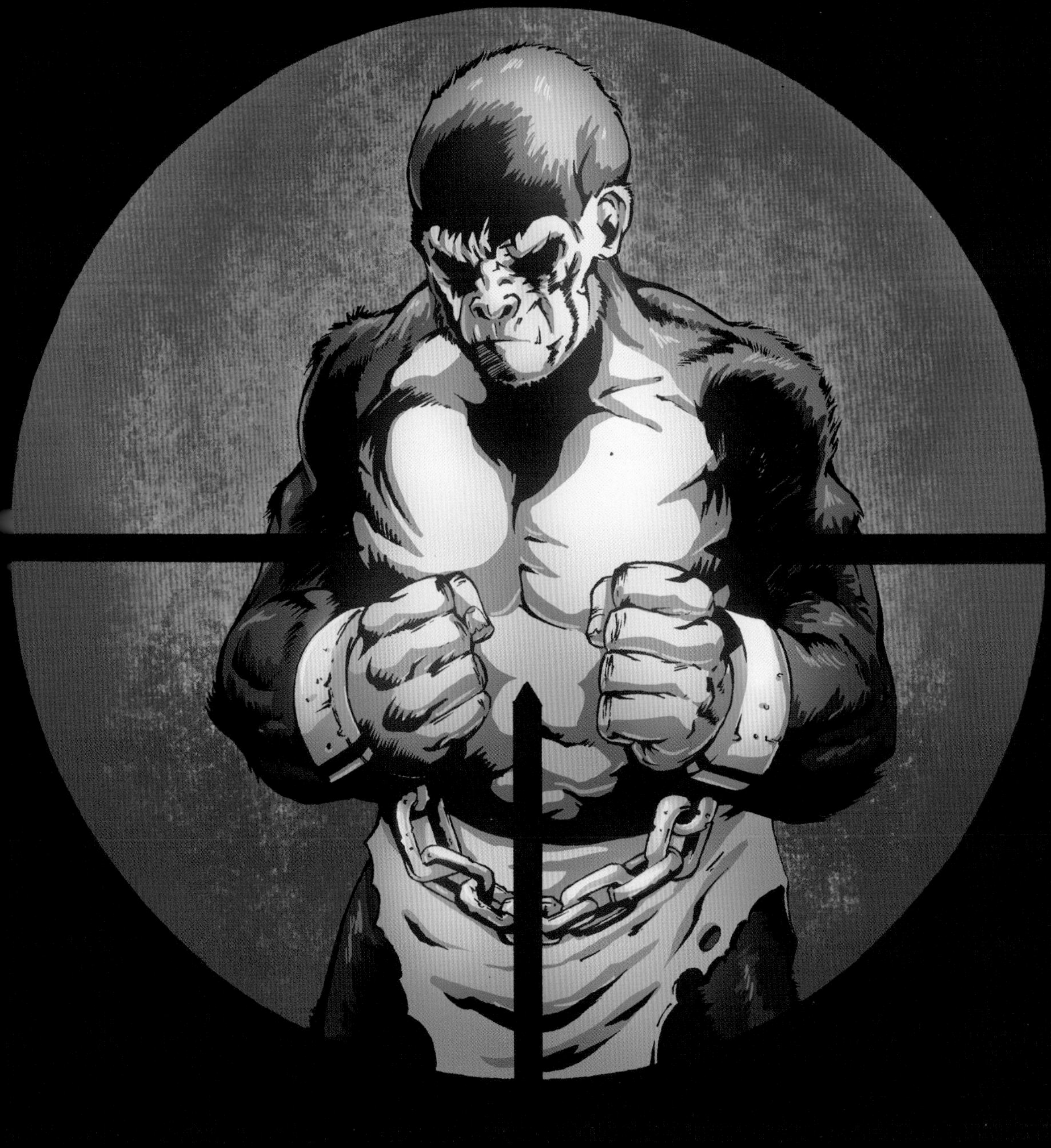

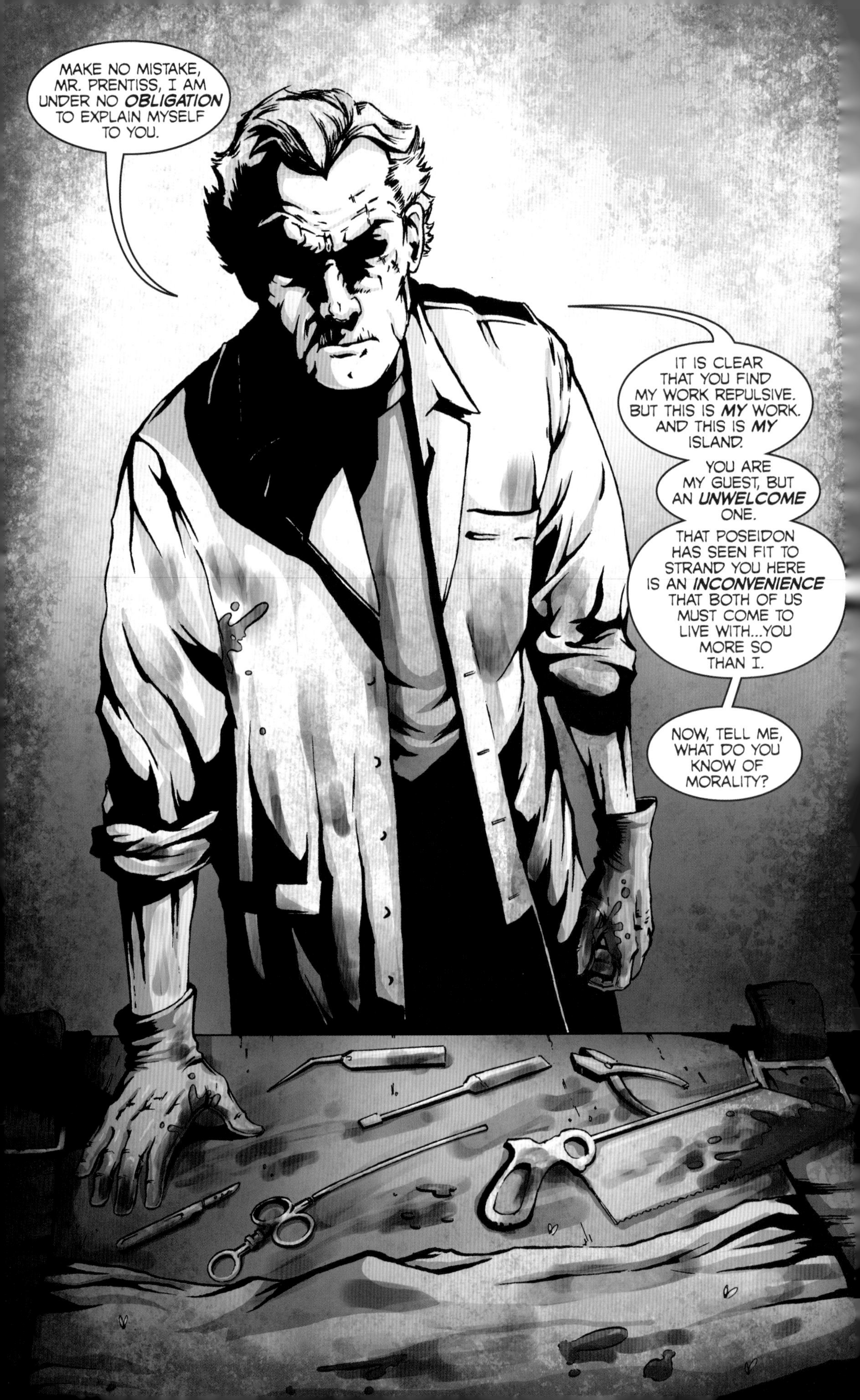
MAKE NO MISTAKE, MR. PRENTISS, I AM UNDER NO OBLIGATION TO EXPLAIN MYSELF TO YOU.
IT IS CLEAR THAT YOU FIND MY WORK REPULSIVE. BUT THIS IS MY WORK. AND THIS IS MY ISLAND.
YOU ARE MY GUEST, BUT AN UNWELCOME ONE.
THAT POSEIDON HAS SEEN FIT TO STRAND YOU HERE IS AN INCONVENIENCE THAT BOTH OF US MUST COME TO LIVE WITH...YOU MORE SO THAN I.
NOW, TELL ME, WHAT DO YOU KNOW OF MORALITY?

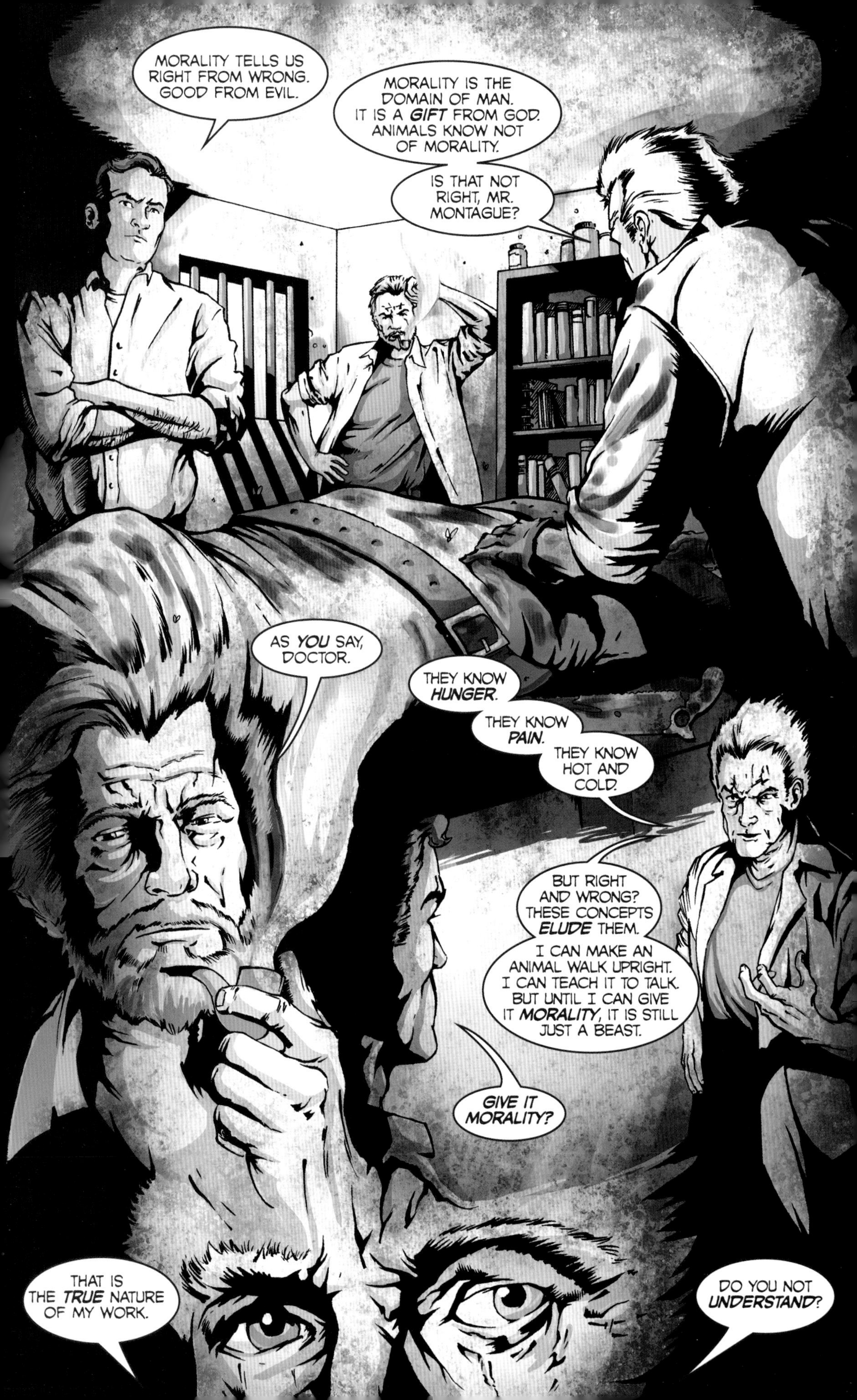

MORALITY TELLS US RIGHT FROM WRONG. GOOD FROM EVIL.
MORALITY IS THE DOMAIN OF MAN. IT IS A *GIFT* FROM GOD. ANIMALS KNOW NOT OF MORALITY.
IS THAT NOT RIGHT, MR. MONTAGUE?
AS *YOU* SAY, DOCTOR.
THEY KNOW *HUNGER*.
THEY KNOW *PAIN*.
THEY KNOW HOT AND COLD.
BUT RIGHT AND WRONG? THESE CONCEPTS *ELUDE* THEM.
I CAN MAKE AN ANIMAL WALK UPRIGHT. I CAN TEACH IT TO TALK. BUT UNTIL I CAN GIVE IT *MORALITY*, IT IS STILL JUST A BEAST.
GIVE IT MORALITY?
THAT IS THE *TRUE* NATURE OF MY WORK.
DO YOU NOT *UNDERSTAND*?

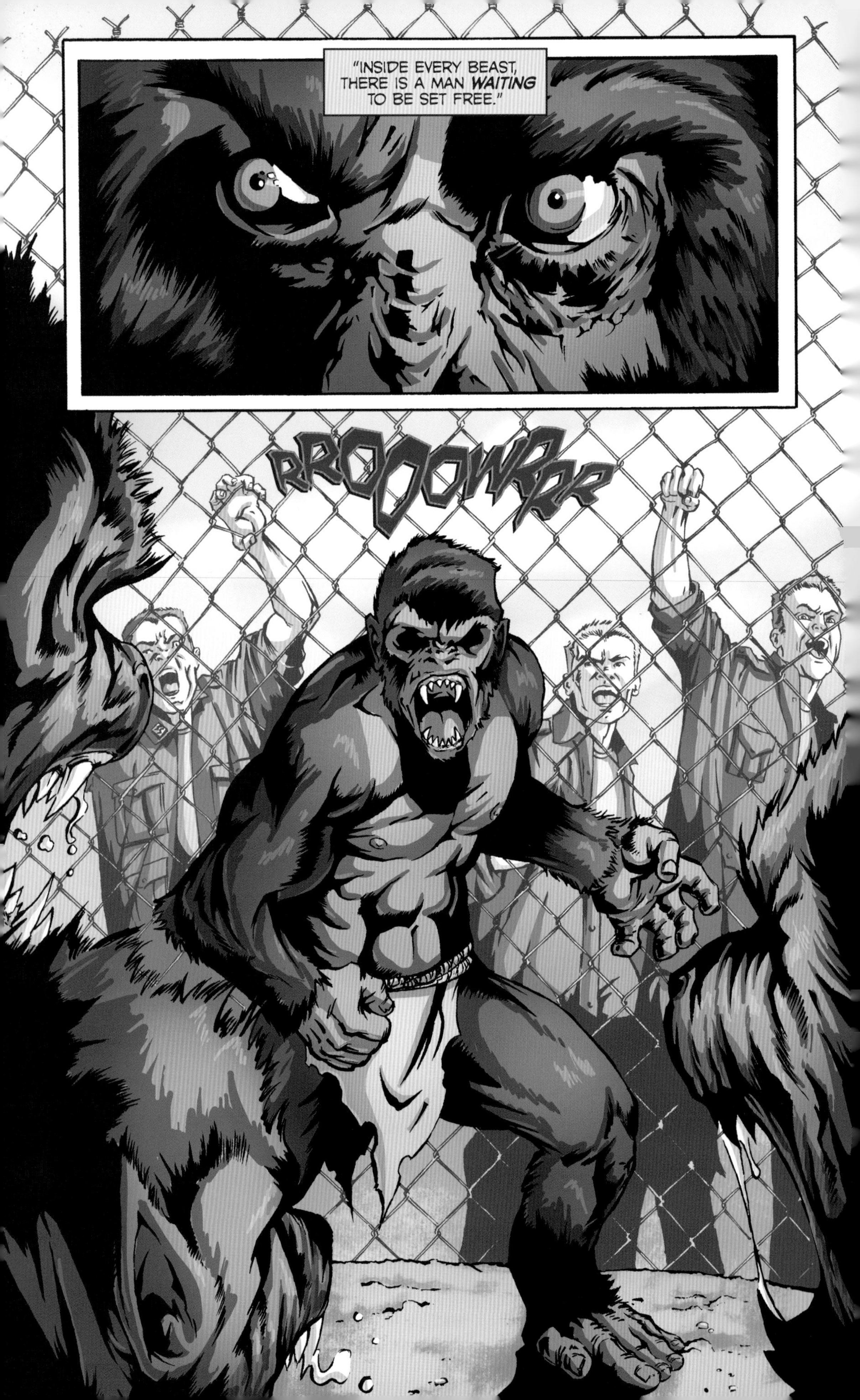
"INSIDE EVERY BEAST, THERE IS A MAN *WAITING* TO BE SET FREE."
RROOOWRRR

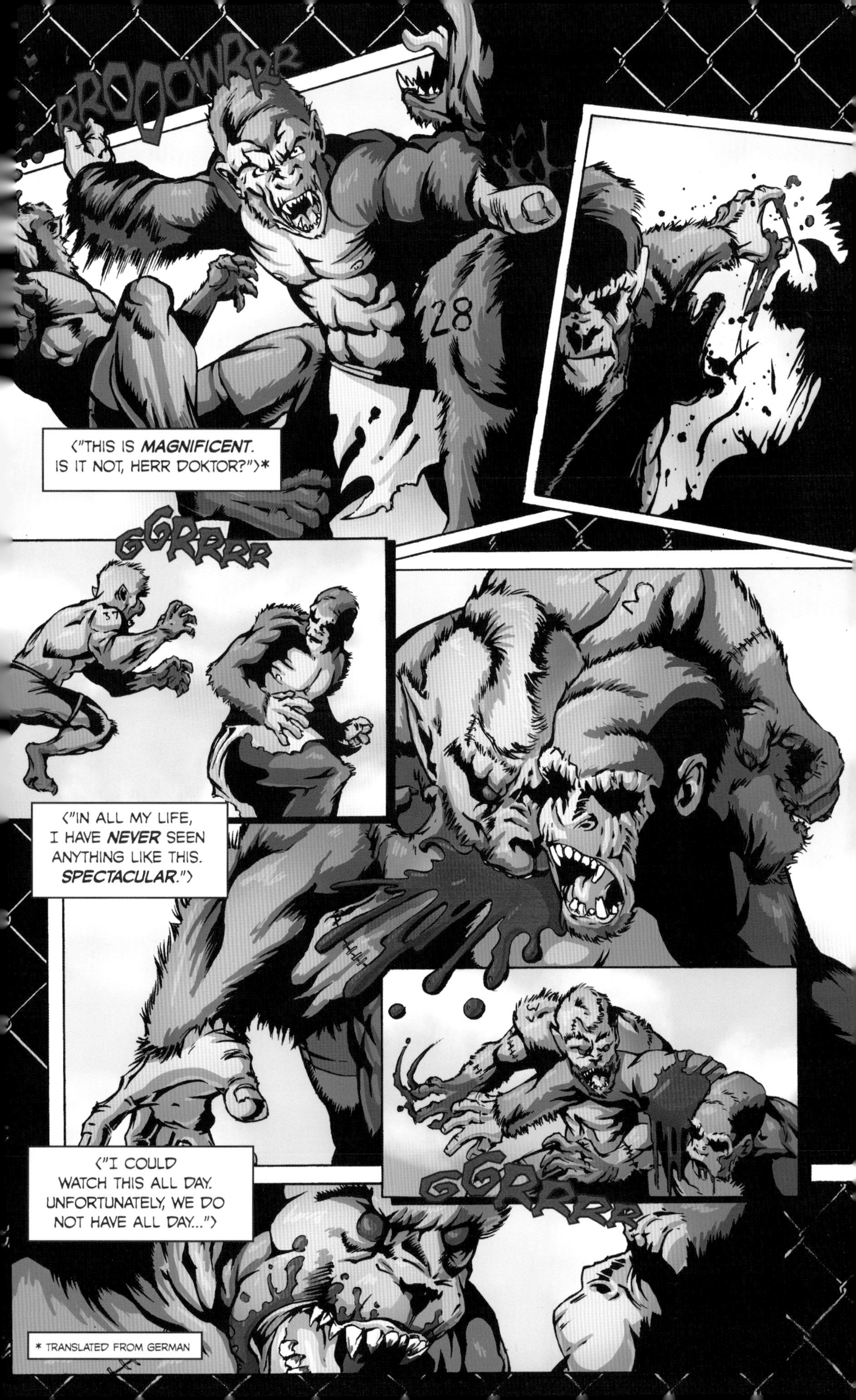
RROOOWRRR
〈"THIS IS MAGNIFICENT. IS IT NOT, HERR DOKTOR?"〉*
GGRRRR
〈"IN ALL MY LIFE, I HAVE NEVER SEEN ANYTHING LIKE THIS. SPECTACULAR."〉
〈"I COULD WATCH THIS ALL DAY. UNFORTUNATELY, WE DO NOT HAVE ALL DAY..."〉
GGRRRR
* TRANSLATED FROM GERMAN

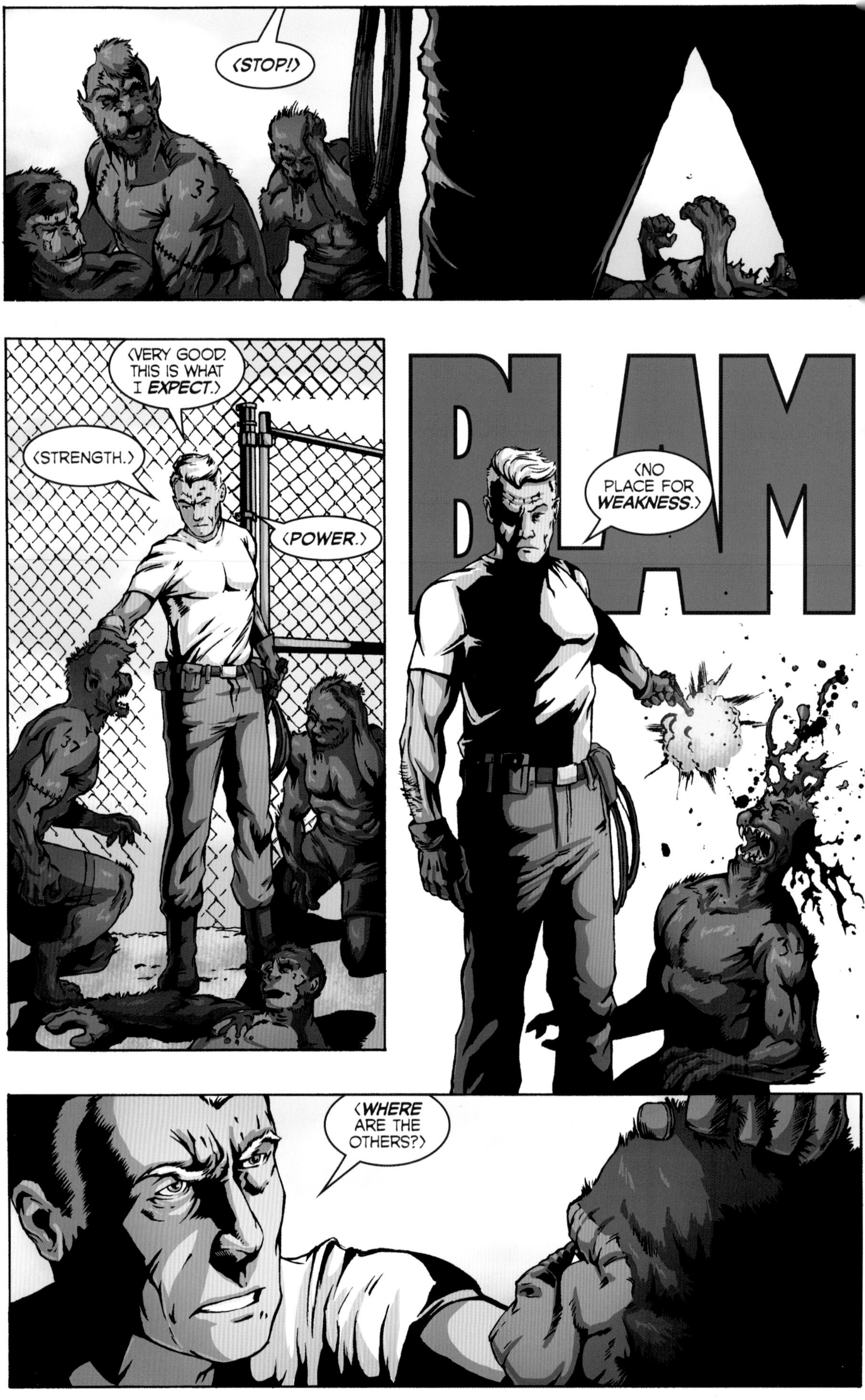
⟨STOP!⟩
⟨VERY GOOD. THIS IS WHAT I EXPECT.⟩
⟨STRENGTH.⟩
⟨POWER.⟩
BLAM
⟨NO PLACE FOR WEAKNESS.⟩
⟨WHERE ARE THE OTHERS?⟩

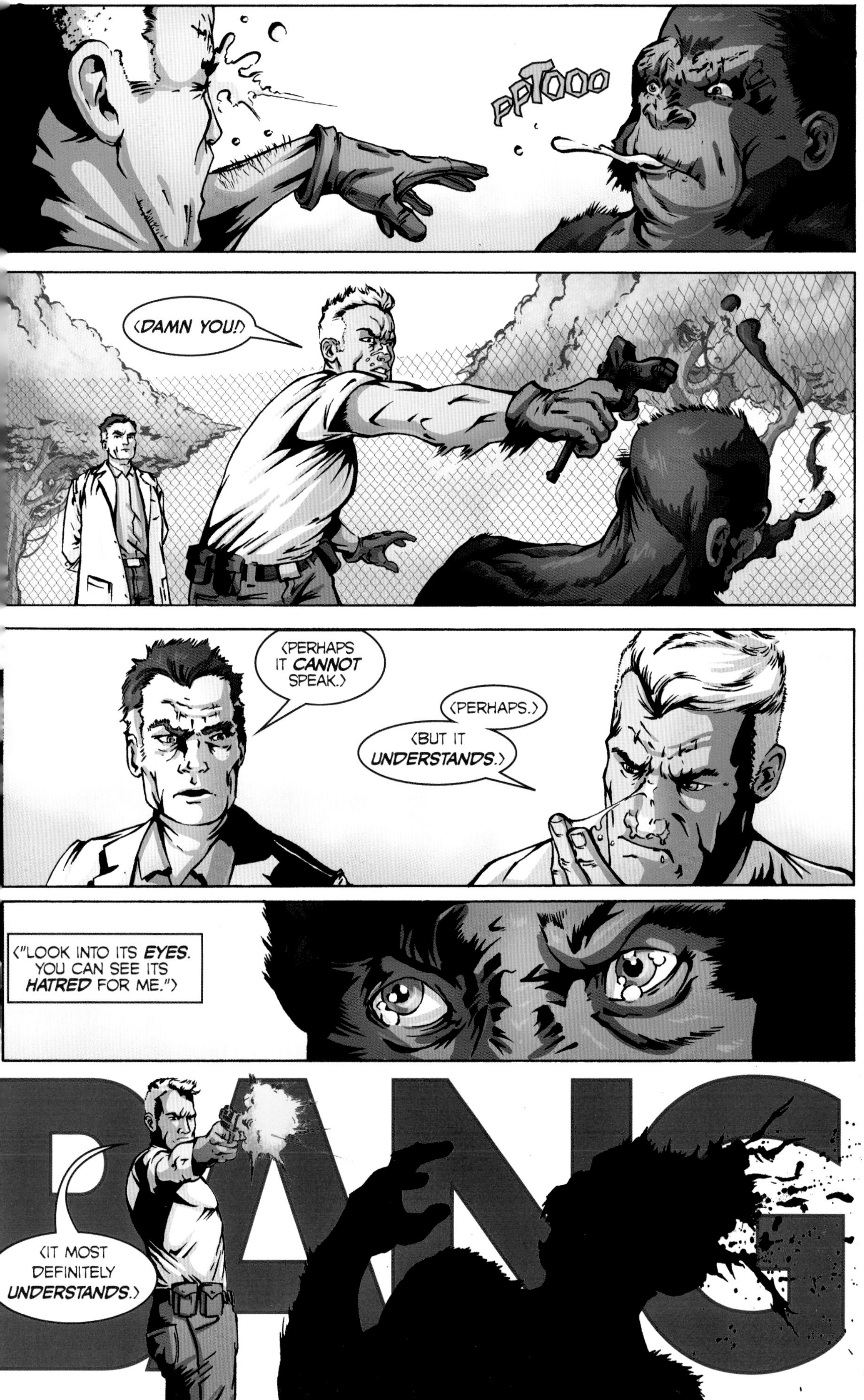

PPTOOO
‹DAMN YOU!›
‹PERHAPS IT *CANNOT* SPEAK.›
‹PERHAPS.›
‹BUT IT *UNDERSTANDS*.›
‹"LOOK INTO ITS *EYES*. YOU CAN SEE ITS *HATRED* FOR ME."›
BANG
‹IT MOST DEFINITELY *UNDERSTANDS*.›

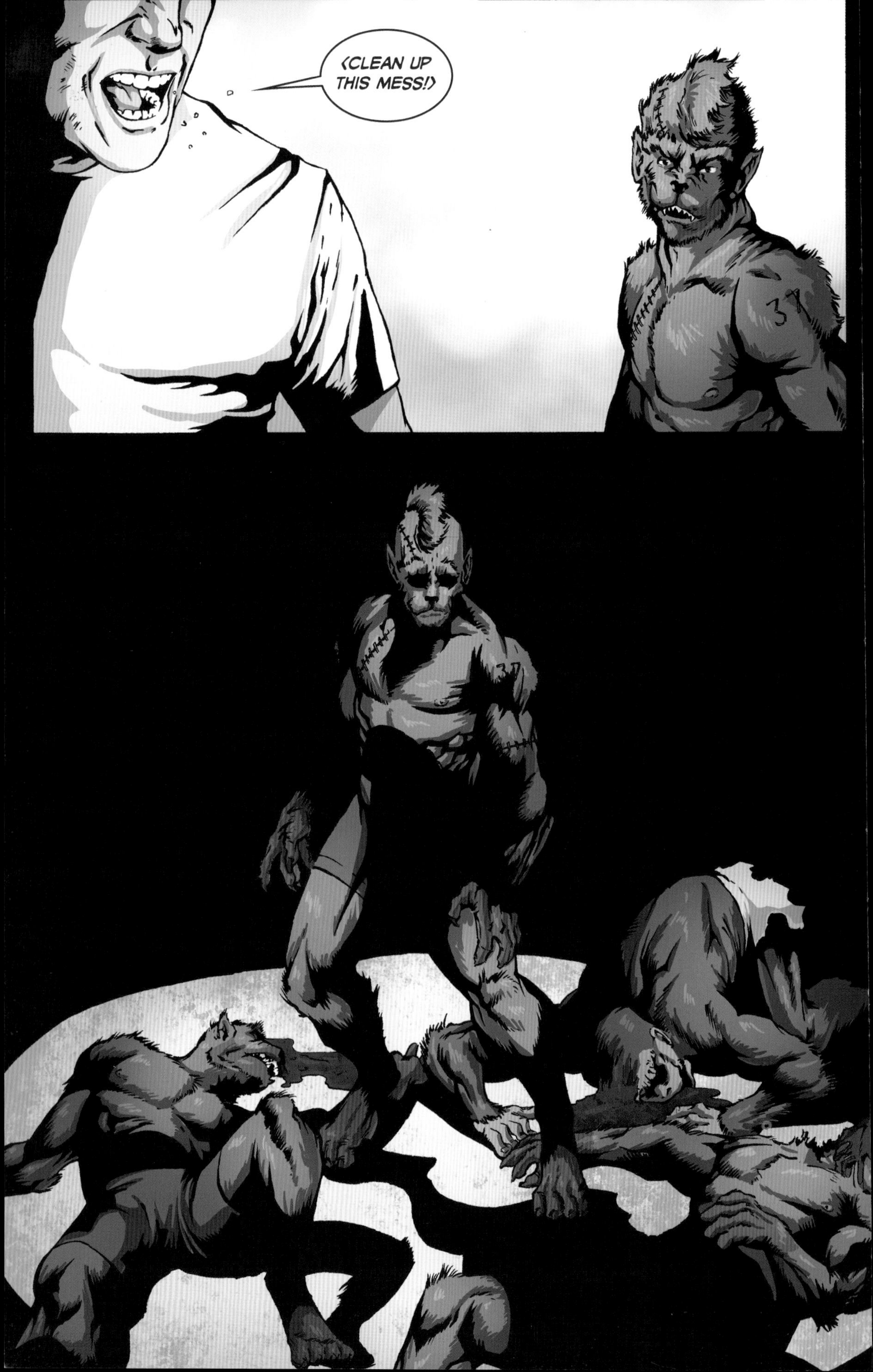

‹CLEAN UP THIS MESS!›

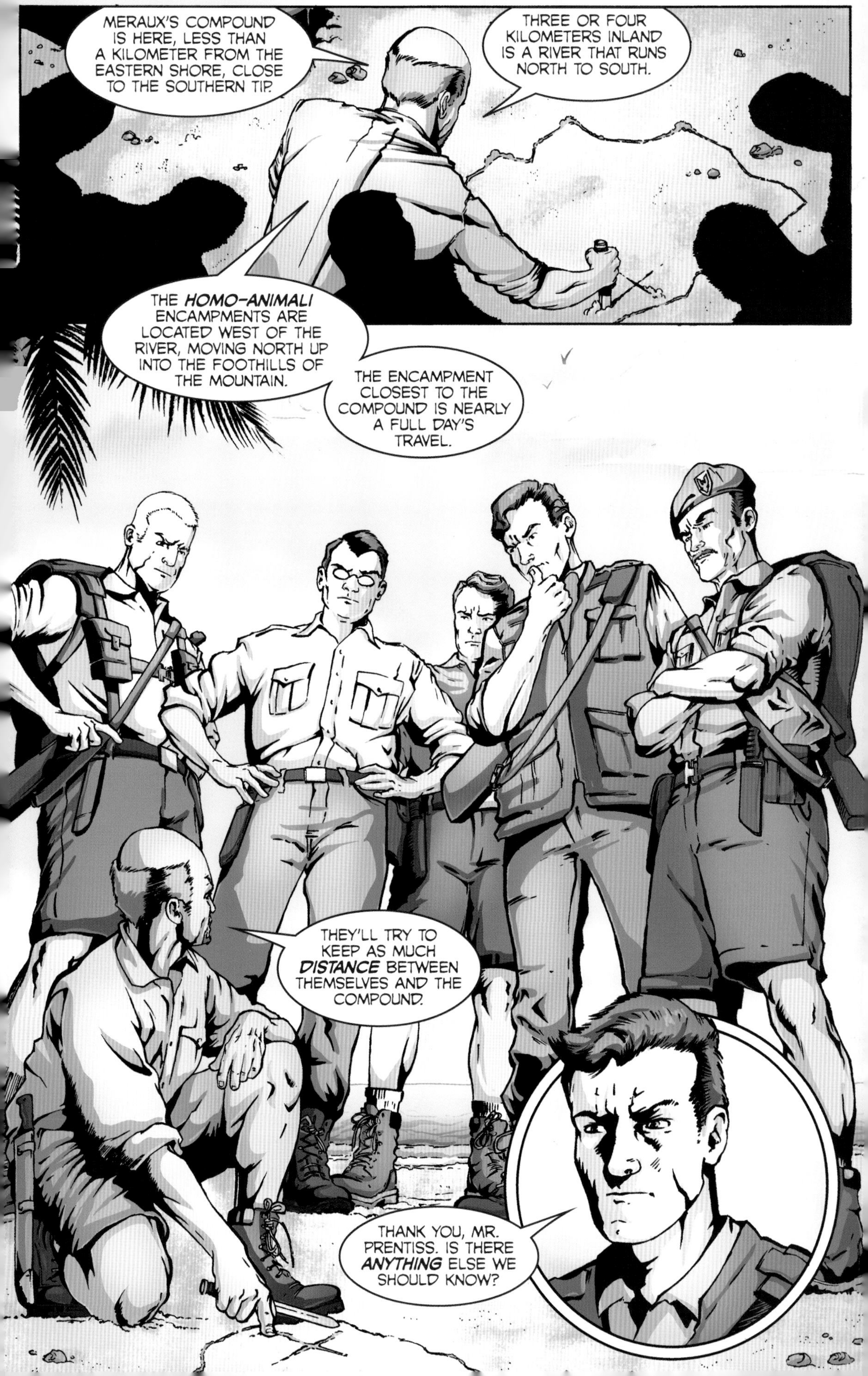
MERAUX'S COMPOUND IS HERE, LESS THAN A KILOMETER FROM THE EASTERN SHORE, CLOSE TO THE SOUTHERN TIP.
THREE OR FOUR KILOMETERS INLAND IS A RIVER THAT RUNS NORTH TO SOUTH.
THE *HOMO-ANIMALI* ENCAMPMENTS ARE LOCATED WEST OF THE RIVER, MOVING NORTH UP INTO THE FOOTHILLS OF THE MOUNTAIN.
THE ENCAMPMENT CLOSEST TO THE COMPOUND IS NEARLY A FULL DAY'S TRAVEL.
THEY'LL TRY TO KEEP AS MUCH *DISTANCE* BETWEEN THEMSELVES AND THE COMPOUND.
THANK YOU, MR. PRENTISS. IS THERE *ANYTHING* ELSE WE SHOULD KNOW?

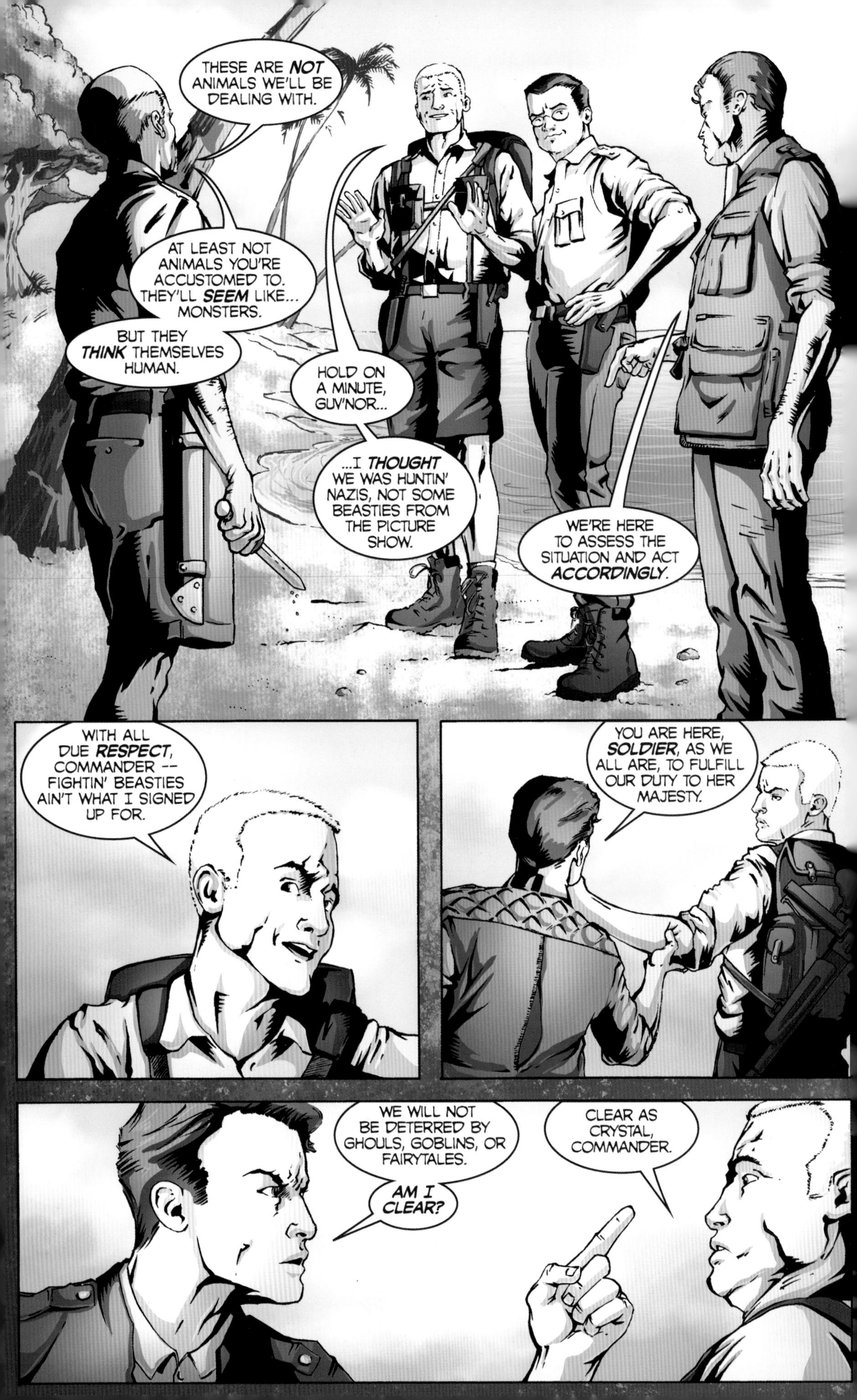
THESE ARE NOT ANIMALS WE'LL BE DEALING WITH.
AT LEAST NOT ANIMALS YOU'RE ACCUSTOMED TO. THEY'LL SEEM LIKE... MONSTERS.
BUT THEY THINK THEMSELVES HUMAN.
HOLD ON A MINUTE, GUV'NOR...
...I THOUGHT WE WAS HUNTIN' NAZIS, NOT SOME BEASTIES FROM THE PICTURE SHOW.
WE'RE HERE TO ASSESS THE SITUATION AND ACT ACCORDINGLY.
WITH ALL DUE RESPECT, COMMANDER -- FIGHTIN' BEASTIES AIN'T WHAT I SIGNED UP FOR.
YOU ARE HERE, SOLDIER, AS WE ALL ARE, TO FULFILL OUR DUTY TO HER MAJESTY.
WE WILL NOT BE DETERRED BY GHOULS, GOBLINS, OR FAIRYTALES.
AM I CLEAR?
CLEAR AS CRYSTAL, COMMANDER.

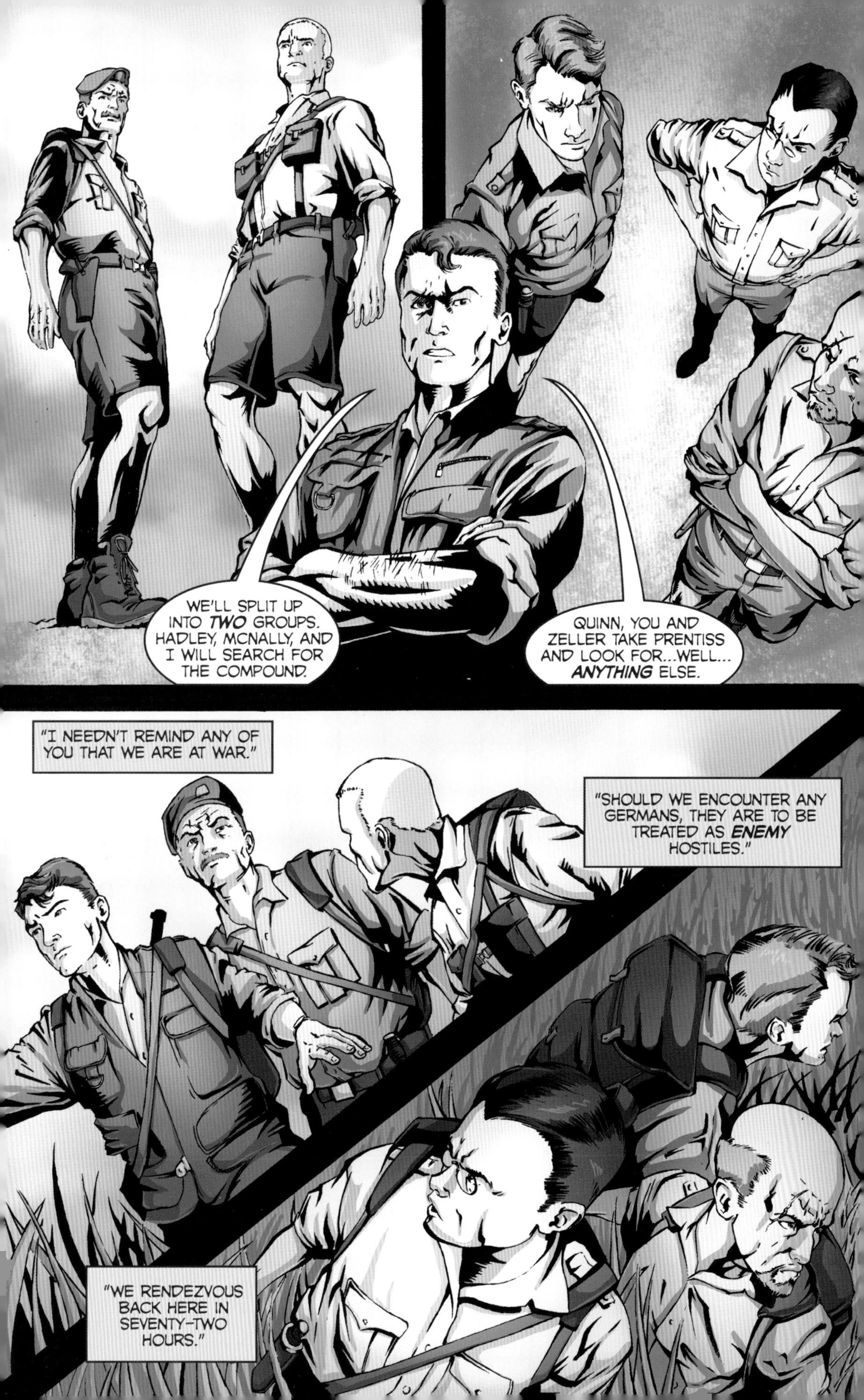
WE'LL SPLIT UP INTO TWO GROUPS. HADLEY, MCNALLY, AND I WILL SEARCH FOR THE COMPOUND.
QUINN, YOU AND ZELLER TAKE PRENTISS AND LOOK FOR...WELL... ANYTHING ELSE.
"I NEEDN'T REMIND ANY OF YOU THAT WE ARE AT WAR."
"SHOULD WE ENCOUNTER ANY GERMANS, THEY ARE TO BE TREATED AS ENEMY HOSTILES."
"WE RENDEZVOUS BACK HERE IN SEVENTY-TWO HOURS."

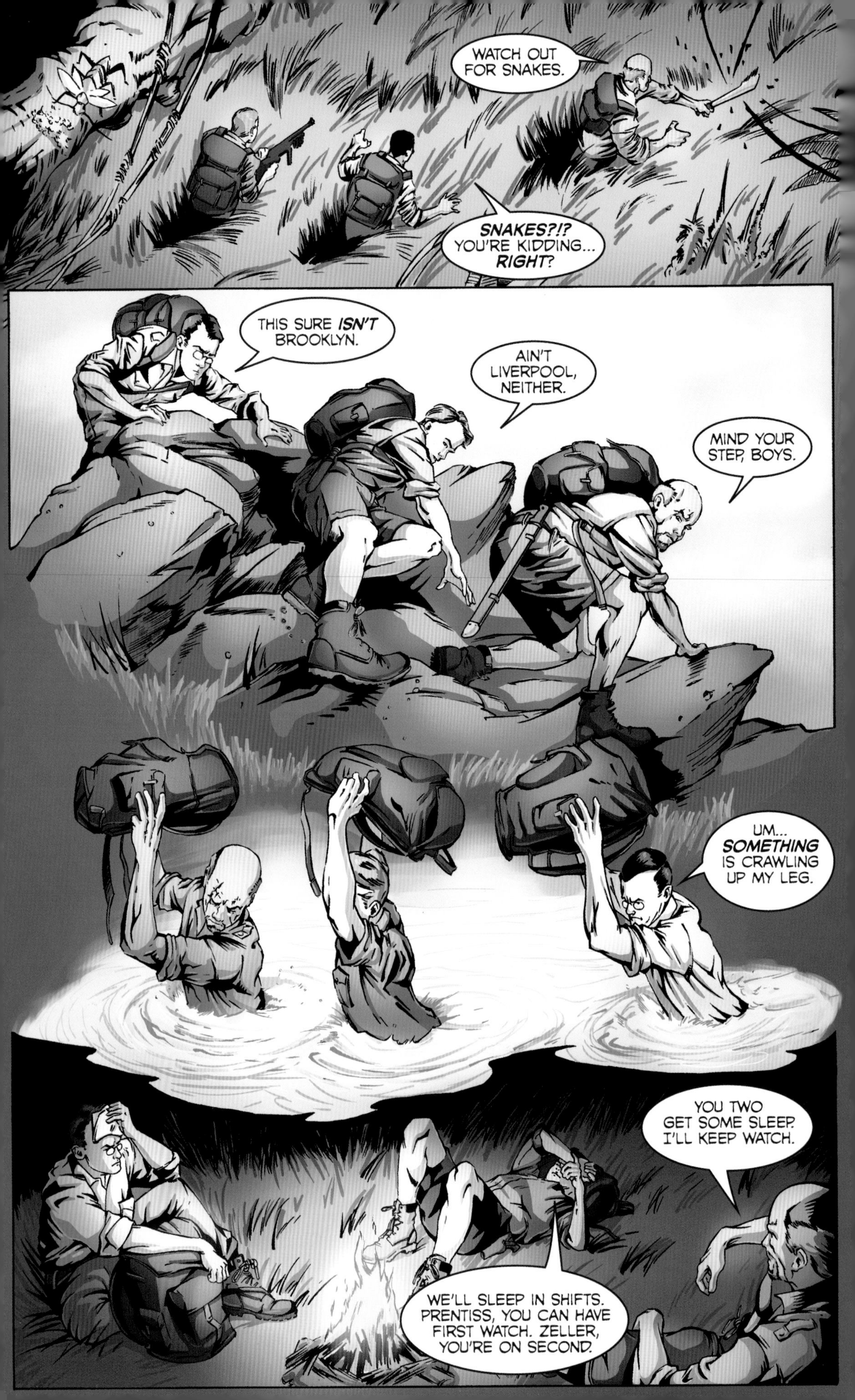
WATCH OUT FOR SNAKES.
SNAKES?!? YOU'RE KIDDING... RIGHT?
THIS SURE ISN'T BROOKLYN.
AIN'T LIVERPOOL, NEITHER.
MIND YOUR STEP, BOYS.
UM... SOMETHING IS CRAWLING UP MY LEG.
YOU TWO GET SOME SLEEP. I'LL KEEP WATCH.
WE'LL SLEEP IN SHIFTS. PRENTISS, YOU CAN HAVE FIRST WATCH. ZELLER, YOU'RE ON SECOND.

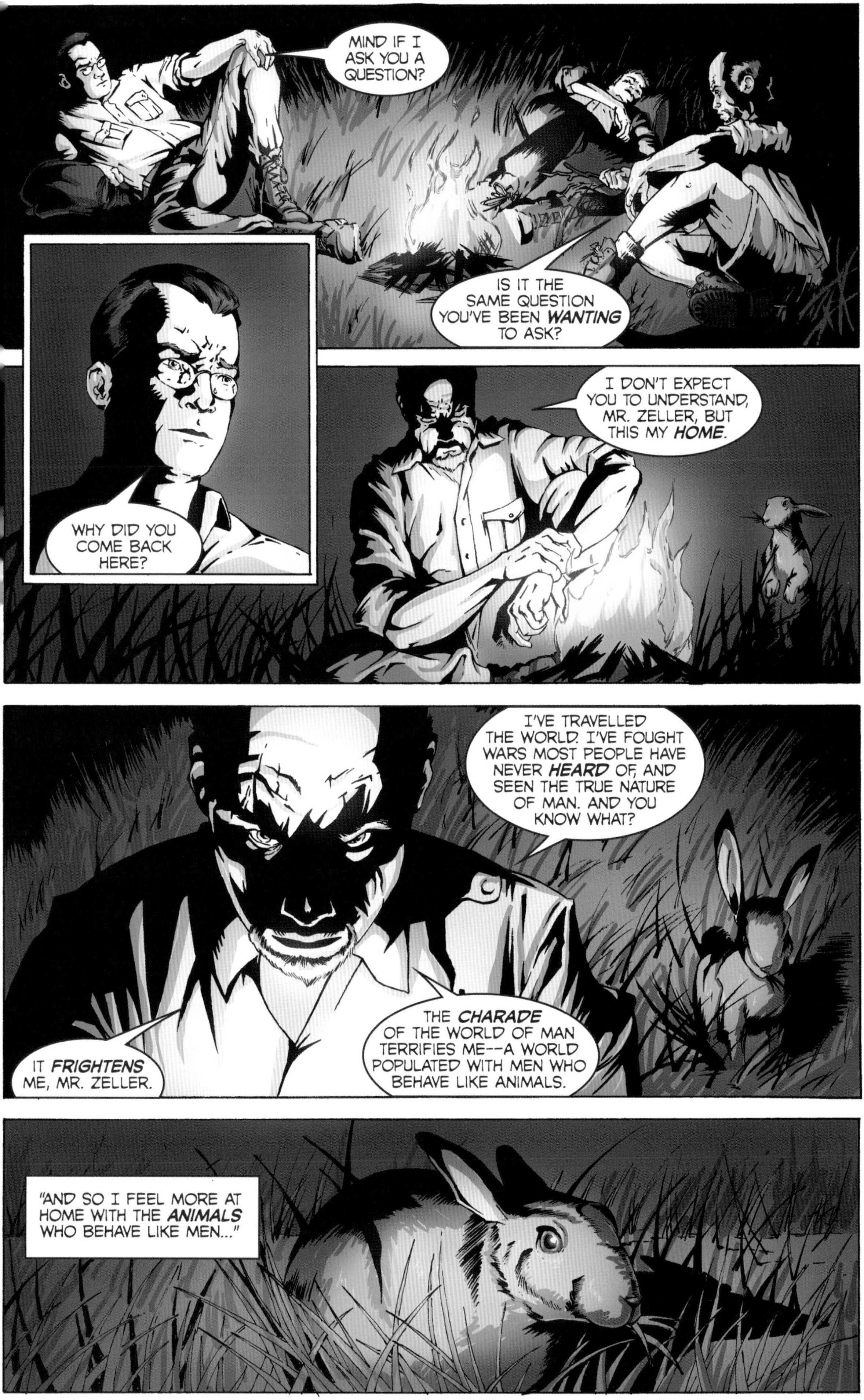

MIND IF I ASK YOU A QUESTION?
IS IT THE SAME QUESTION YOU'VE BEEN *WANTING* TO ASK?
WHY DID YOU COME BACK HERE?
I DON'T EXPECT YOU TO UNDERSTAND, MR. ZELLER, BUT THIS MY *HOME*.
I'VE TRAVELLED THE WORLD. I'VE FOUGHT WARS MOST PEOPLE HAVE NEVER *HEARD* OF, AND SEEN THE TRUE NATURE OF MAN. AND YOU KNOW WHAT?
IT *FRIGHTENS* ME, MR. ZELLER.
THE *CHARADE* OF THE WORLD OF MAN TERRIFIES ME--A WORLD POPULATED WITH MEN WHO BEHAVE LIKE ANIMALS.
"AND SO I FEEL MORE AT HOME WITH THE *ANIMALS* WHO BEHAVE LIKE MEN..."

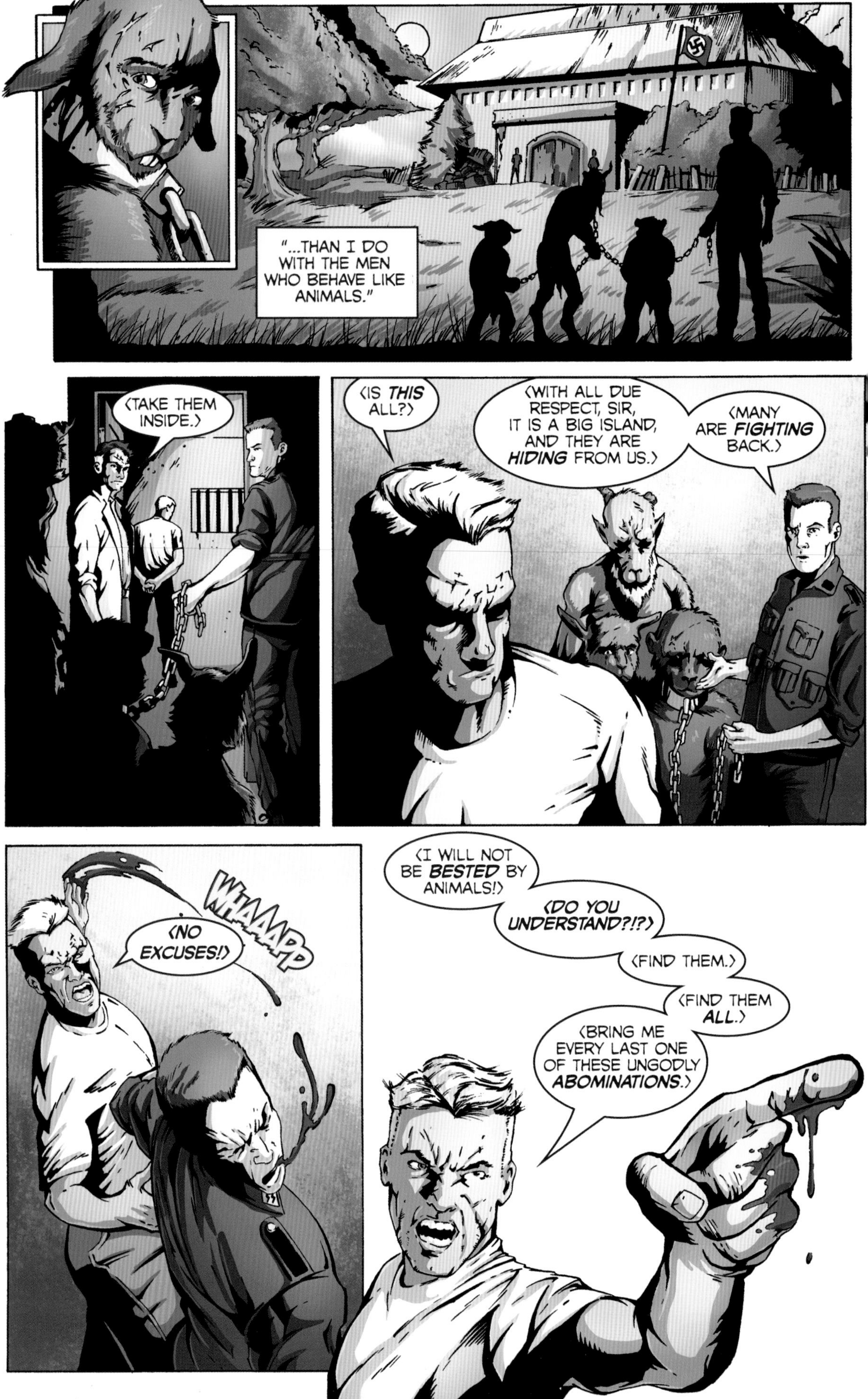
"...THAN I DO WITH THE MEN WHO BEHAVE LIKE ANIMALS."
‹TAKE THEM INSIDE.›
‹IS THIS ALL?›
‹WITH ALL DUE RESPECT, SIR, IT IS A BIG ISLAND, AND THEY ARE HIDING FROM US.›
‹MANY ARE FIGHTING BACK.›
WHAAAPP
‹NO EXCUSES!›
‹I WILL NOT BE BESTED BY ANIMALS!›
‹DO YOU UNDERSTAND?!?›
‹FIND THEM.›
‹FIND THEM ALL.›
‹BRING ME EVERY LAST ONE OF THESE UNGODLY ABOMINATIONS.›

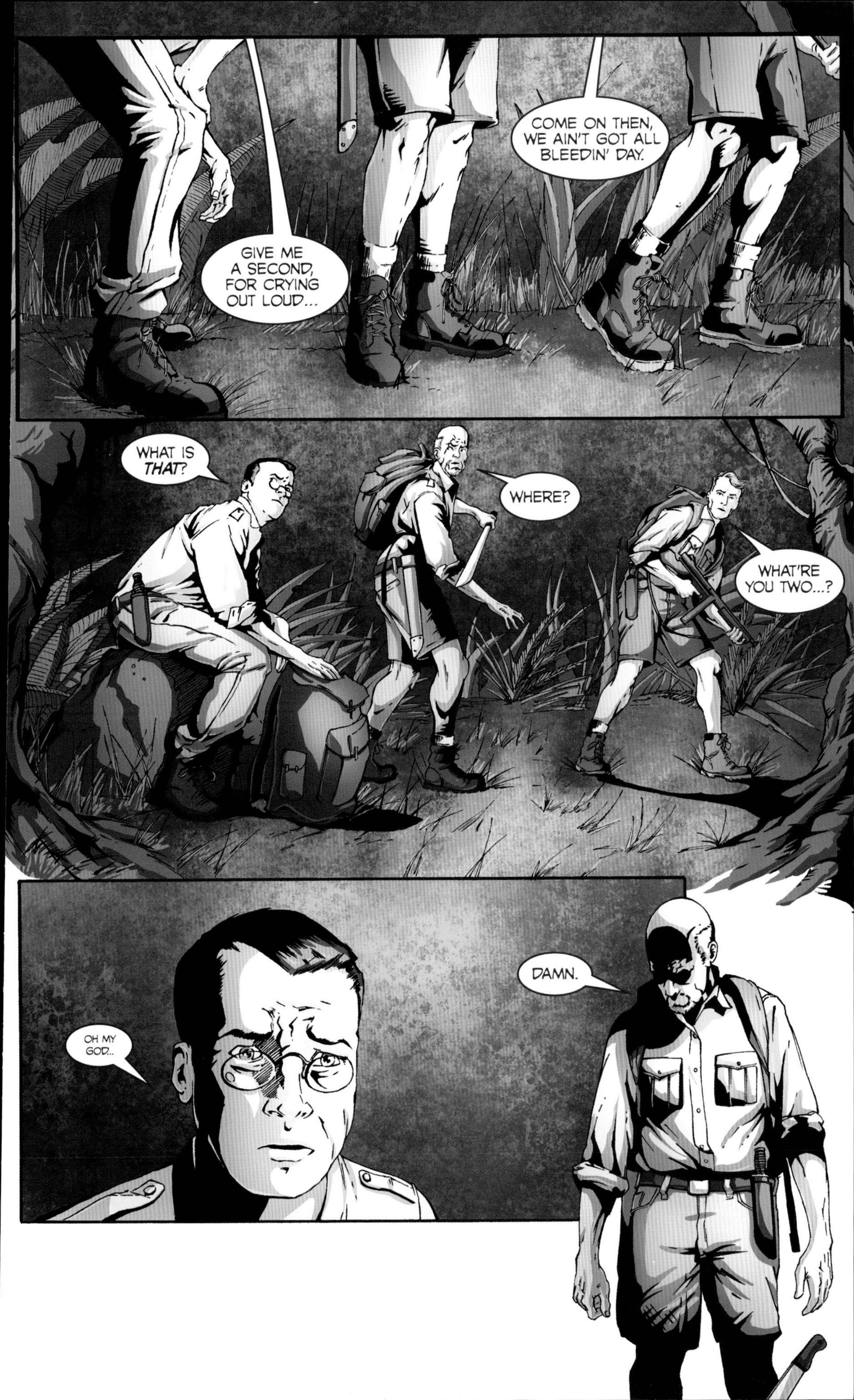
GIVE ME A SECOND, FOR CRYING OUT LOUD...
COME ON THEN, WE AIN'T GOT ALL BLEEDIN' DAY.
WHAT IS *THAT*?
WHERE?
WHAT'RE YOU TWO...?
OH MY GOD...
DAMN.

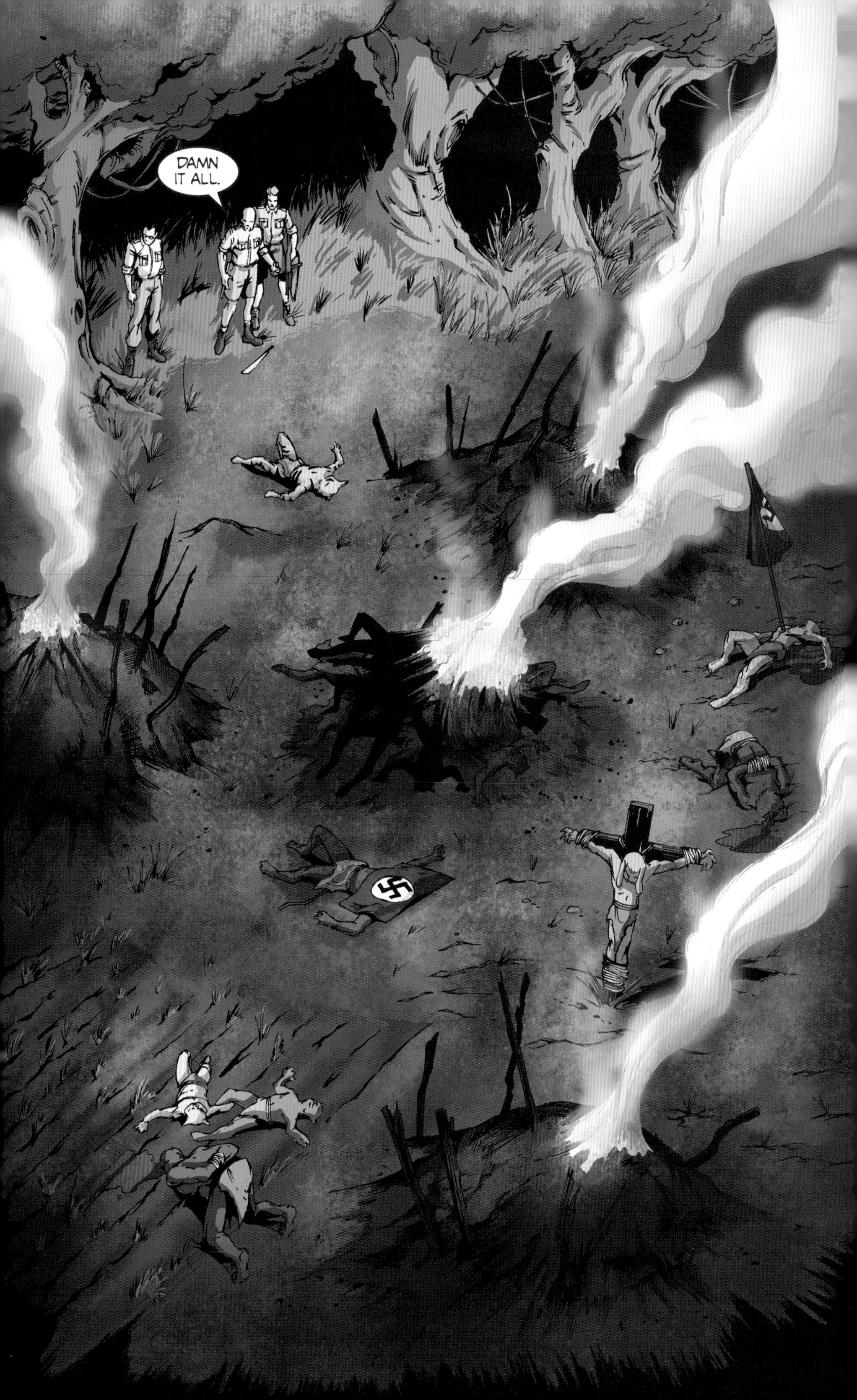
DAMN IT ALL.

Zeller, A. - Correspondence

TOP SECRET

THIS IS A COVER SHEET

BASIC SECURITY REQUIREMENTS ARE CONTAINED IN AR 380-5

THE UNAUTHORIZED DISCLOSURE OF THE INFORMATION CONTAINED IN THE ATTACHED DOCUMENT(S) COULD RESULT IN EXCEPTIONALLY GRAVE DANGER TO THE UNITED STATES

RESPONSIBILITY OF PERSONS HANDLING THE ATTACHED DOCUMENT(S)

1. Enter on DA Form 969 your name and the date you had access to the document(s).
2. Exercise the necessary safeguards to prevent unauthorized disclosure by never leaving the document(s) unattended except when properly secured in a locked safe.
3. Transfer the document(s) only to persons who need to know and who possess the required security clearance.
4. Obtain a receipt whenever relinquishing control of the document(s).

STORAGE

Store as prescribed in AR 380-5.

REPRODUCTION

TOP SECRET material may be copied, extracted, or reproduced only when the classifying authority has authorized such actions.

DISPOSITION

This cover sheet should be removed when document(s) are filed in a permanent file, declassified, destroyed, or mailed.

(This cover sheet is unclassified when separated from classified documents)

TOP SECRET

DA LABEL 24
1 FEB 59

PREVIOUS EDITIONS OF THIS LABEL ARE OBSOLETE

AGL (1) 4-59-40M-71603

Department of the Navy
Office of Naval Intelligence
1650 Pennsylvania Avenue N.W.
Washington, D.C. 20502

<u>TOP SECRET</u>   Oct. 8, 1939

From: Lt. Zeller, Naval Intelligence
To: Gen. Musgrove, Army Intelligence

Subject: Intercepted German Correspondence/Photographs

Gen. Musgrove,

Having shared my conclusions with Col. Eaton, I feel it
most important to follow up on the matter involving the
German communiqué intercepted last month in Panama. I
have studied the photographs, and though I am at a loss
to identify what is in the pictures, I am certain that it
is not an actor in make-up, as has been suggested. While I
agree that make-up can be used to transform actors into
what appear to be hideous monsters, this is not what we
are dealing with.

I have taken the liberty of sending along several exam-
ples of what make-up is capable of achieving, which I
encourage you to compare with the photos we intercepted.
It is clear that whatever is in the German photos is not
an actor like Boris Karloff or Bela Lugosi in make-up.
This can only lead to the conclusion that we are dealing
with something beyond our scope of understanding. As you
know all too well, the Nazis have a reputation of
experimenting with the unknown and the supernatural (as
evidenced several years ago with the situation in Egypt),
and it is for this reason I strongly recommend that we
treat "Operation: Kreatürlich Soldaten" as a viable
threat.

Chapter Four

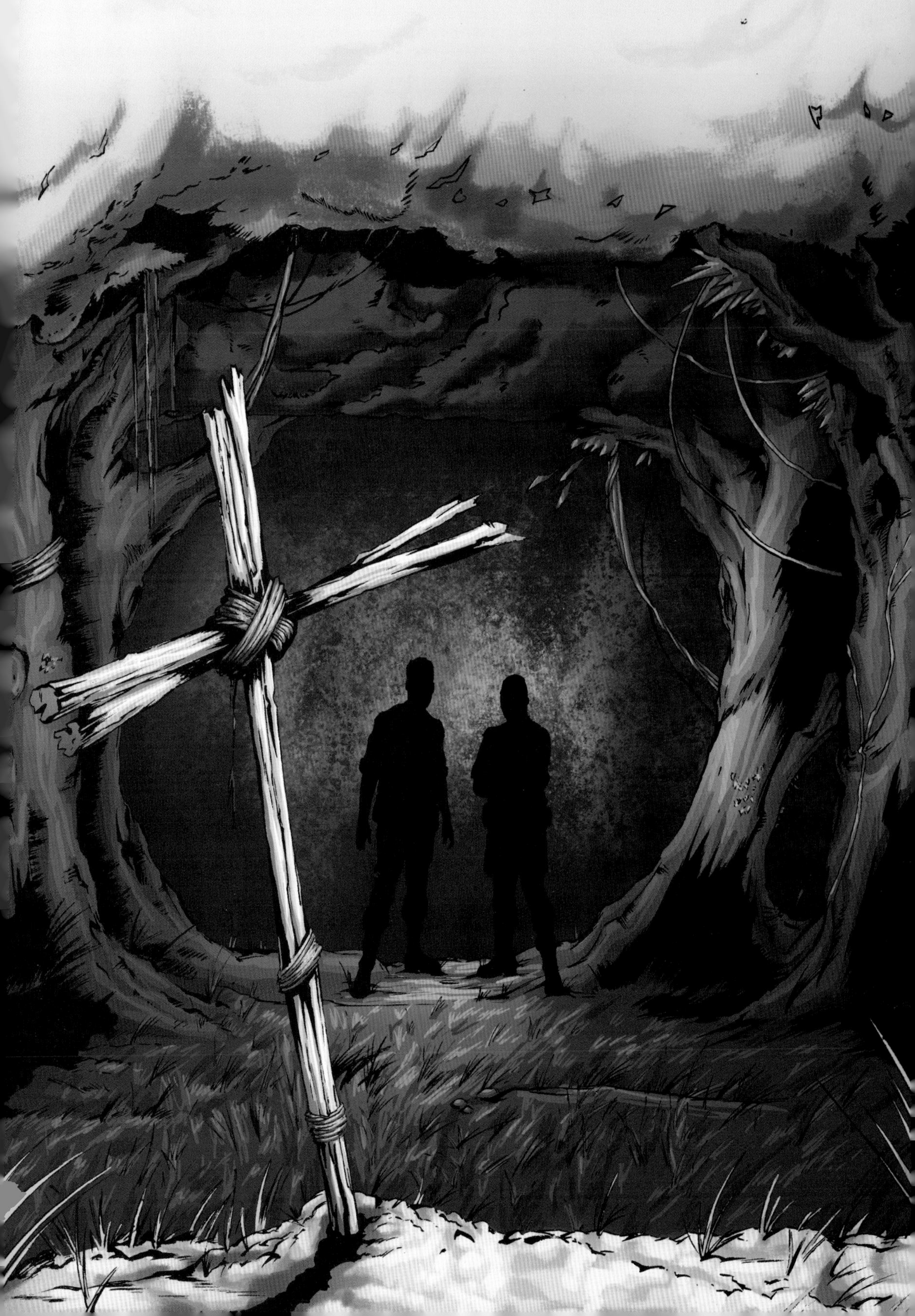

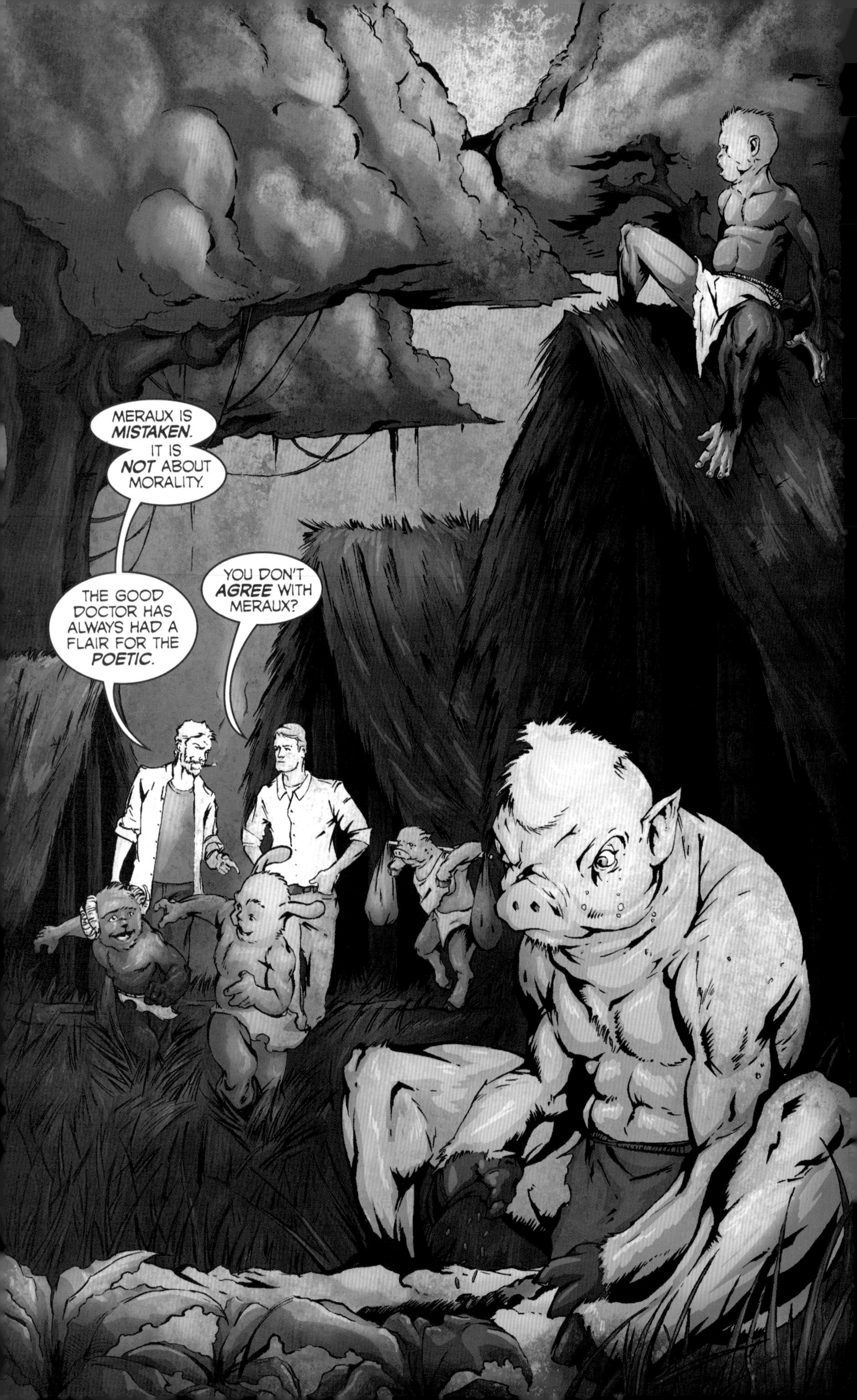
MERAUX IS MISTAKEN. IT IS NOT ABOUT MORALITY.
THE GOOD DOCTOR HAS ALWAYS HAD A FLAIR FOR THE POETIC.
YOU DON'T AGREE WITH MERAUX?

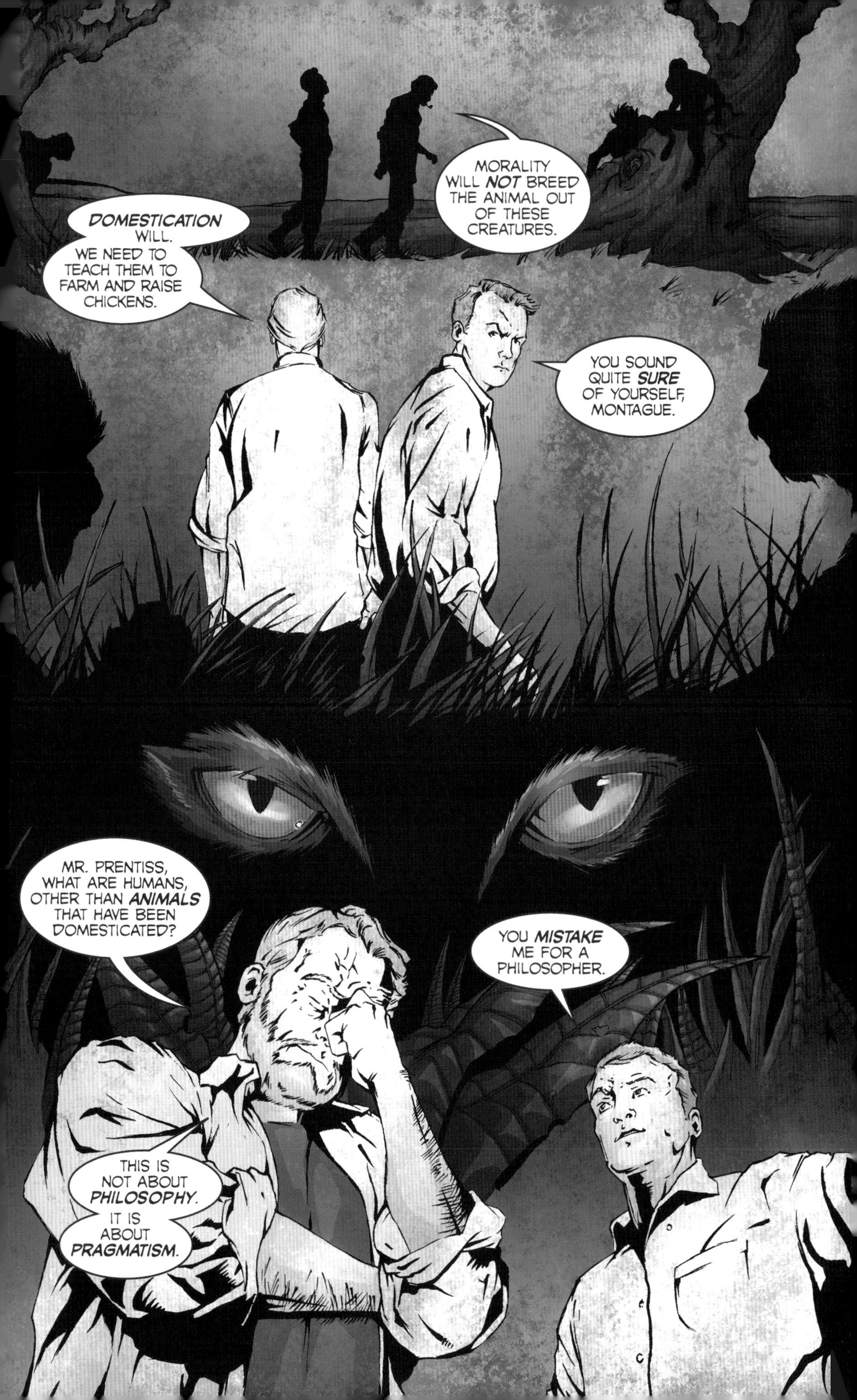
MORALITY WILL **NOT** BREED THE ANIMAL OUT OF THESE CREATURES.
DOMESTICATION WILL.
WE NEED TO TEACH THEM TO FARM AND RAISE CHICKENS.
YOU SOUND QUITE ***SURE*** OF YOURSELF, MONTAGUE.
MR. PRENTISS, WHAT ARE HUMANS, OTHER THAN ***ANIMALS*** THAT HAVE BEEN DOMESTICATED?
YOU ***MISTAKE*** ME FOR A PHILOSOPHER.
THIS IS NOT ABOUT ***PHILOSOPHY***.
IT IS ABOUT ***PRAGMATISM***.

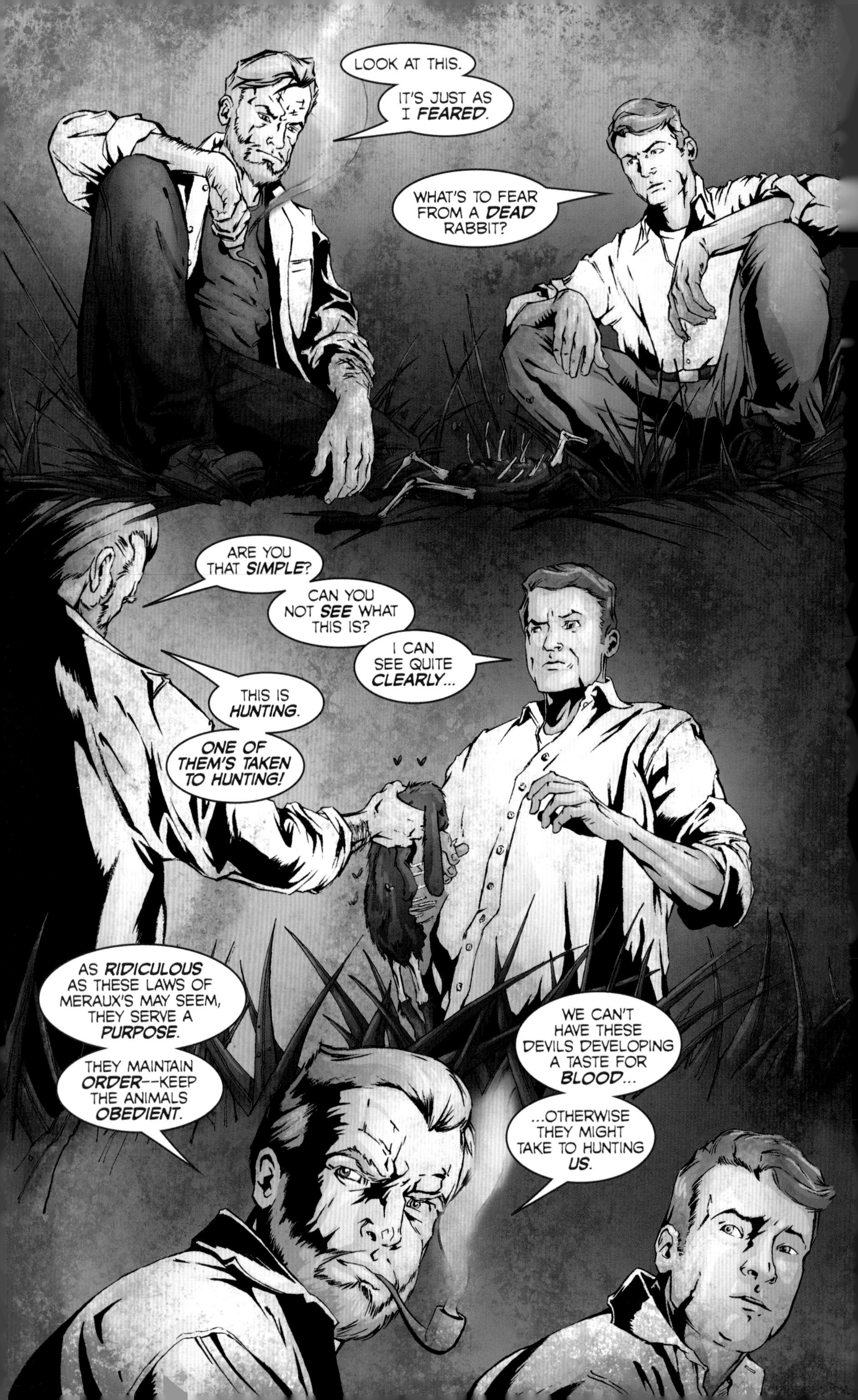
LOOK AT THIS.
IT'S JUST AS I FEARED.
WHAT'S TO FEAR FROM A DEAD RABBIT?
ARE YOU THAT SIMPLE?
CAN YOU NOT SEE WHAT THIS IS?
I CAN SEE QUITE CLEARLY...
THIS IS HUNTING.
ONE OF THEM'S TAKEN TO HUNTING!
AS RIDICULOUS AS THESE LAWS OF MERAUX'S MAY SEEM, THEY SERVE A PURPOSE.
THEY MAINTAIN ORDER--KEEP THE ANIMALS OBEDIENT.
WE CAN'T HAVE THESE DEVILS DEVELOPING A TASTE FOR BLOOD...
...OTHERWISE THEY MIGHT TAKE TO HUNTING US.

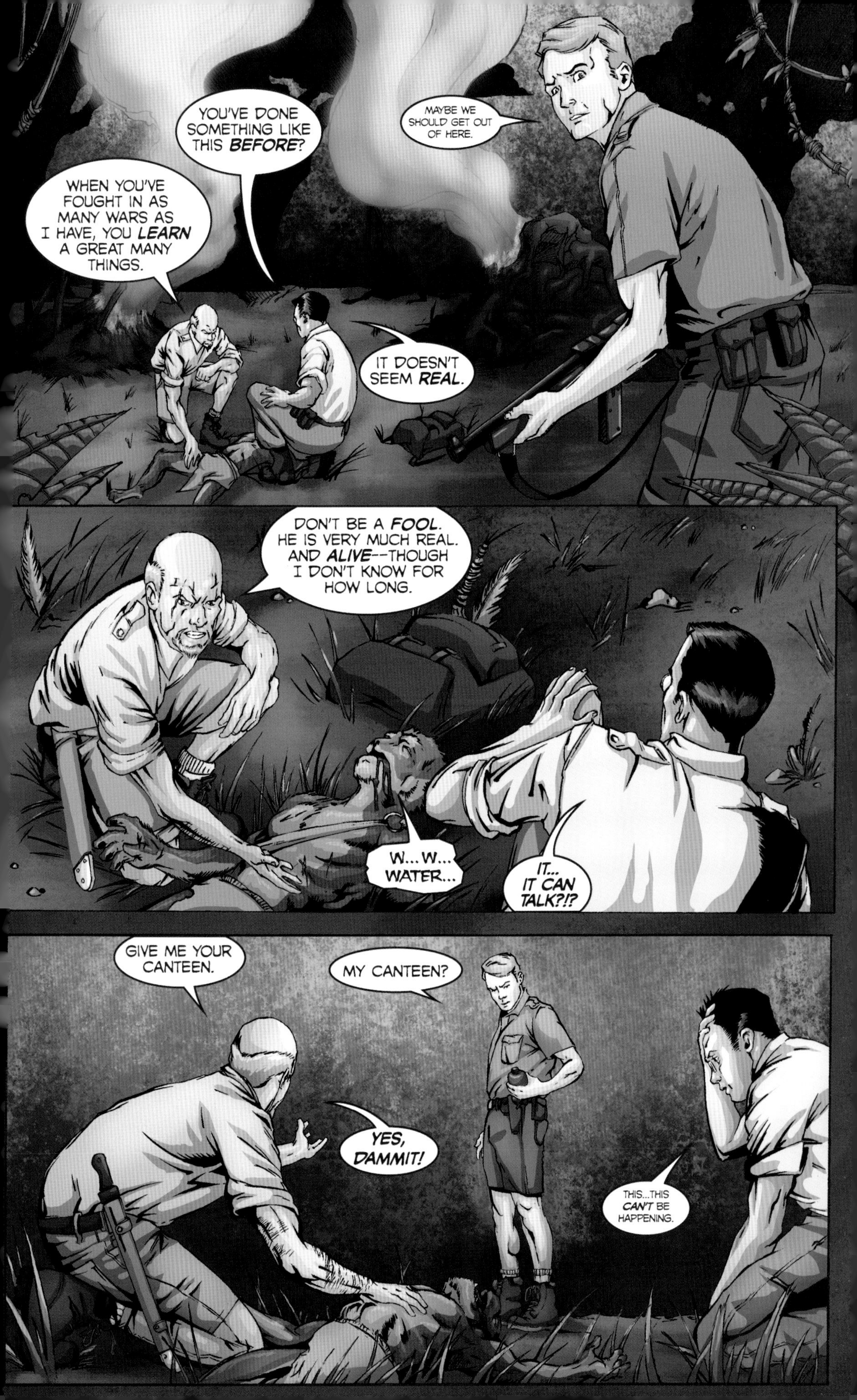
WHEN YOU'VE FOUGHT IN AS MANY WARS AS I HAVE, YOU LEARN A GREAT MANY THINGS.
YOU'VE DONE SOMETHING LIKE THIS BEFORE?
MAYBE WE SHOULD GET OUT OF HERE.
IT DOESN'T SEEM REAL.
DON'T BE A FOOL. HE IS VERY MUCH REAL. AND ALIVE--THOUGH I DON'T KNOW FOR HOW LONG.
W... W... WATER...
IT... IT CAN TALK?!?
GIVE ME YOUR CANTEEN.
MY CANTEEN?
YES, DAMMIT!
THIS...THIS CAN'T BE HAPPENING.

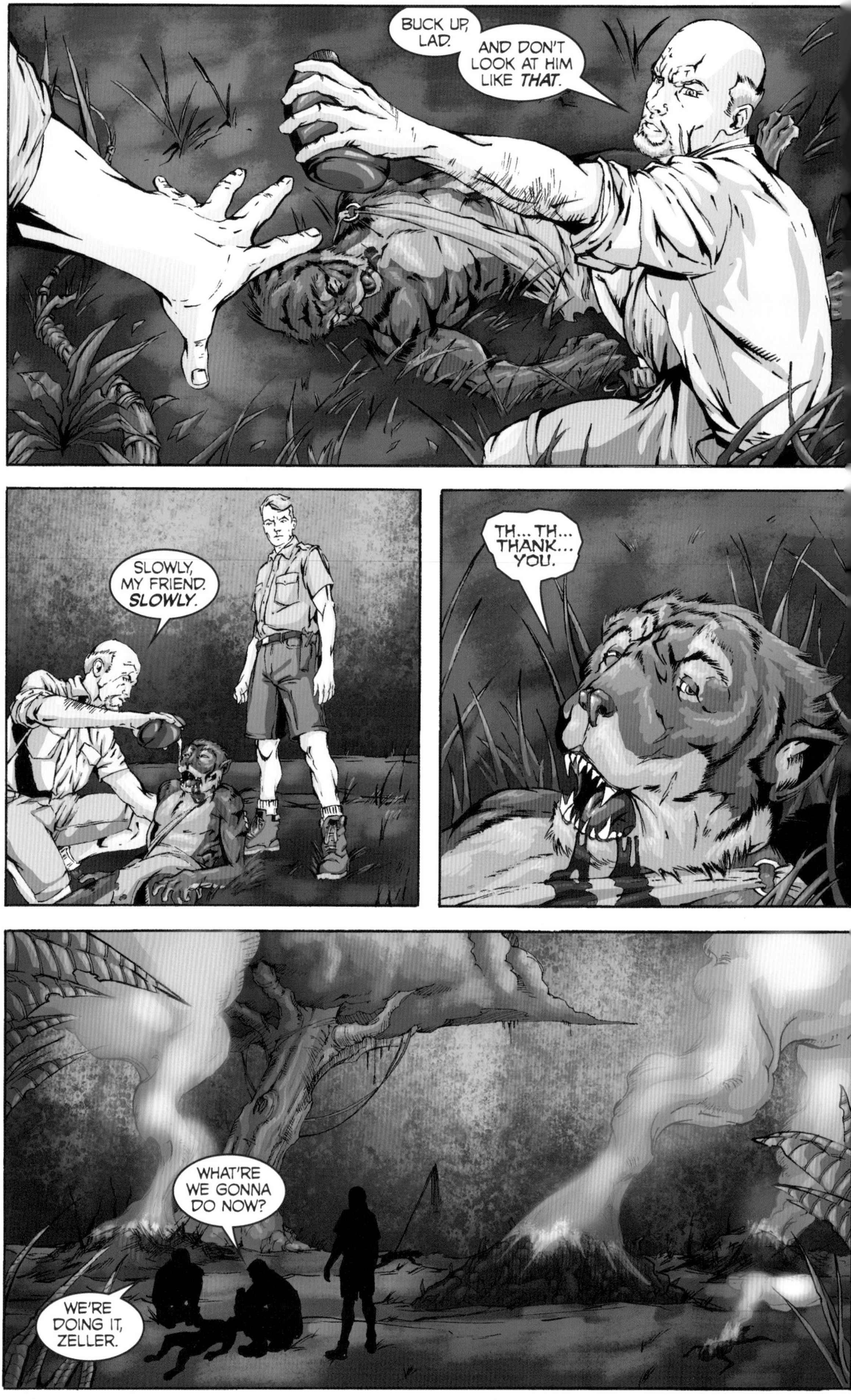
BUCK UP, LAD.
AND DON'T LOOK AT HIM LIKE *THAT*.
SLOWLY, MY FRIEND. ***SLOWLY***.
TH... TH... THANK... YOU.
WHAT'RE WE GONNA DO NOW?
WE'RE DOING IT, ZELLER.

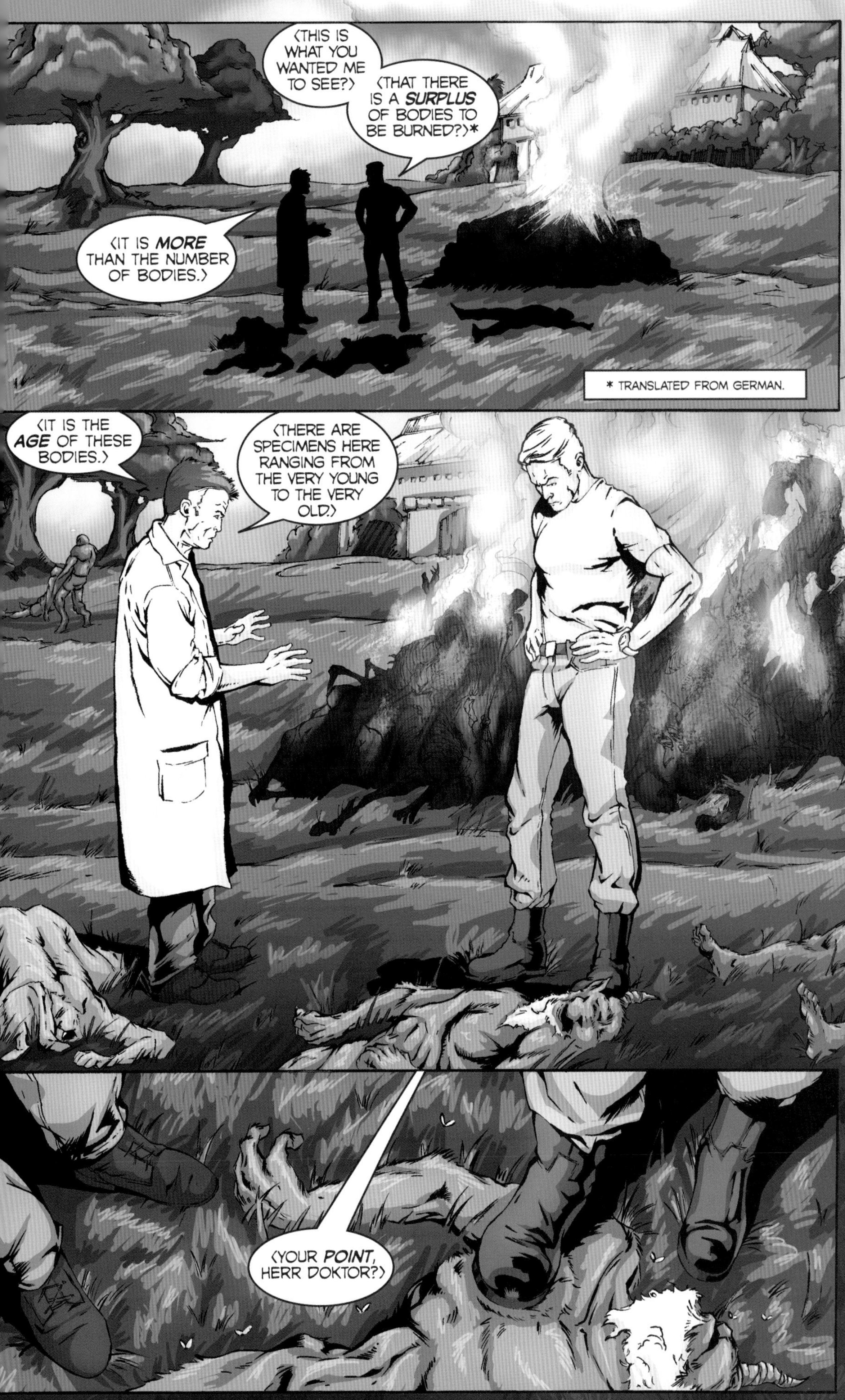
<THIS IS WHAT YOU WANTED ME TO SEE?>
<THAT THERE IS A ***SURPLUS*** OF BODIES TO BE BURNED?>*
<IT IS ***MORE*** THAN THE NUMBER OF BODIES.>
* TRANSLATED FROM GERMAN.
<IT IS THE ***AGE*** OF THESE BODIES.>
<THERE ARE SPECIMENS HERE RANGING FROM THE VERY YOUNG TO THE VERY OLD.>
<YOUR ***POINT***, HERR DOKTOR?>

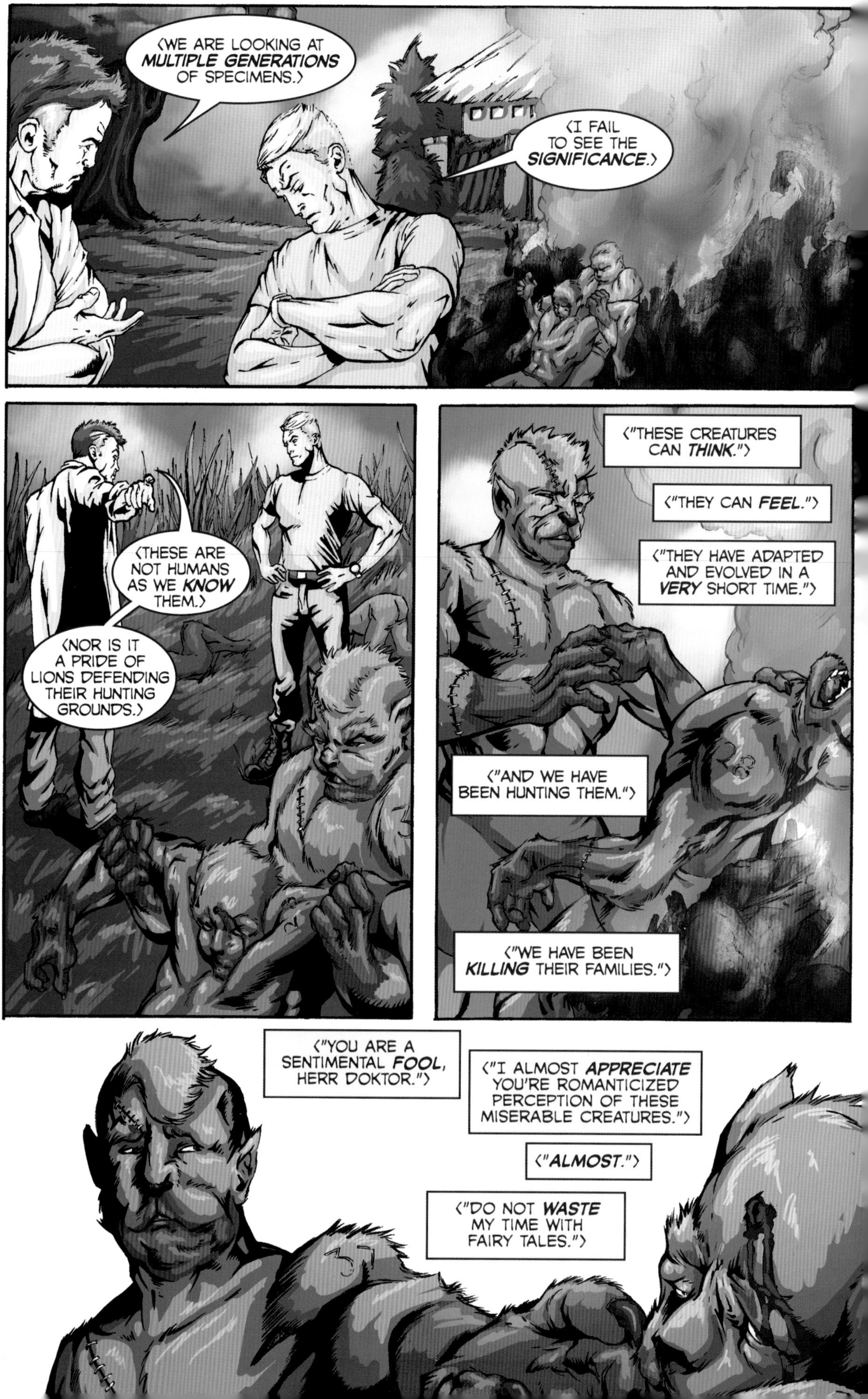
‹WE ARE LOOKING AT MULTIPLE GENERATIONS OF SPECIMENS.›
‹I FAIL TO SEE THE SIGNIFICANCE.›
‹THESE ARE NOT HUMANS AS WE KNOW THEM.›
‹NOR IS IT A PRIDE OF LIONS DEFENDING THEIR HUNTING GROUNDS.›
‹"THESE CREATURES CAN THINK."›
‹"THEY CAN FEEL."›
‹"THEY HAVE ADAPTED AND EVOLVED IN A VERY SHORT TIME."›
‹"AND WE HAVE BEEN HUNTING THEM."›
‹"WE HAVE BEEN KILLING THEIR FAMILIES."›
‹"YOU ARE A SENTIMENTAL FOOL, HERR DOKTOR."›
‹"I ALMOST APPRECIATE YOU'RE ROMANTICIZED PERCEPTION OF THESE MISERABLE CREATURES."›
‹"ALMOST."›
‹"DO NOT WASTE MY TIME WITH FAIRY TALES."›

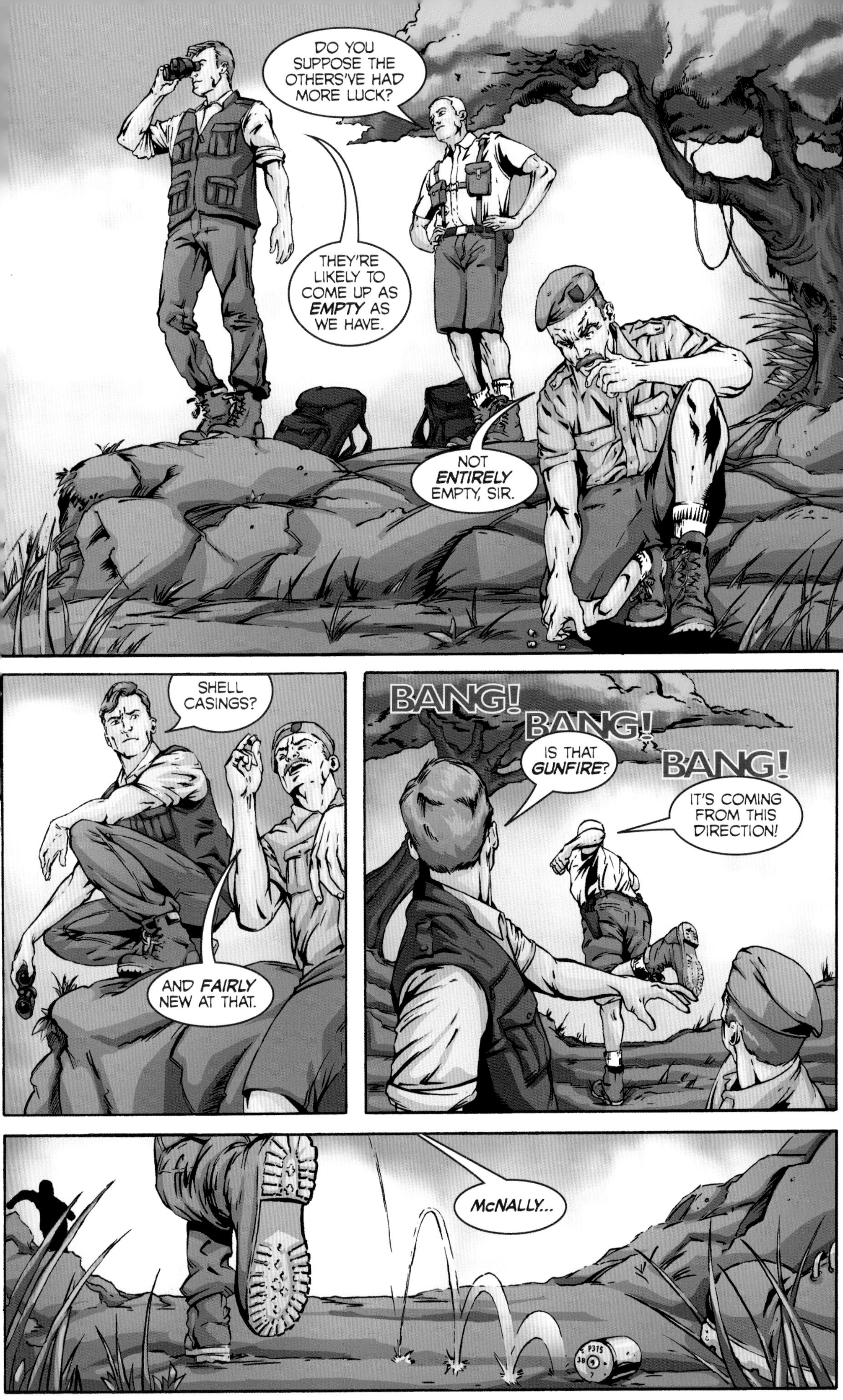
DO YOU SUPPOSE THE OTHERS'VE HAD MORE LUCK?
THEY'RE LIKELY TO COME UP AS EMPTY AS WE HAVE.
NOT ENTIRELY EMPTY, SIR.
SHELL CASINGS?
AND FAIRLY NEW AT THAT.
BANG!
BANG!
IS THAT GUNFIRE?
BANG!
IT'S COMING FROM THIS DIRECTION!
McNALLY...

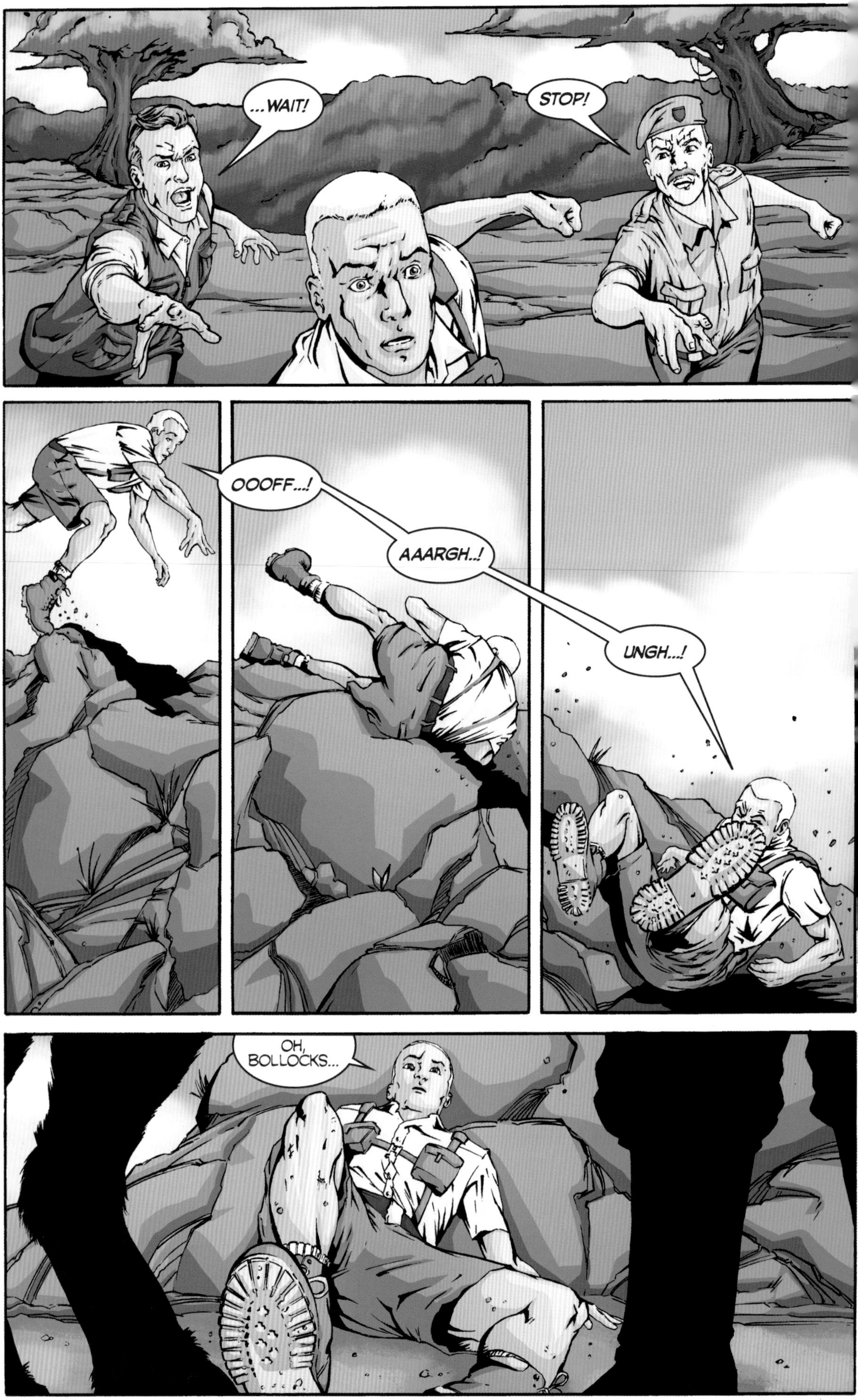
...WAIT!
STOP!
OOOFF...!
AAARGH..!
UNGH...!
OH, BOLLOCKS...

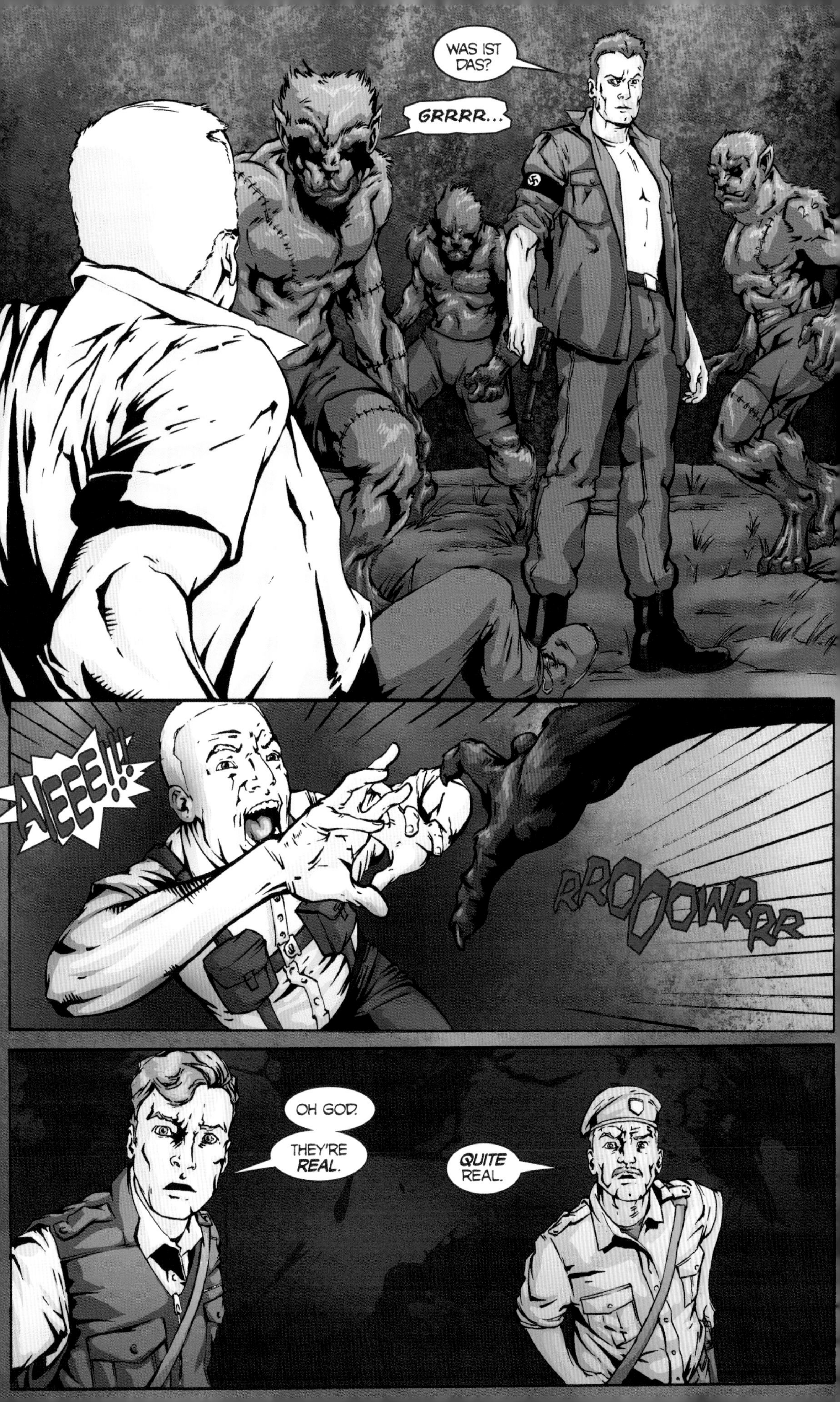
WAS IST DAS?
GRRRR...
AIEEE!!!
RROOOOWRRRR
OH GOD.
THEY'RE *REAL*.
QUITE REAL.

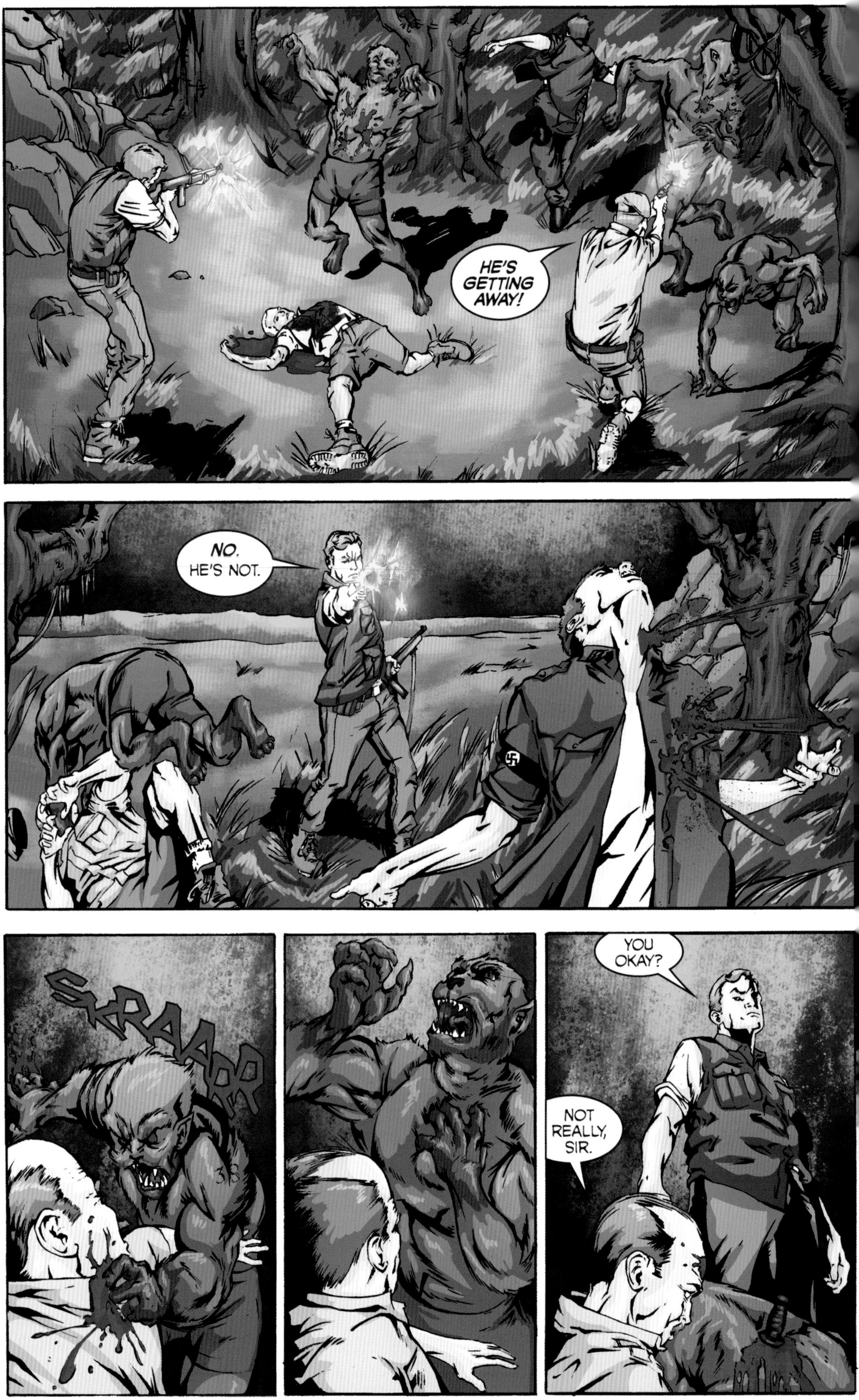
HE'S GETTING AWAY!
NO. HE'S NOT.
SKRAAARR
YOU OKAY?
NOT REALLY, SIR.

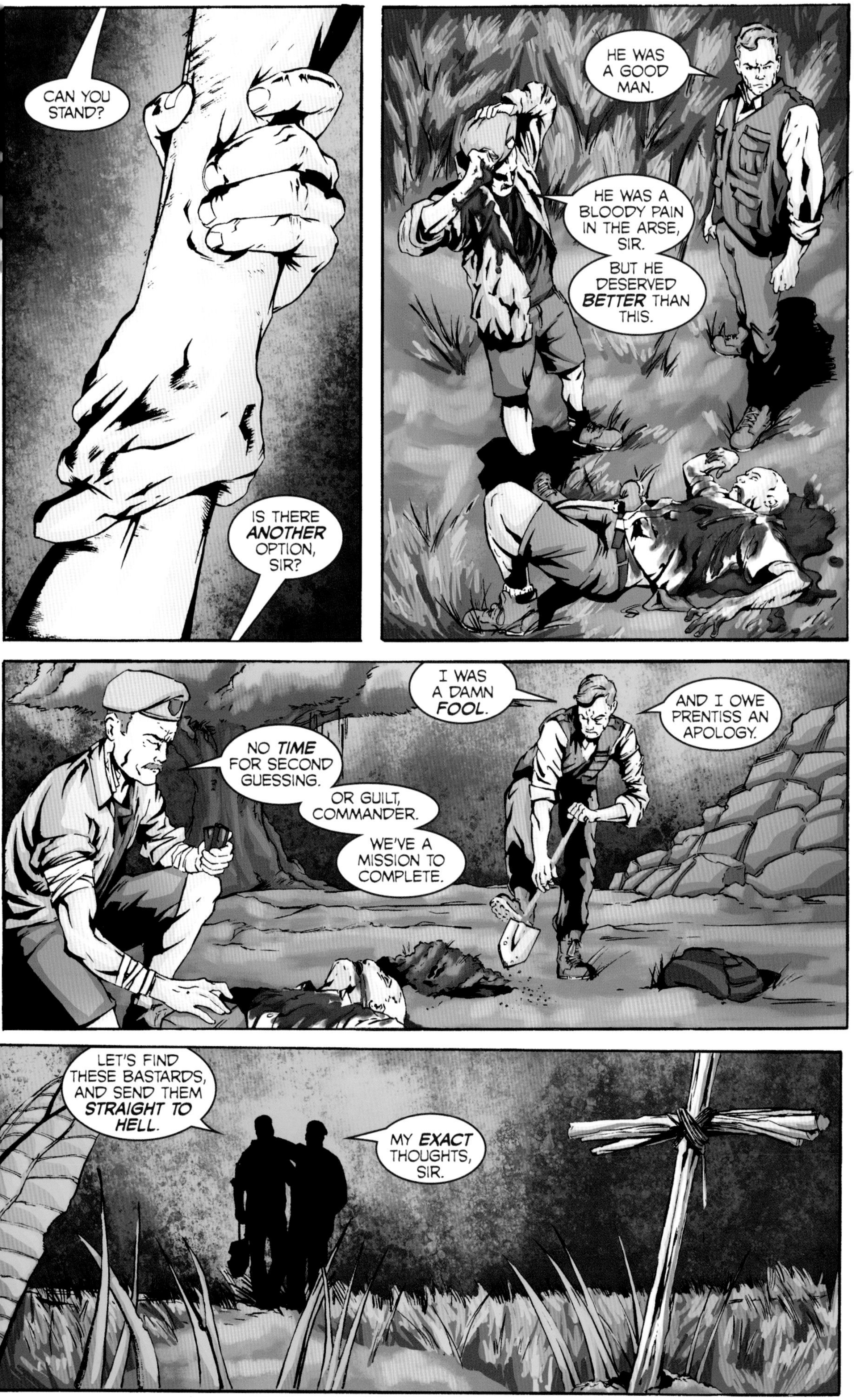
CAN YOU STAND?
IS THERE ANOTHER OPTION, SIR?
HE WAS A GOOD MAN.
HE WAS A BLOODY PAIN IN THE ARSE, SIR.
BUT HE DESERVED BETTER THAN THIS.
I WAS A DAMN FOOL.
AND I OWE PRENTISS AN APOLOGY.
NO TIME FOR SECOND GUESSING.
OR GUILT, COMMANDER.
WE'VE A MISSION TO COMPLETE.
LET'S FIND THESE BASTARDS, AND SEND THEM STRAIGHT TO HELL.
MY EXACT THOUGHTS, SIR.

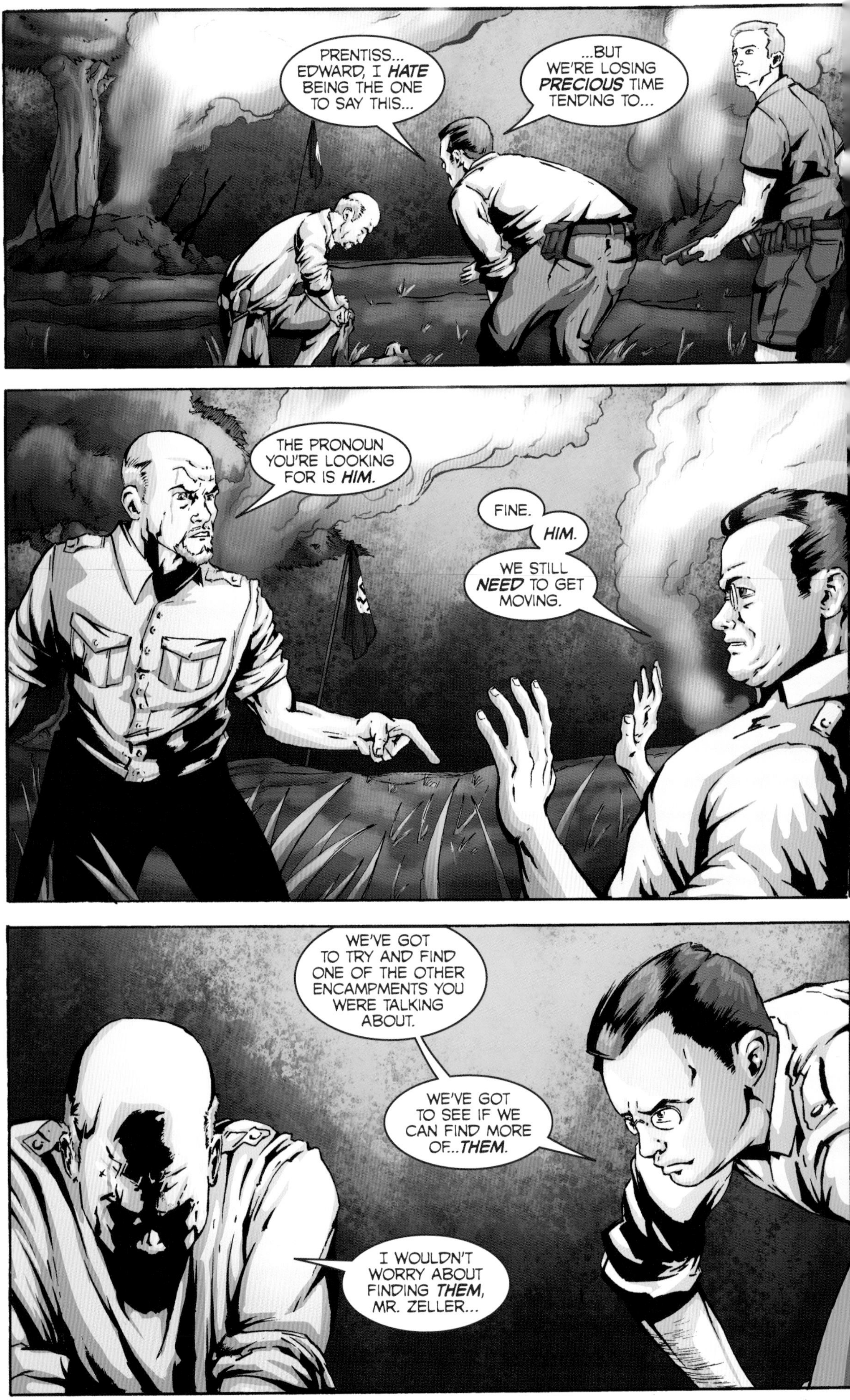
PRENTISS... EDWARD, I *HATE* BEING THE ONE TO SAY THIS...
...BUT WE'RE LOSING *PRECIOUS* TIME TENDING TO...
THE PRONOUN YOU'RE LOOKING FOR IS *HIM*.
FINE.
HIM.
WE STILL *NEED* TO GET MOVING.
WE'VE GOT TO TRY AND FIND ONE OF THE OTHER ENCAMPMENTS YOU WERE TALKING ABOUT.
WE'VE GOT TO SEE IF WE CAN FIND MORE OF...*THEM*.
I WOULDN'T WORRY ABOUT FINDING *THEM*, MR. ZELLER...

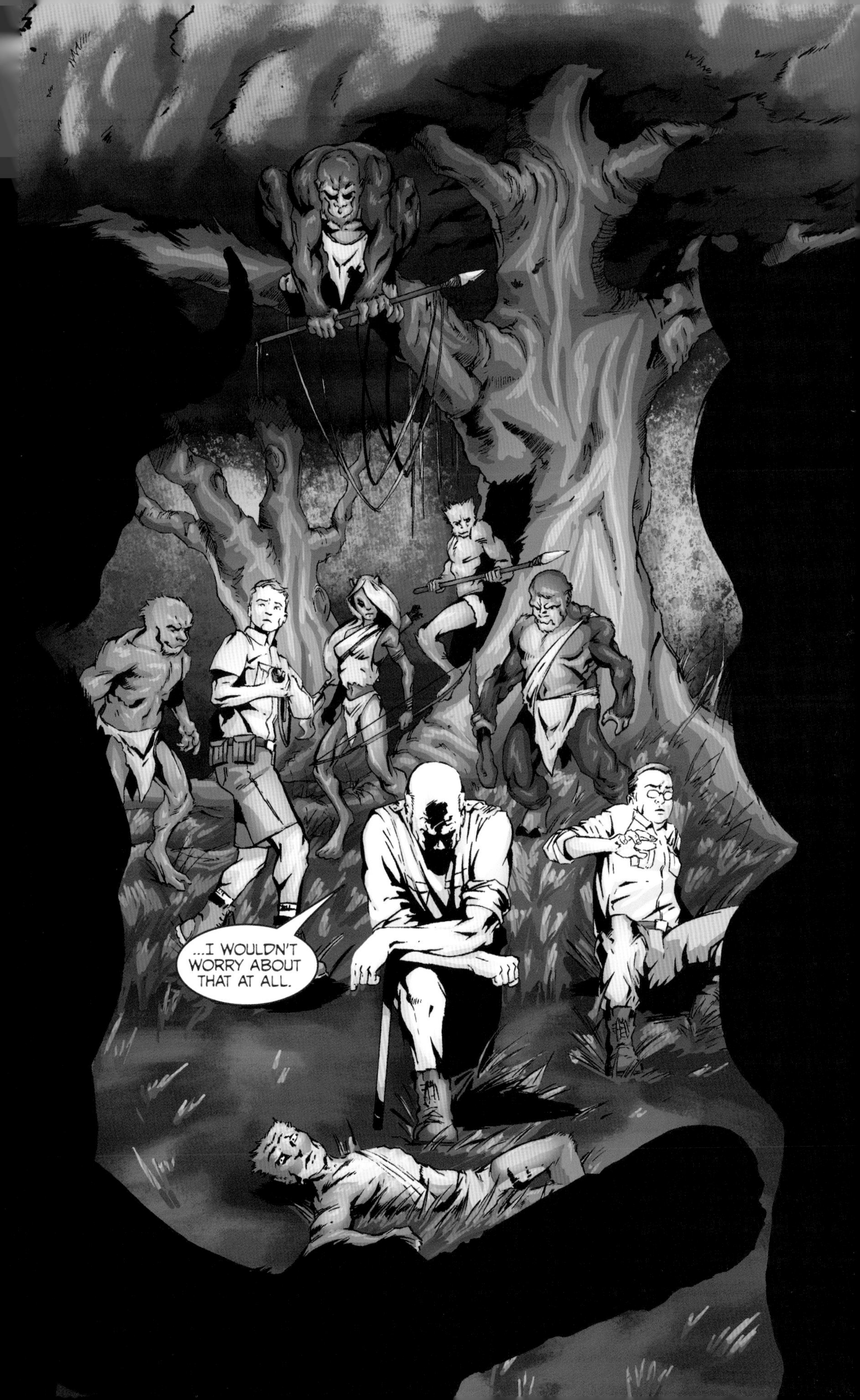
...I WOULDN'T WORRY ABOUT THAT AT ALL.

TOP SECRET

THIS IS A COVER SHEET

BASIC SECURITY REQUIREMENTS ARE CONTAINED IN AR 380–5

THE UNAUTHORIZED DISCLOSURE OF THE INFORMATION CONTAINED IN THE ATTACHED DOCUMENT(S) COULD RESULT IN EXCEPTIONALLY GRAVE DANGER TO THE UNITED STATES

RESPONSIBILITY OF PERSONS HANDLING THE ATTACHED DOCUMENT(S)

1. Enter on DA Form 969 your name and the date you had access to the document(s).
2. Exercise the necessary safeguards to prevent unauthorized disclosure by never leaving the document(s) unattended except when properly secured in a locked safe.
3. Transfer the document(s) only to persons who need to know and who possess the required security clearance.
4. Obtain a receipt whenever relinquishing control of the document(s).

STORAGE

Store as prescribed in AR 380–5.

REPRODUCTION

TOP SECRET material may be copied, extracted, or reproduced only when the classifying authority has authorized such actions.

DISPOSITION

This cover sheet should be removed when document(s) are filed in a permanent file, declassified, destroyed, or mailed.

(This cover sheet is unclassified when separated from classified documents)

TOP SECRET

Prentiss, E. - Journal

TOP SECRET

September ? 1894

Though I know not the full duration of my stay thus far, of this I am certain, more than a full month has passed. I know this from having tracked the stages of the moon. I know that it is some time in the month of September, though again, the exact date eludes me. If either Meraux of Montague keeps track of the date, they do not feel compelled to share such information. Likewise, when I inquire as to when the next supply vessel shall weigh anchor, both my host and his dutiful assistant remain evasive.

Neither Meraux nor Montague seem to know how many of these creatures inhabit the island. I myself have identified no less than sixty-two different creatures in one of the villages alone. There are at least three villages that I know of (and possibly a fourth), making it reasonable to postulate that there are in excess of one hundred of these beasts roaming the island.

Five-Men and Big-Thinks --

These are the names they use describe those with more intelligence. I believe the name Five-Man is derived from the fact that humans have five fingers, and I have never heard them use the term for anyone other than Meraux, Montague, or myself. Most of those they call Big-Thinks appear to be from the primate family.

TOP SECRET

My concern lies within the obvious difference in temperaments amongst the villages. One of the villages in particular is populated solely by what can only be described as aggressive predators. These predators, who reside far to the north, have displayed antagonistic tendencies toward the other villages. Several of these predators have shown open hostility toward me, and I worry it is only a matter of time before their animalistic nature comes to the fore, resulting in grave consequences. Meraux, however, assures me that all of his "children" are absolutely devout in their abstinence of violence. I pray that this remains true, at least until I can find a way off this accursed island of Dr. Meraux.

The Northern Tribe --

In nature, the females are often the hunters. I suspect this may be the case with some of the homo-animalia. Against the orders of Meraux, and the advice of Montague, I have taken to observing the northern tribe.

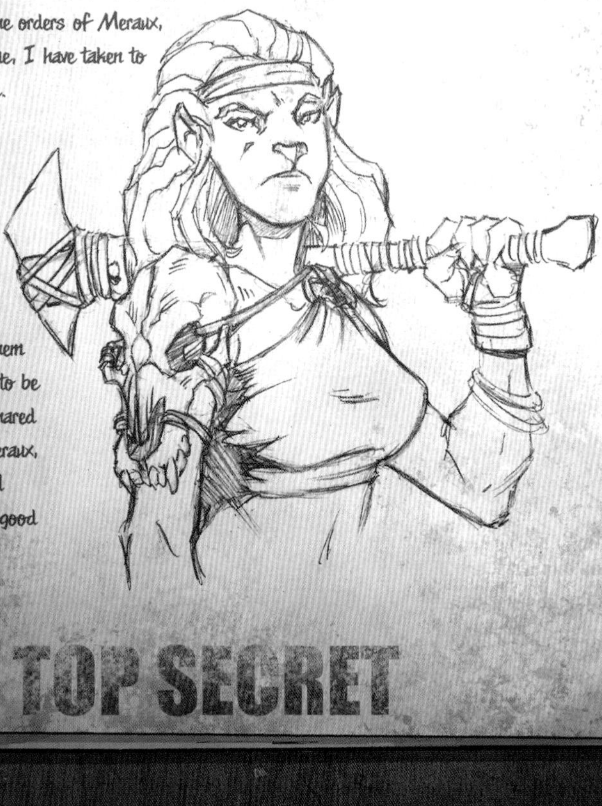

I have spotted some of them hunting, and many appear to be female (?). I have not shared these observations with Meraux, so as to spare these pitiful monstrosities a trip to the good doctor's House of Pain.

TOP SECRET

TOP SECRET

The more aggressive homo-animalia all appear to be feline in origin (tigers, jaguars, panthers, etc.). There is one in particular -- a jaguar, I believe -- that has demonstrated considerable hostility toward me. Montague has warned me to avoid these more unruly devils (his name, not mine).

As time progresses, I have come to feel more comfortable around many of the homo-animalia. The notable exception being these jungle cats, which seem slow to give up their predator instincts.

TOP SECRET

CHAPTER FIVE

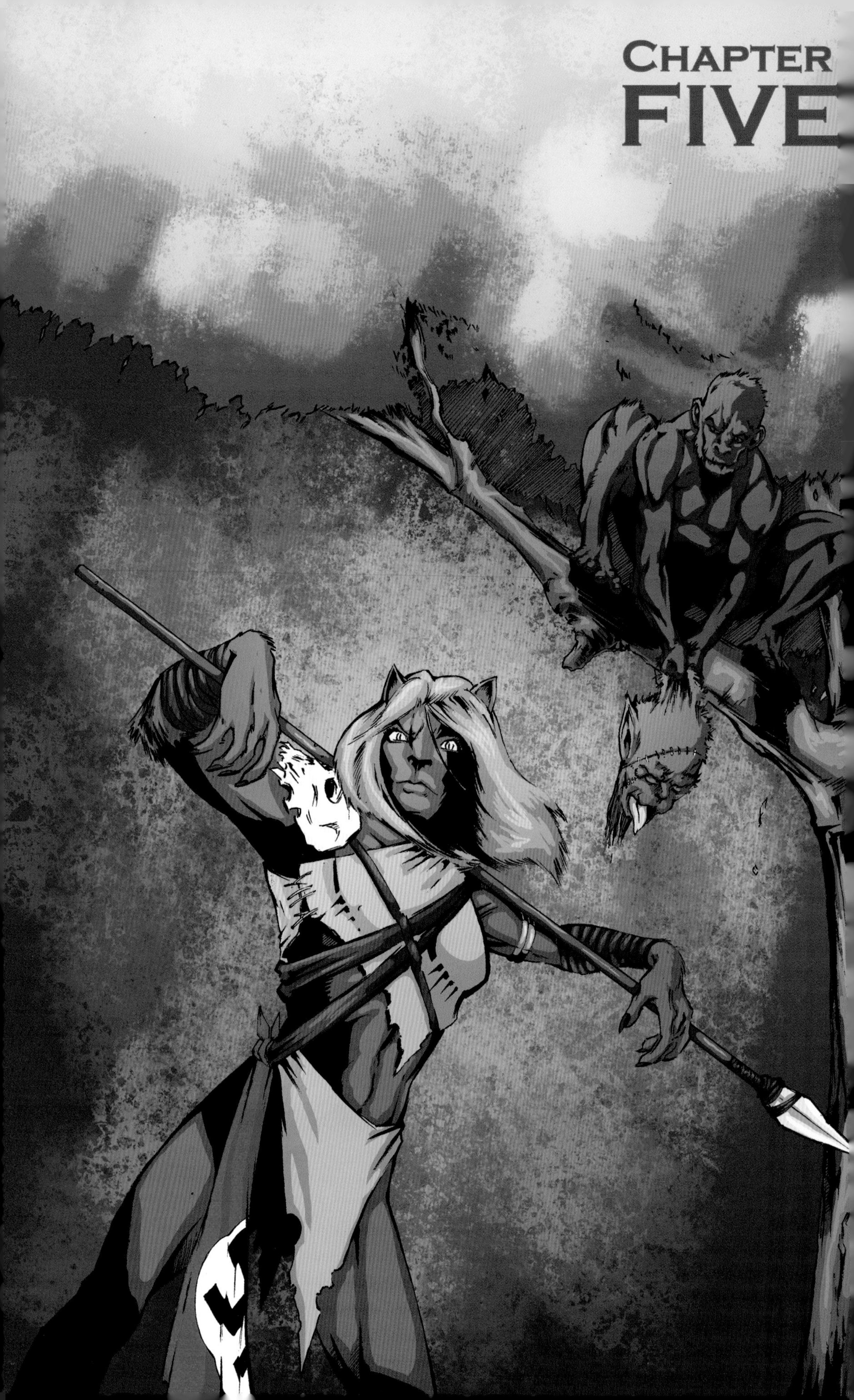

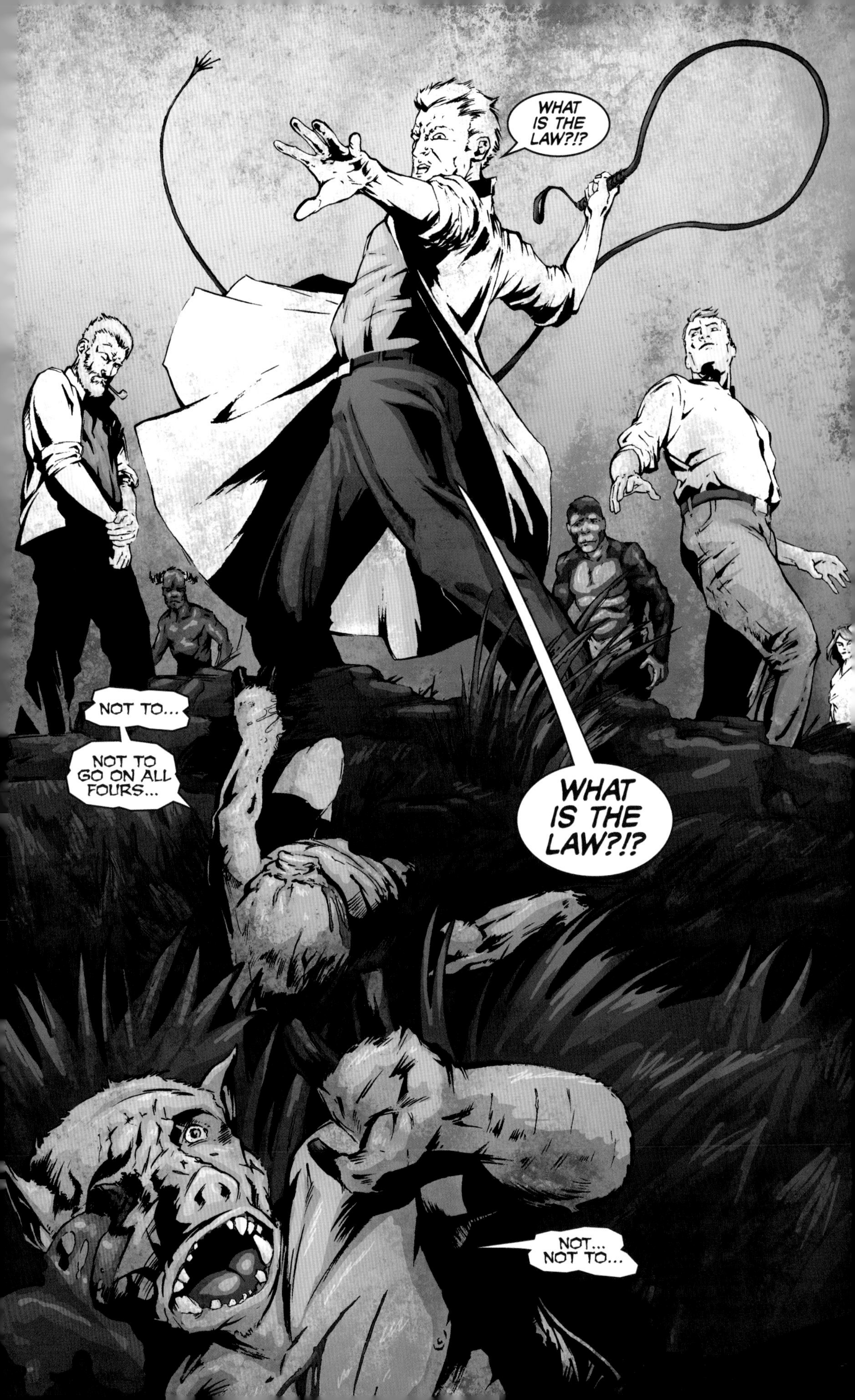
WHAT IS THE LAW?!?
NOT TO...
NOT TO GO ON ALL FOURS...
WHAT IS THE LAW?!?
NOT... NOT TO...

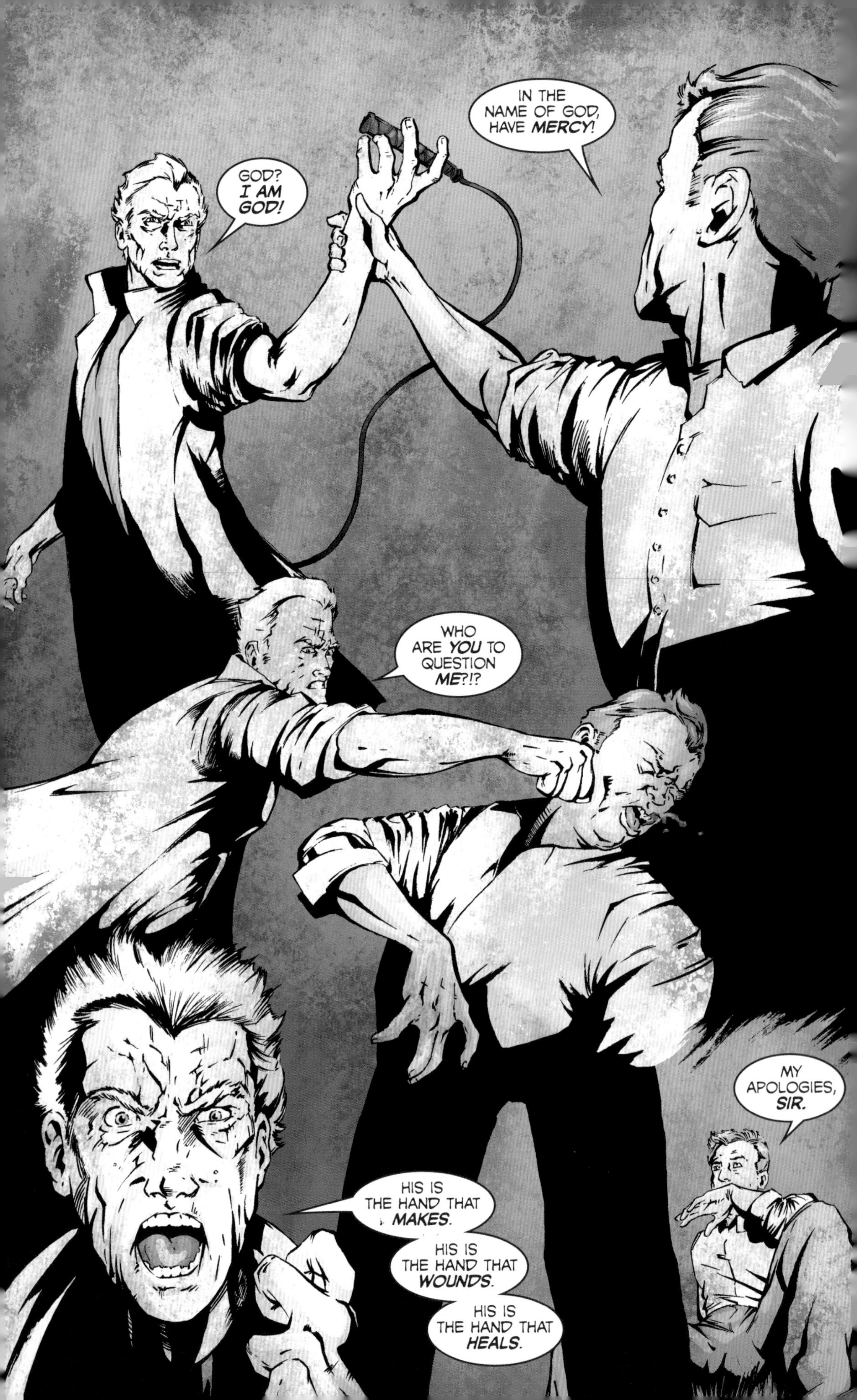
IN THE NAME OF GOD, HAVE MERCY!
GOD? I AM GOD!
WHO ARE YOU TO QUESTION ME?!?
MY APOLOGIES, SIR.
HIS IS THE HAND THAT MAKES.
HIS IS THE HAND THAT WOUNDS.
HIS IS THE HAND THAT HEALS.

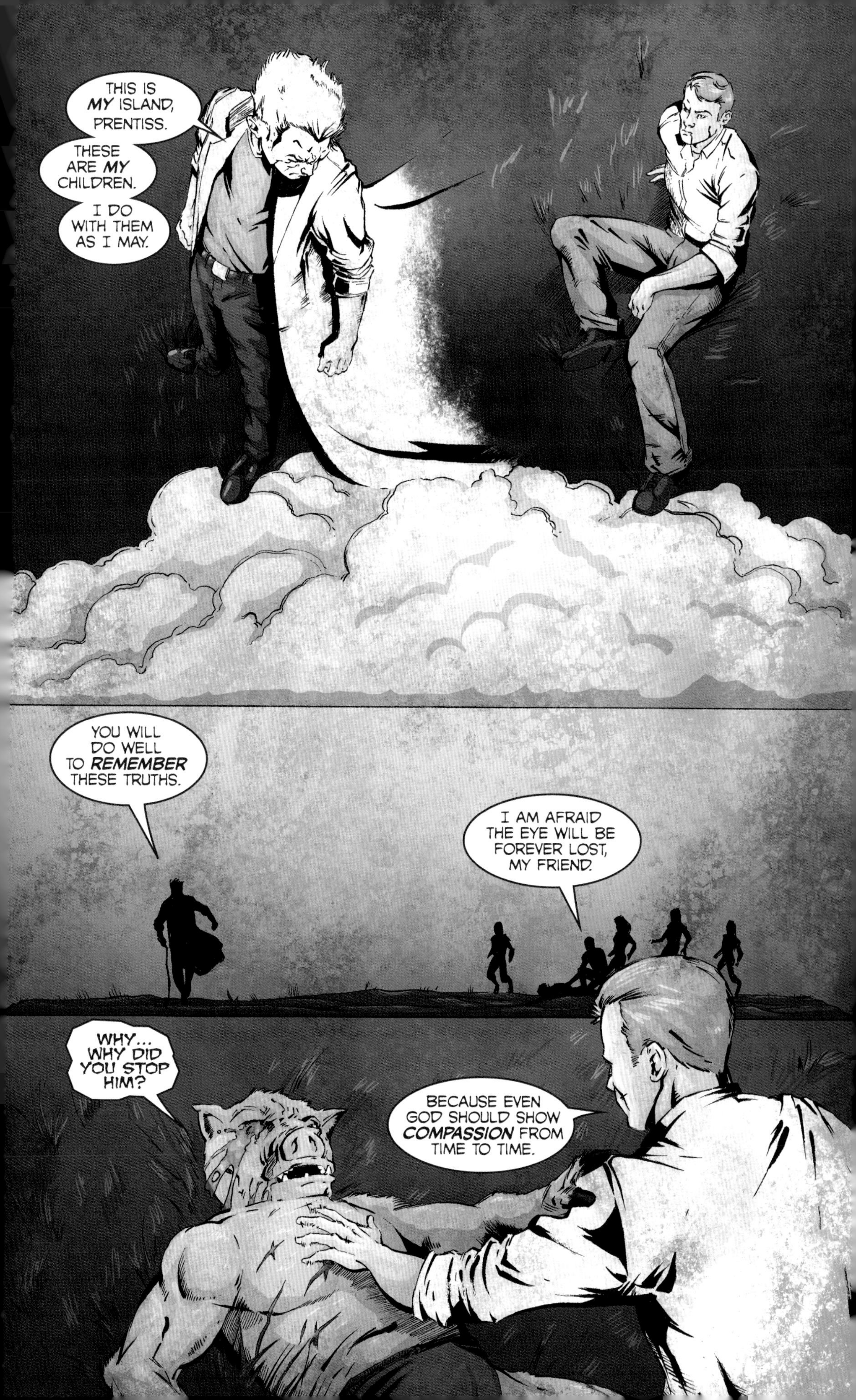
THIS IS MY ISLAND, PRENTISS.
THESE ARE MY CHILDREN.
I DO WITH THEM AS I MAY.
YOU WILL DO WELL TO REMEMBER THESE TRUTHS.
I AM AFRAID THE EYE WILL BE FOREVER LOST, MY FRIEND.
WHY... WHY DID YOU STOP HIM?
BECAUSE EVEN GOD SHOULD SHOW COMPASSION FROM TIME TO TIME.

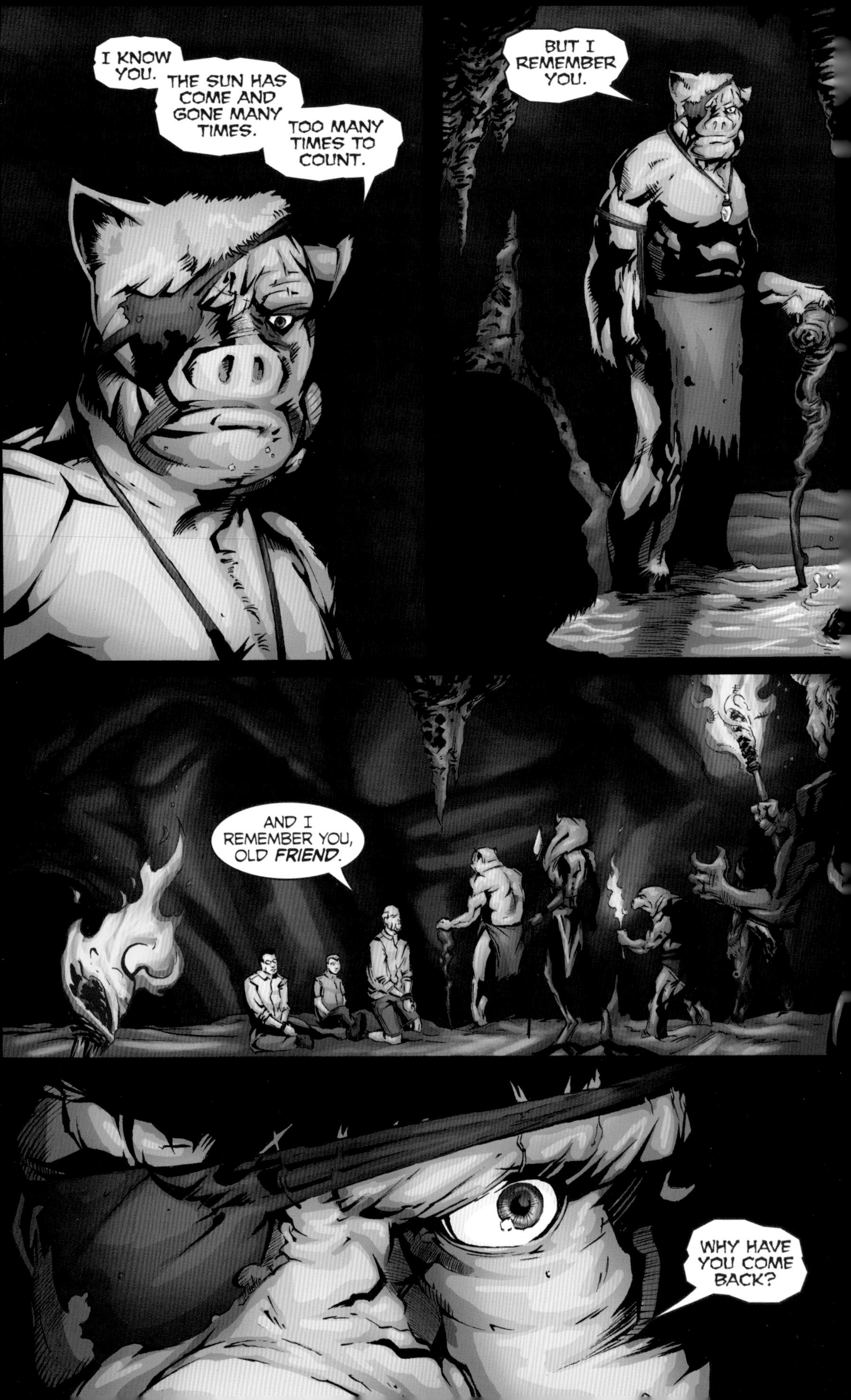
I KNOW YOU.
THE SUN HAS COME AND GONE MANY TIMES.
TOO MANY TIMES TO COUNT.
BUT I REMEMBER YOU.
AND I REMEMBER YOU, OLD FRIEND.
WHY HAVE YOU COME BACK?

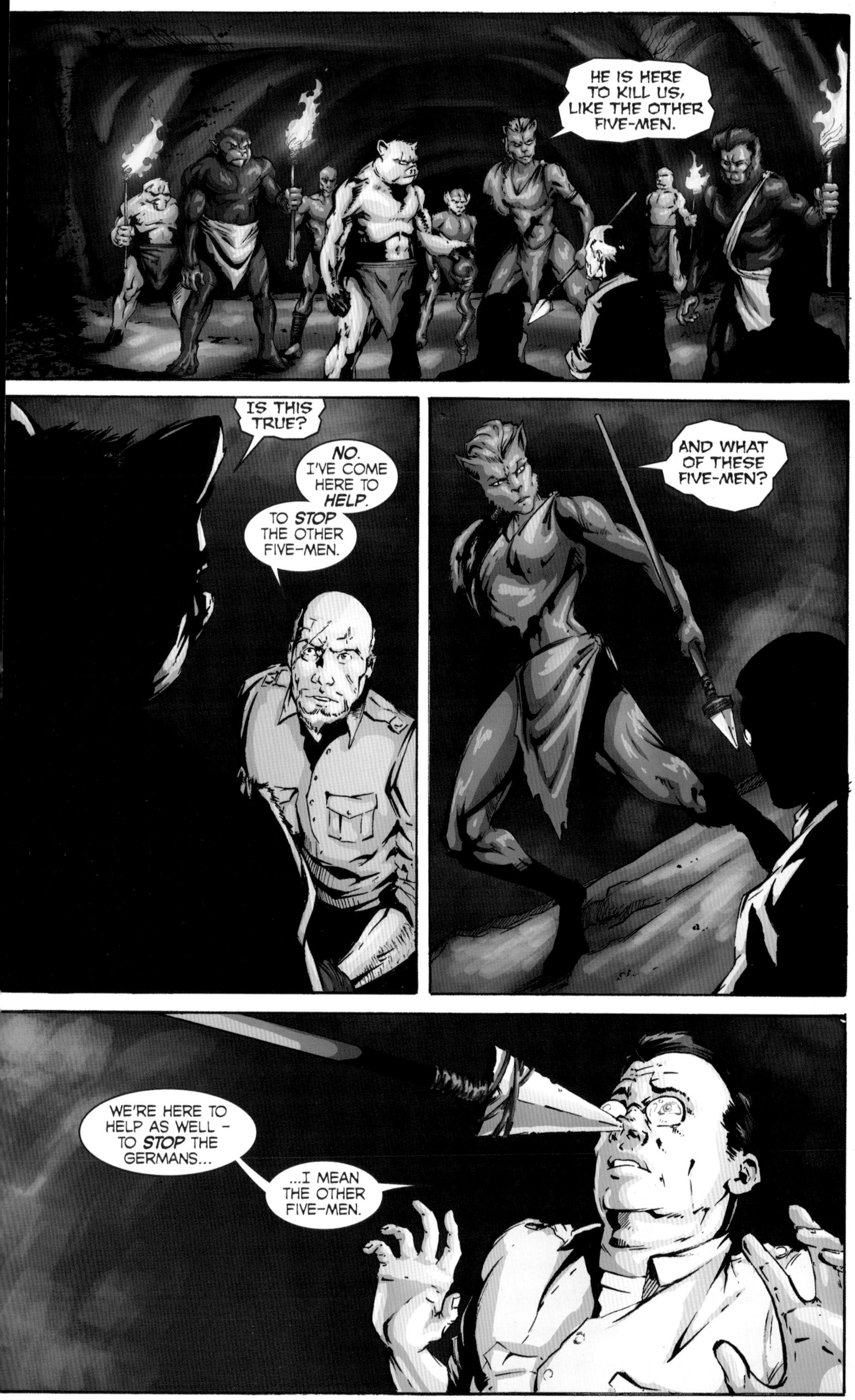
HE IS HERE TO KILL US, LIKE THE OTHER FIVE-MEN.
IS THIS TRUE?
NO. I'VE COME HERE TO HELP.
TO STOP THE OTHER FIVE-MEN.
AND WHAT OF THESE FIVE-MEN?
WE'RE HERE TO HELP AS WELL - TO STOP THE GERMANS...
...I MEAN THE OTHER FIVE-MEN.

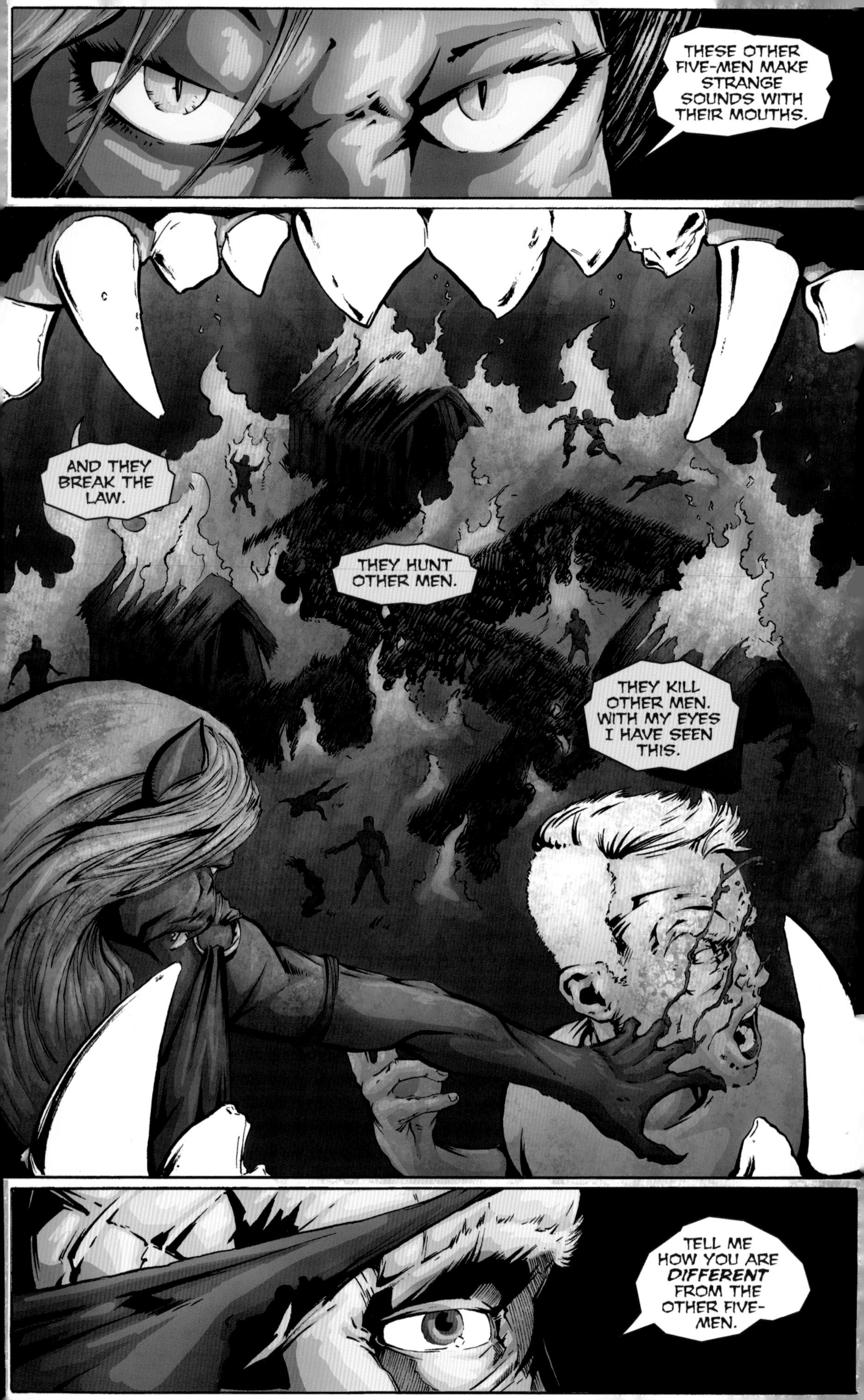
THESE OTHER FIVE-MEN MAKE STRANGE SOUNDS WITH THEIR MOUTHS.
AND THEY BREAK THE LAW.
THEY HUNT OTHER MEN.
THEY KILL OTHER MEN. WITH MY EYES I HAVE SEEN THIS.
TELL ME HOW YOU ARE *DIFFERENT* FROM THE OTHER FIVE-MEN.

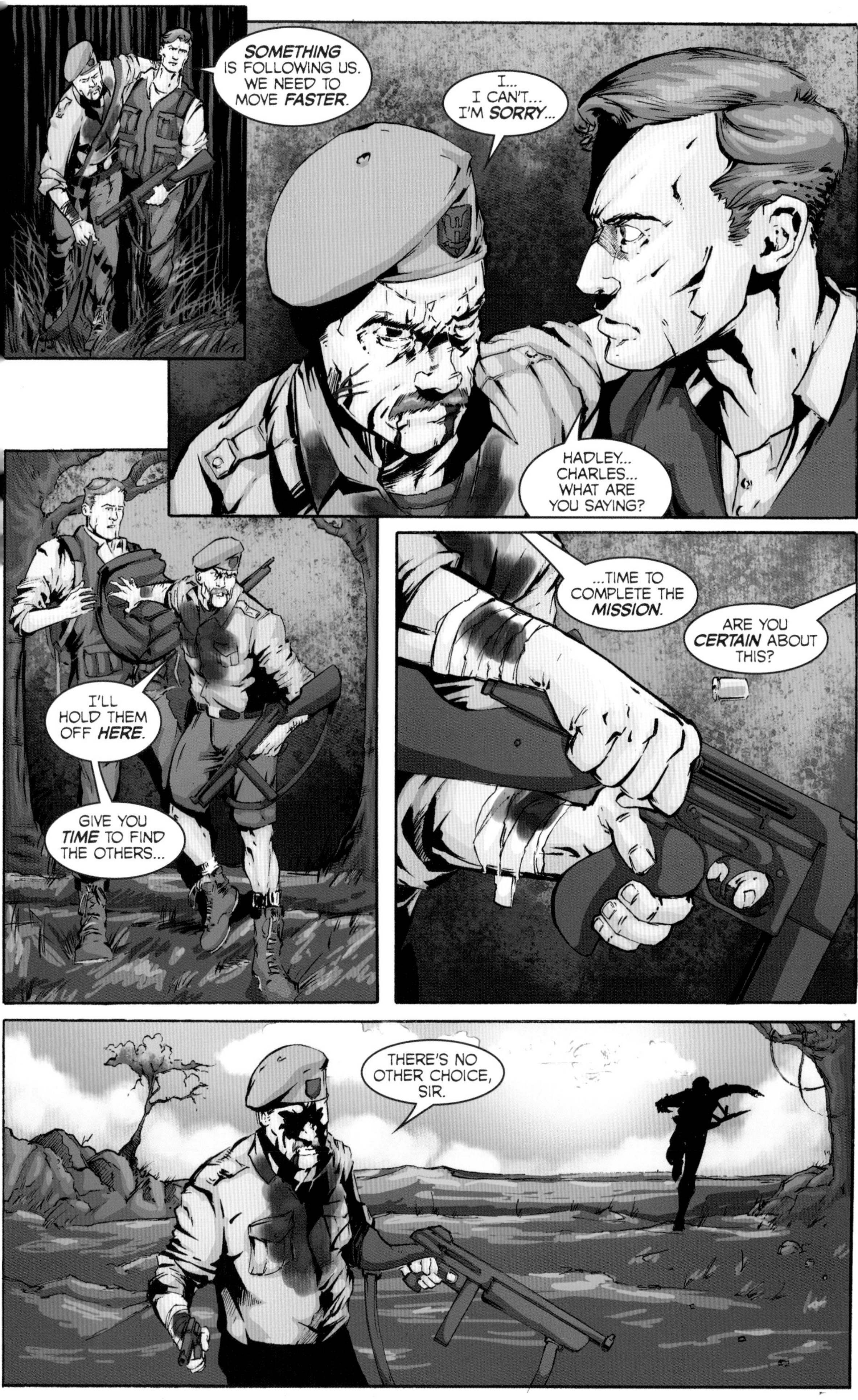
SOMETHING IS FOLLOWING US. WE NEED TO MOVE FASTER.
I... I CAN'T... I'M SORRY...
HADLEY... CHARLES... WHAT ARE YOU SAYING?
I'LL HOLD THEM OFF HERE.
GIVE YOU TIME TO FIND THE OTHERS...
...TIME TO COMPLETE THE MISSION.
ARE YOU CERTAIN ABOUT THIS?
THERE'S NO OTHER CHOICE, SIR.

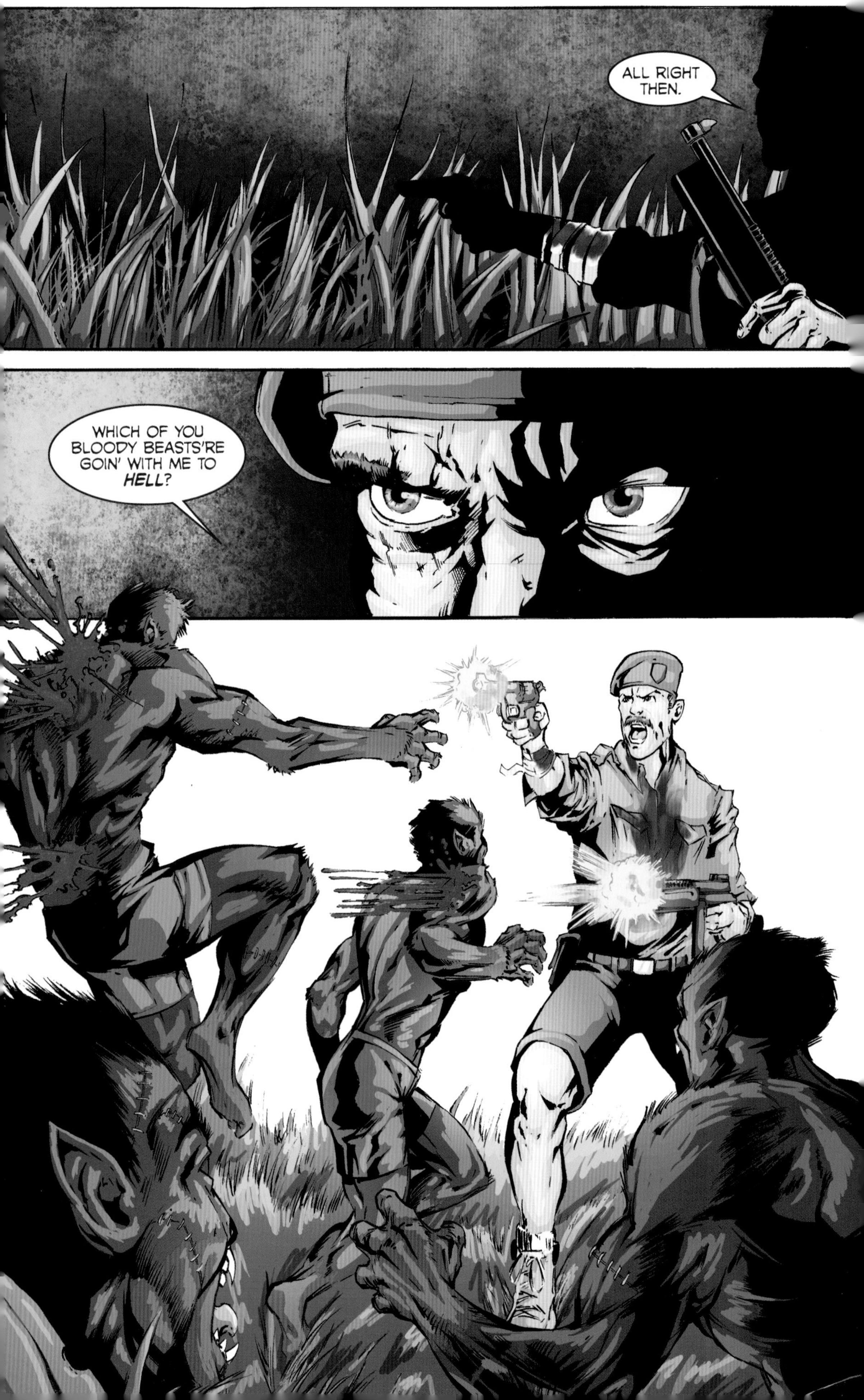
ALL RIGHT THEN.
WHICH OF YOU BLOODY BEASTS'RE GOIN' WITH ME TO *HELL*?

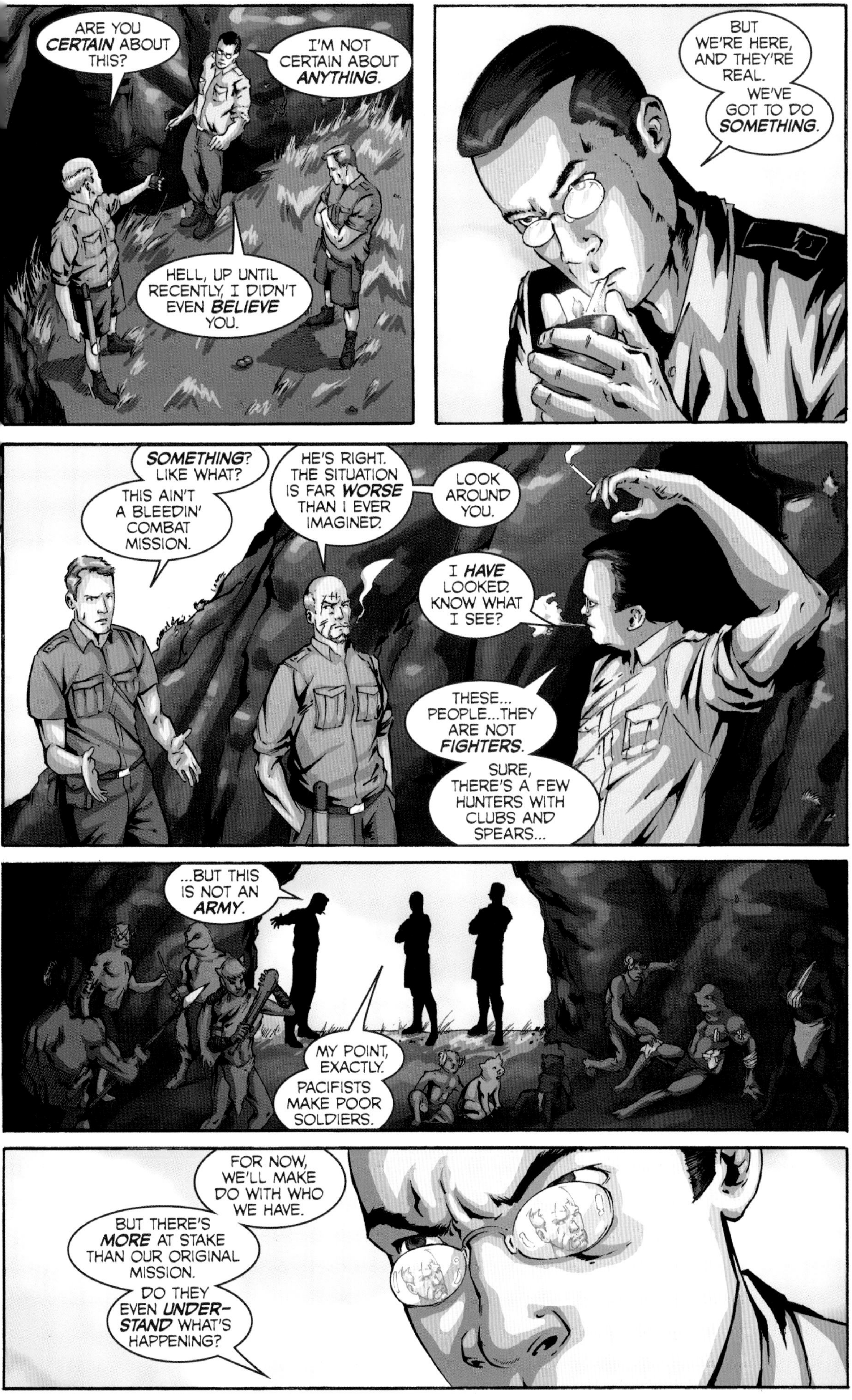

ARE YOU *CERTAIN* ABOUT THIS?
I'M NOT CERTAIN ABOUT *ANYTHING*.
HELL, UP UNTIL RECENTLY, I DIDN'T EVEN *BELIEVE* YOU.
BUT WE'RE HERE, AND THEY'RE REAL.
WE'VE GOT TO DO *SOMETHING*.
SOMETHING? LIKE WHAT?
THIS AIN'T A BLEEDIN' COMBAT MISSION.
HE'S RIGHT. THE SITUATION IS FAR *WORSE* THAN I EVER IMAGINED.
LOOK AROUND YOU.
I *HAVE* LOOKED. KNOW WHAT I SEE?
THESE... PEOPLE...THEY ARE NOT *FIGHTERS*.
SURE, THERE'S A FEW HUNTERS WITH CLUBS AND SPEARS...
...BUT THIS IS NOT AN *ARMY*.
MY POINT, EXACTLY.
PACIFISTS MAKE POOR SOLDIERS.
FOR NOW, WE'LL MAKE DO WITH WHO WE HAVE.
BUT THERE'S *MORE* AT STAKE THAN OUR ORIGINAL MISSION.
DO THEY EVEN *UNDER-STAND* WHAT'S HAPPENING?

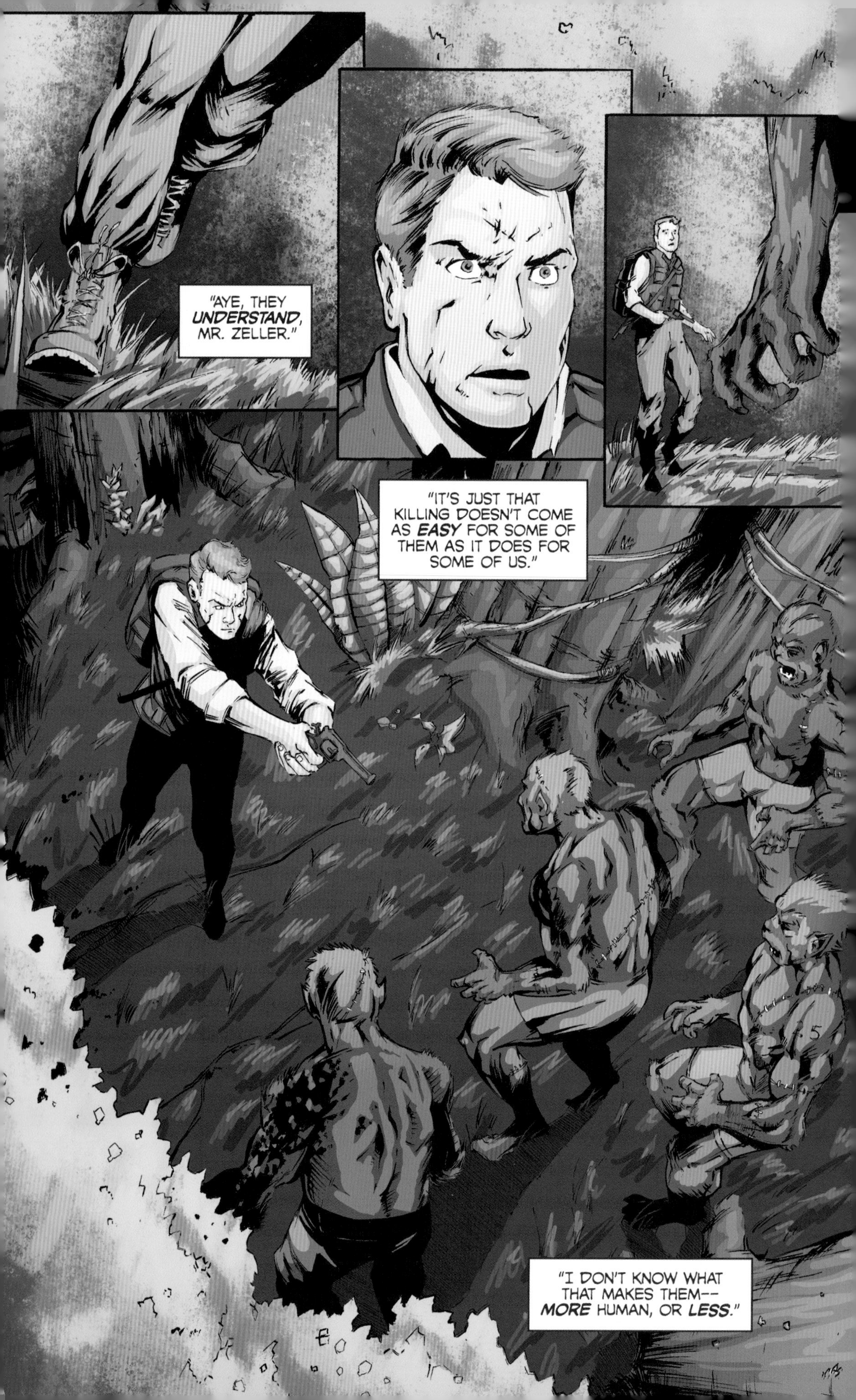
"AYE, THEY UNDERSTAND, MR. ZELLER."
"IT'S JUST THAT KILLING DOESN'T COME AS EASY FOR SOME OF THEM AS IT DOES FOR SOME OF US."
"I DON'T KNOW WHAT THAT MAKES THEM-- MORE HUMAN, OR LESS."

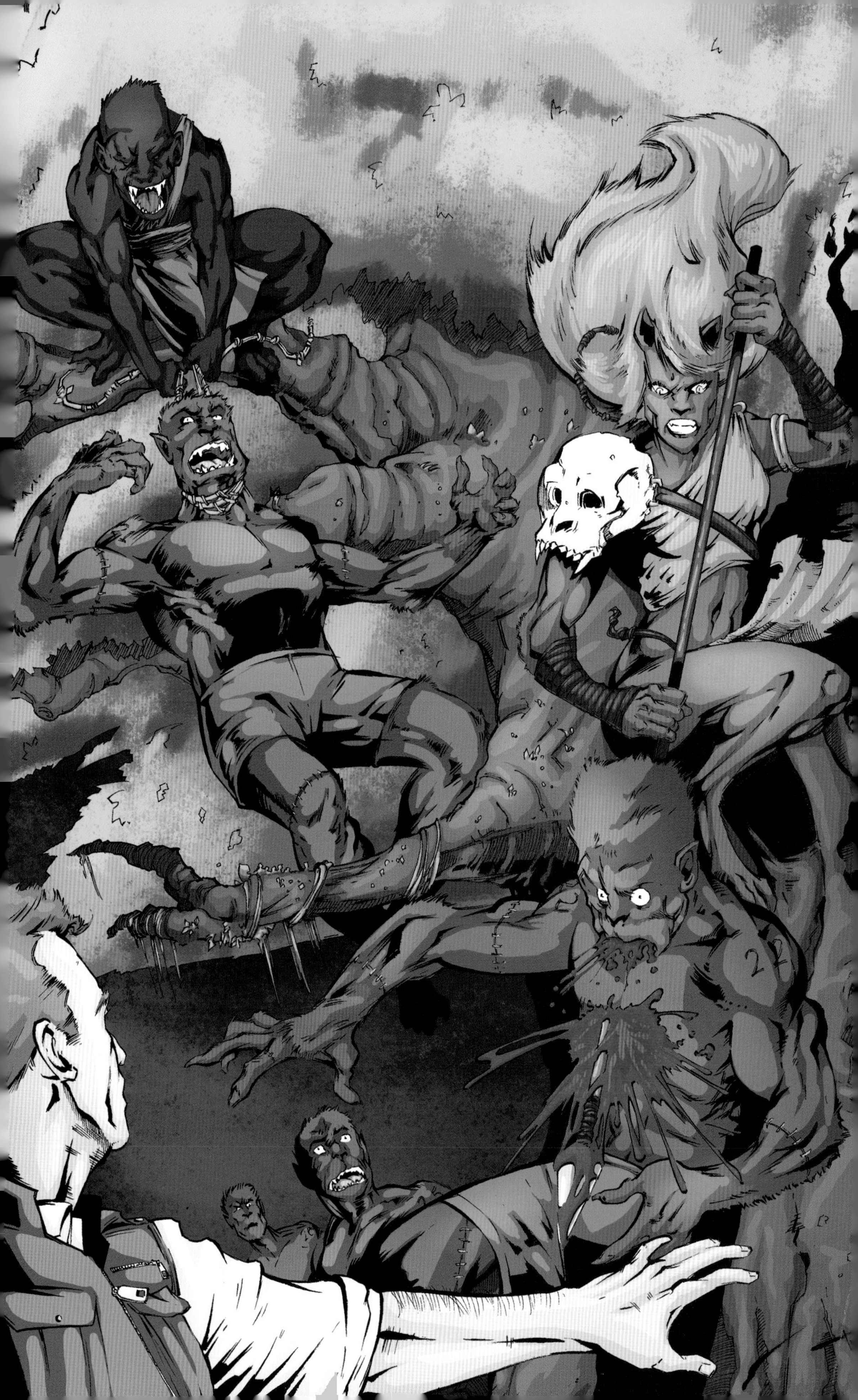

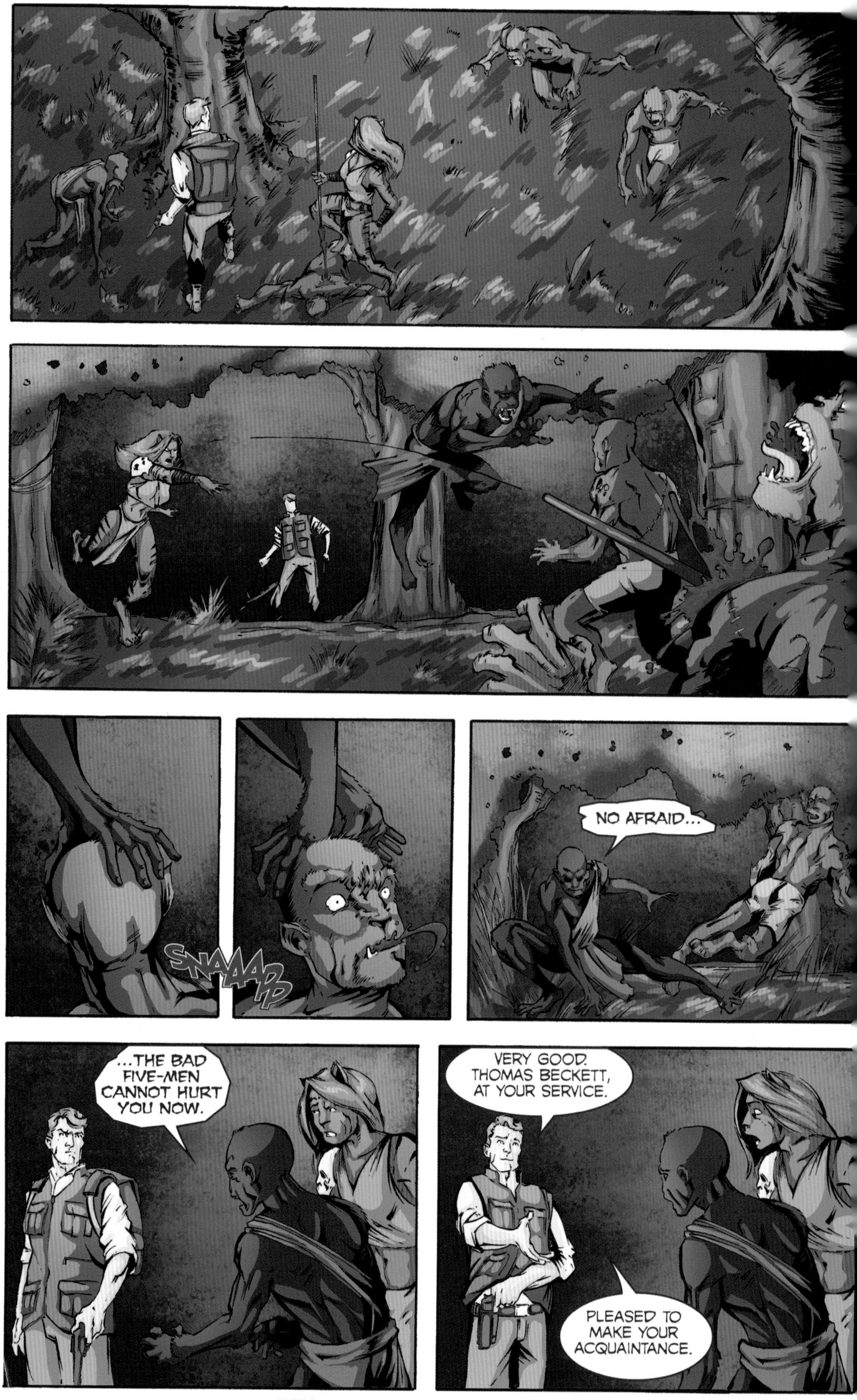
SNAAAP
NO AFRAID...
...THE BAD FIVE-MEN CANNOT HURT YOU NOW.
VERY GOOD. THOMAS BECKETT, AT YOUR SERVICE.
PLEASED TO MAKE YOUR ACQUAINTANCE.

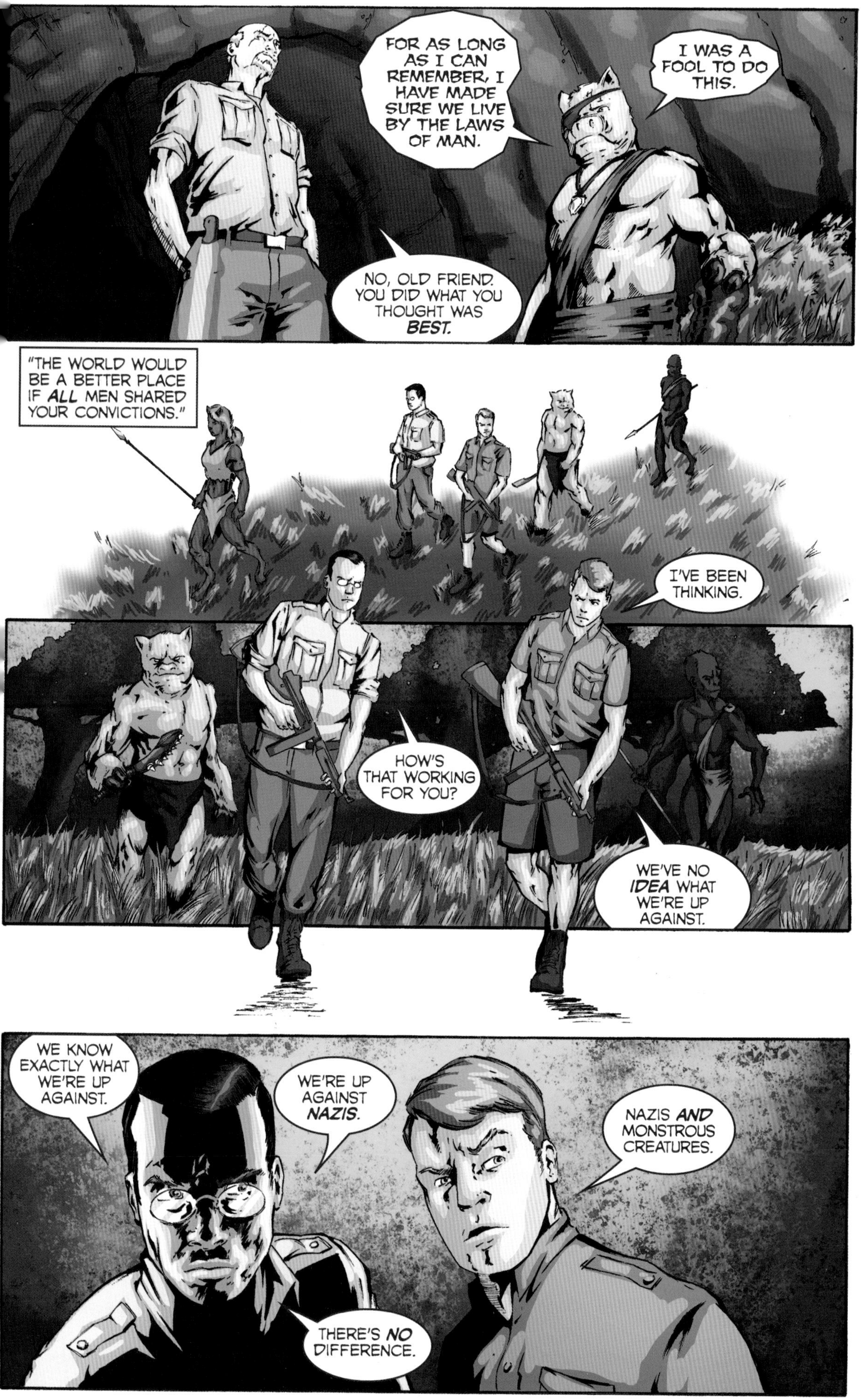

FOR AS LONG AS I CAN REMEMBER, I HAVE MADE SURE WE LIVE BY THE LAWS OF MAN.
I WAS A FOOL TO DO THIS.
NO, OLD FRIEND. YOU DID WHAT YOU THOUGHT WAS ***BEST.***
"THE WORLD WOULD BE A BETTER PLACE IF ***ALL*** MEN SHARED YOUR CONVICTIONS."
I'VE BEEN THINKING.
HOW'S THAT WORKING FOR YOU?
WE'VE NO ***IDEA*** WHAT WE'RE UP AGAINST.
WE KNOW EXACTLY WHAT WE'RE UP AGAINST.
WE'RE UP AGAINST ***NAZIS.***
NAZIS ***AND*** MONSTROUS CREATURES.
THERE'S ***NO*** DIFFERENCE.

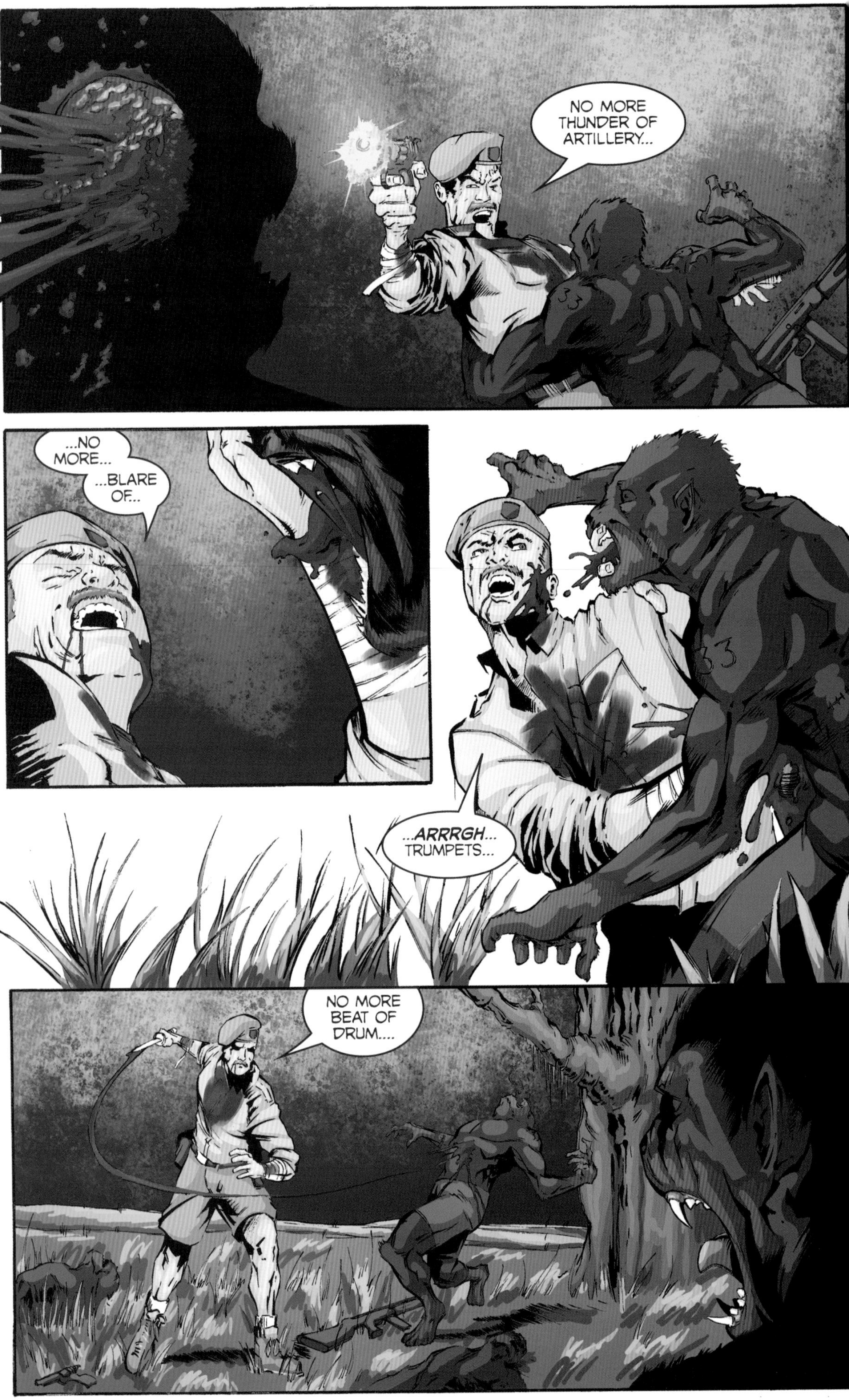
NO MORE THUNDER OF ARTILLERY...
...NO MORE...
...BLARE OF...
...ARRRGH... TRUMPETS...
NO MORE BEAT OF DRUM....

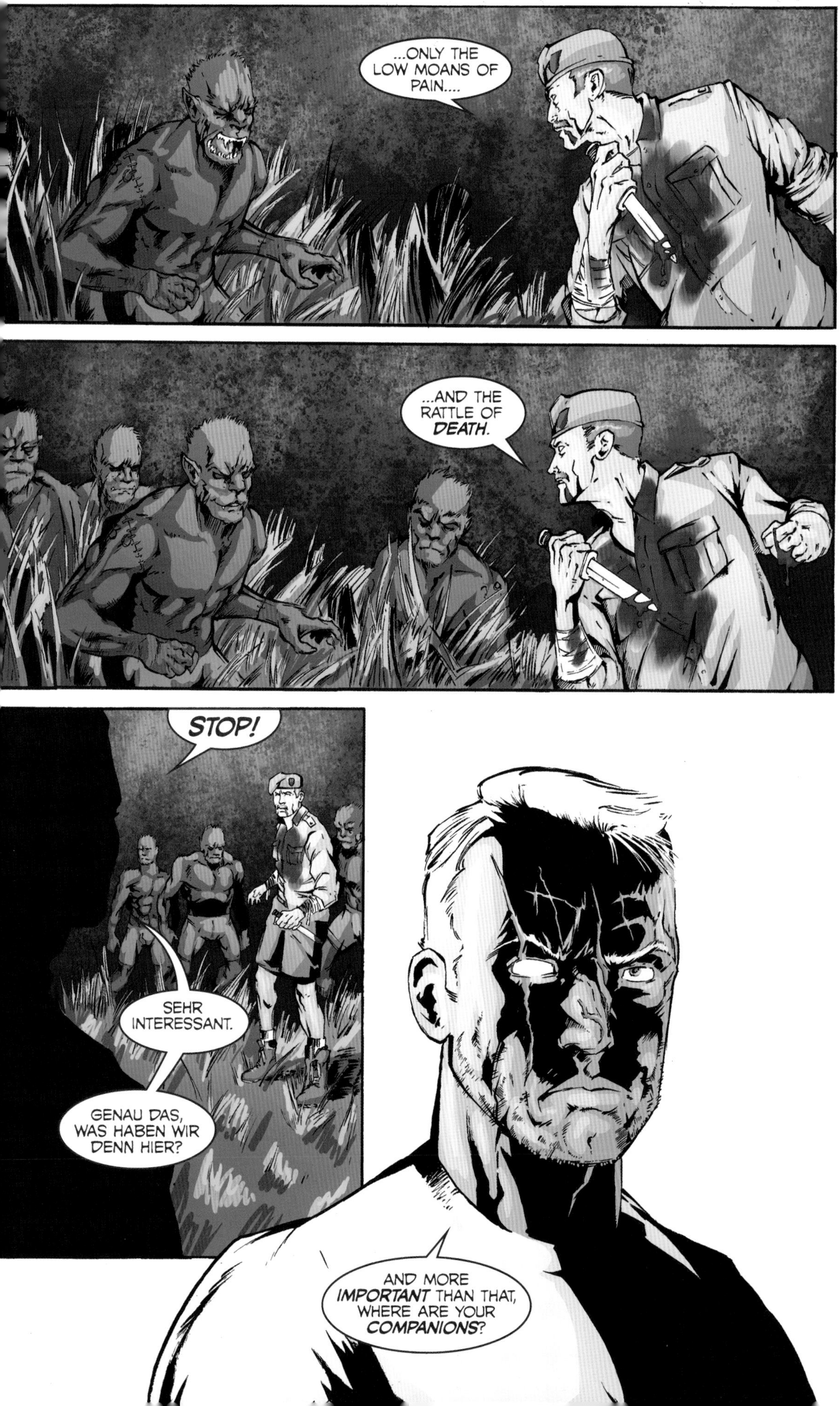
...ONLY THE LOW MOANS OF PAIN....
...AND THE RATTLE OF DEATH.
STOP!
SEHR INTERESSANT.
GENAU DAS, WAS HABEN WIR DENN HIER?
AND MORE IMPORTANT THAN THAT, WHERE ARE YOUR COMPANIONS?

TOP SECRET

THIS IS A COVER SHEET

BASIC SECURITY REQUIREMENTS ARE CONTAINED IN AR 380-5

THE UNAUTHORIZED DISCLOSURE OF THE INFORMATION CONTAINED IN THE ATTACHED DOCUMENT(S) COULD RESULT IN EXCEPTIONALLY GRAVE DANGER TO THE UNITED STATES

RESPONSIBILITY OF PERSONS HANDLING THE ATTACHED DOCUMENT(S)

1. Enter on DA Form 969 your name and the date you had access to the document(s).
2. Exercise the necessary safeguards to prevent unauthorized disclosure by never leaving the document(s) unattended except when properly secured in a locked safe.
3. Transfer the document(s) only to persons who need to know and who possess the required security clearance.
4. Obtain a receipt whenever relinquishing control of the document(s).

STORAGE

Store as prescribed in AR 380-5.

REPRODUCTION

TOP SECRET material may be copied, extracted, or reproduced only when the classifying authority has authorized such actions.

DISPOSITION

This cover sheet should be removed when document(s) are filed in a permanent file, declassified, destroyed, or mailed.

(This cover sheet is unclassified when separated from classified documents)

TOP SECRET

DA LABEL 24
1 FEB 59

PREVIOUS EDITIONS OF THIS LABEL ARE OBSOLETE

AGL (1) 4-59-40M-71603

Prentiss, E. - Journal

TOP SECRET

November ? 1894

As of late, the extent of Meraux's madness has become increasingly clear. Likewise, Montague's faculties must be called into question. Much of his time is spent under the influence of some homemade spirits derived from various fermented fruits.

Furthermore, I suspect that Montague has been consorting with some of the female homo-animalia. Though it sickens me to think of this, I must also consider the possible some may have bore his offspring. There is, in fact, a population of these creatures that I have identified as not having been created within Meraux's lab, but are rather the result of these beings mating. This does not seem to bother Meraux, and the fact that I suspect several of these younger homo-animalia have their origins within the loins of Montague...it is must troubling indeed. Clearly, both men have ventured far from the realm of rational thought.

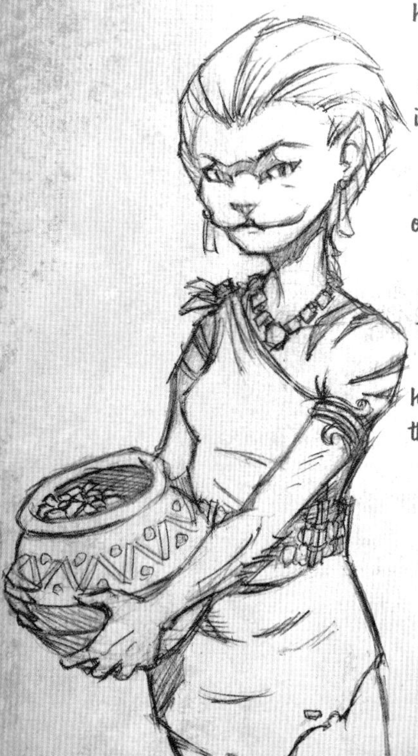

Second Generation --

The more time I spend among them, the more I notice those that are quite young. They do not bare the scars of those created under Meraux's knife. This can only mean that they are the result of the creatures breeding. Indeed, it is not uncommon to see them interacting as a family or a community. There is more complexity to these beings than I had originally assumed.

TOP SECRET

TOP SECRET

I have begun to fashion a raft, though that description may be too complimentary of my work. My fear that a supply vessel will not arrive with any haste, has driven me to building this raft, which I am keeping secret from Meraux, though I believe Montague has his suspicions. My concern lies not with the seaworthiness of my raft, or even in a supply of provisions, it is in not having a chart for navigation. Shall I merely set sail, heading toward the rising sun, hoping to reach Panama? Such a voyage seems like the futile attempt of man who has parted company with his sanity. And yet, to drift aimlessly on the Pacific, hoping that the currents carry me to Panama, seems far more steeped within the realm of reason and sanity than staying on this island.

I must admit, however, that I have grown fond of some of these creatures. Perhaps this is in response to the sadistic nature of Meraux's abuse. Is it possible that the way he treats his "children" has stirred within me my own paternal feelings? Indeed, I have challenged the way he abuses these poor wretches, which has only served to inflame his wrath.

Though if I am to be honest in the fondness I feel, and to speculate as to where it originates, the trespasses of Meraux (and the molestations of Montague) are only part of what informs my feelings. Despite their appearance, these creatures are more than the monstrous façade that would define them. They are not human. By that same measure, they are neither animal. They are something I have never encountered, nor do I suspect I will ever encounter again, save for the dreams that will likely stay with me the remainder of my days.

To say that I will miss these odd beings who have, by fate's cruel circumstance, become my companions for all these months, would be untrue. Indeed, some of them I fear beyond words, and will be content to done with them (as I suspect they would like to be done with me). But there shall be a few, the company of which I have grown fond of, that will be kept in my prayers (should I ever pray gain). For as soon as I make my escape, they will be left here with Meraux, and he, more so than they, is the real monster.

TOP SECRET

Chapter Six

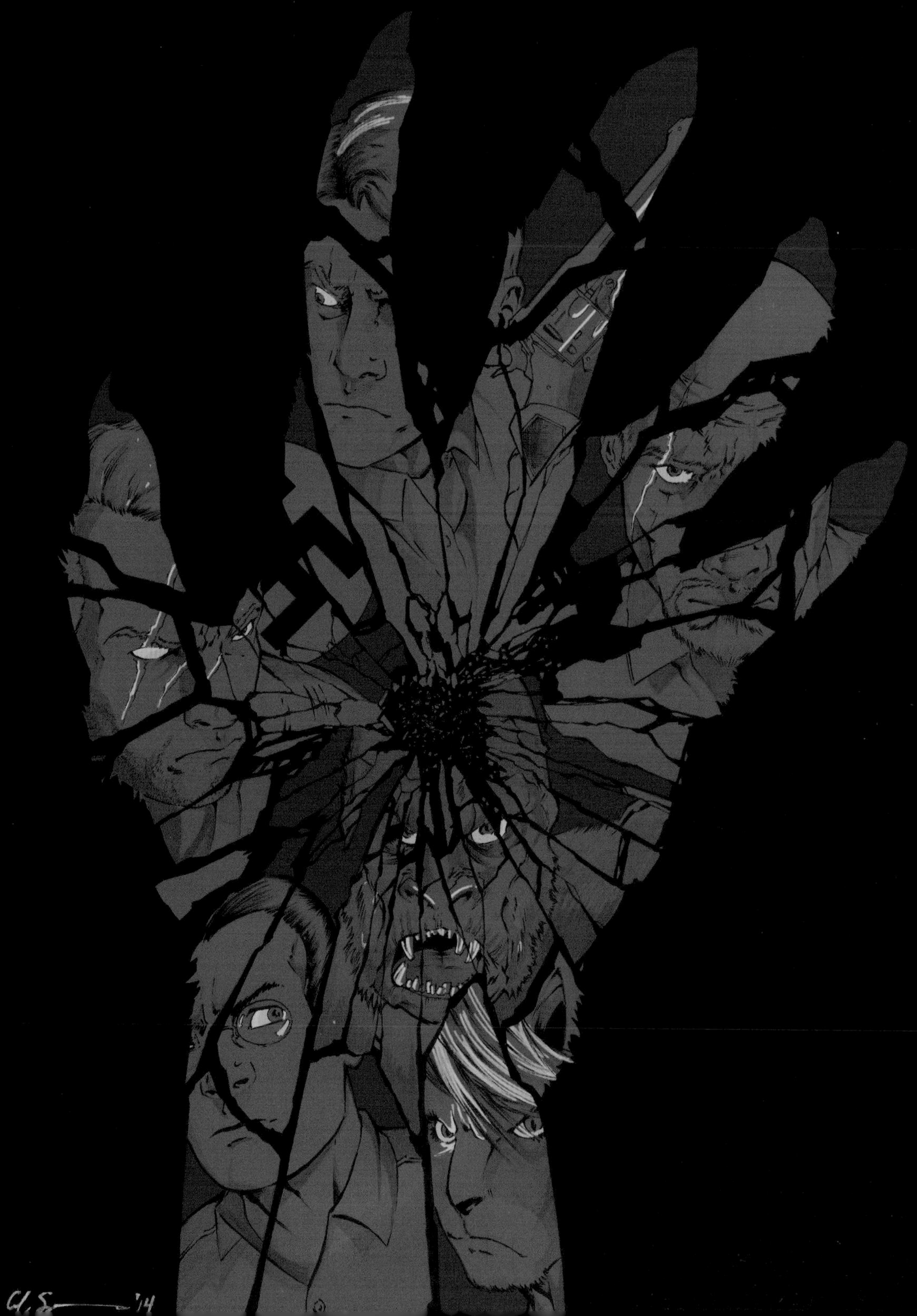

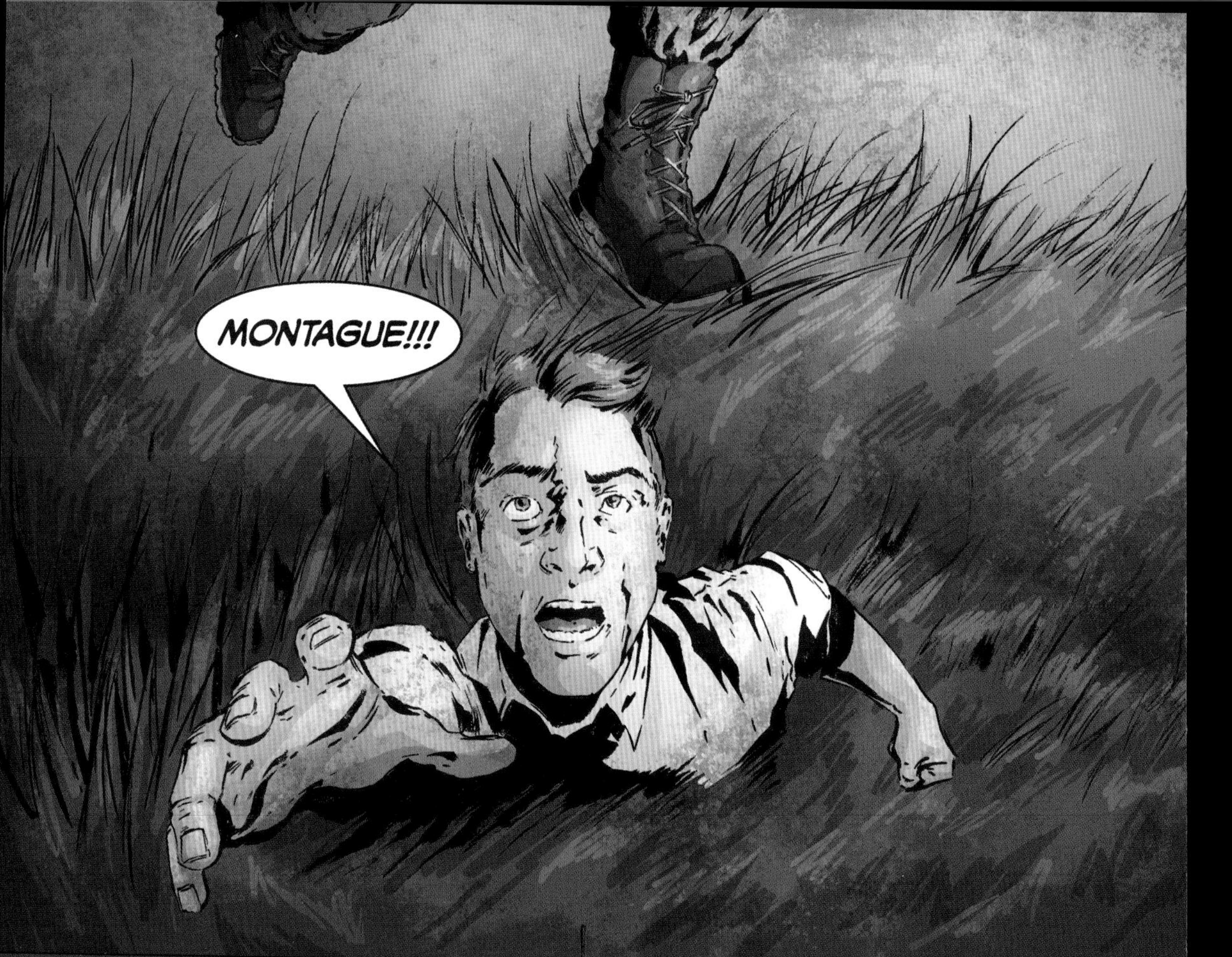
MONTAGUE!!!

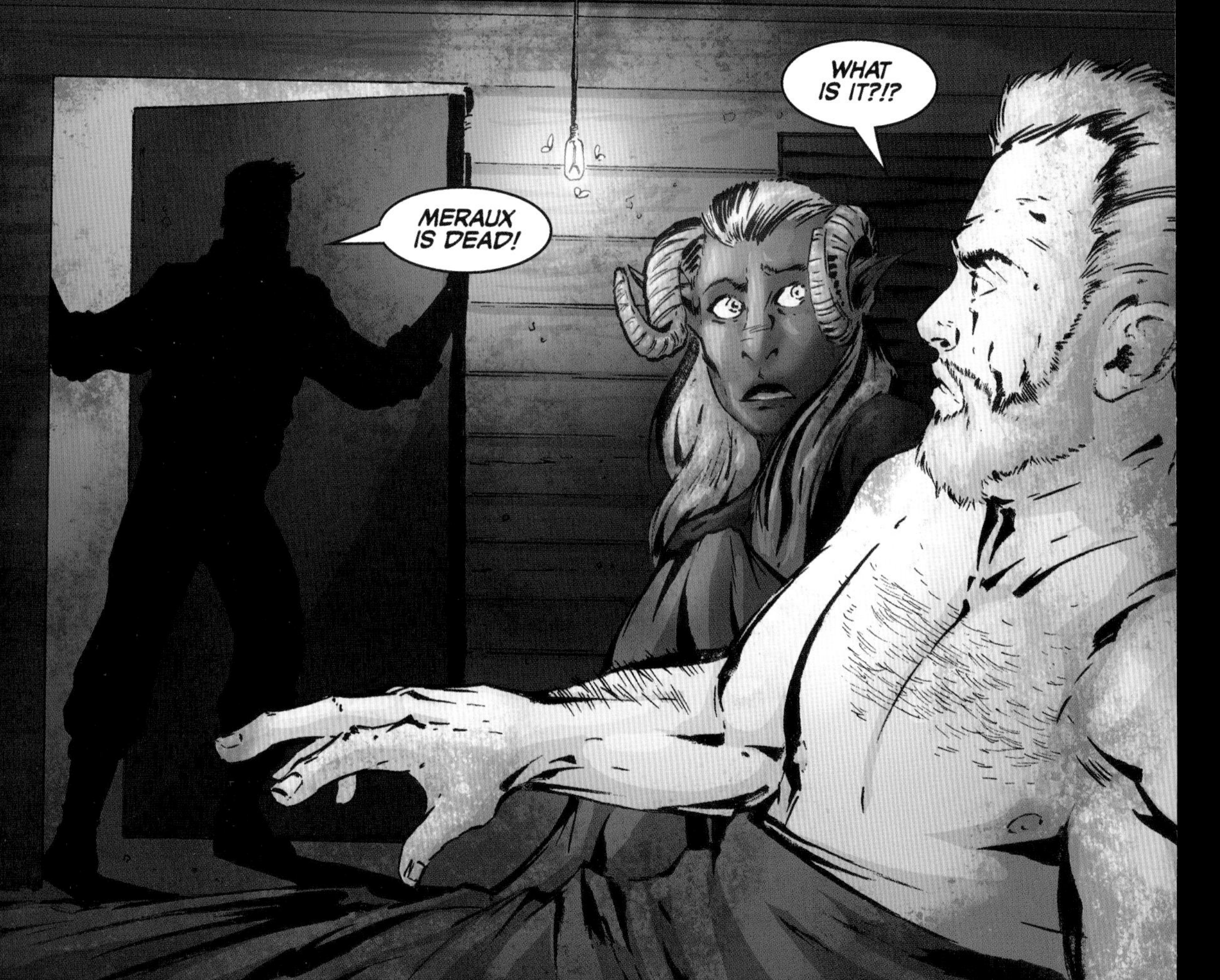
WHAT IS IT?!?
MERAUX IS DEAD!

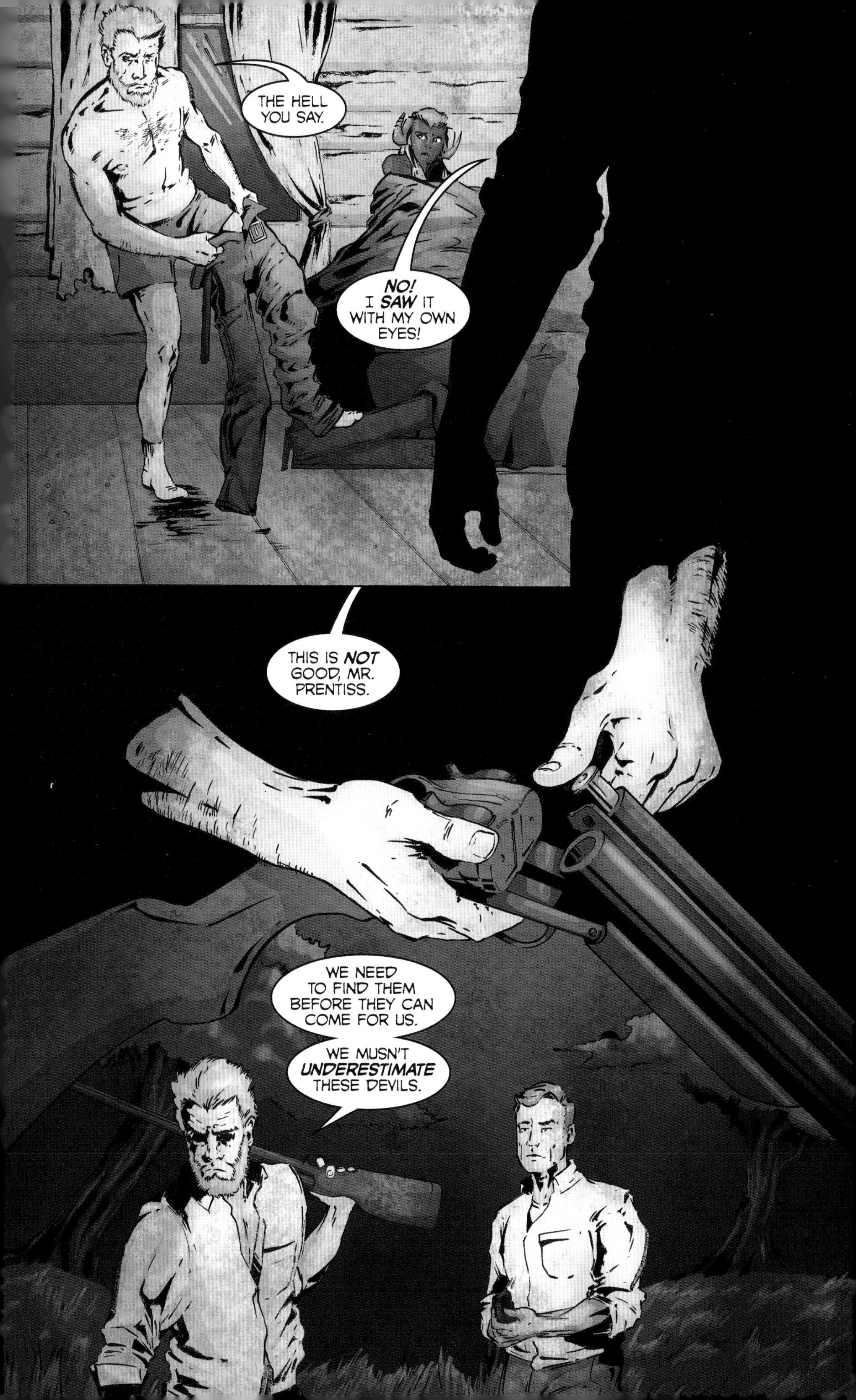
THE HELL YOU SAY.
NO! I SAW IT WITH MY OWN EYES!
THIS IS NOT GOOD, MR. PRENTISS.
WE NEED TO FIND THEM BEFORE THEY CAN COME FOR US.
WE MUSN'T UNDERESTIMATE THESE DEVILS.

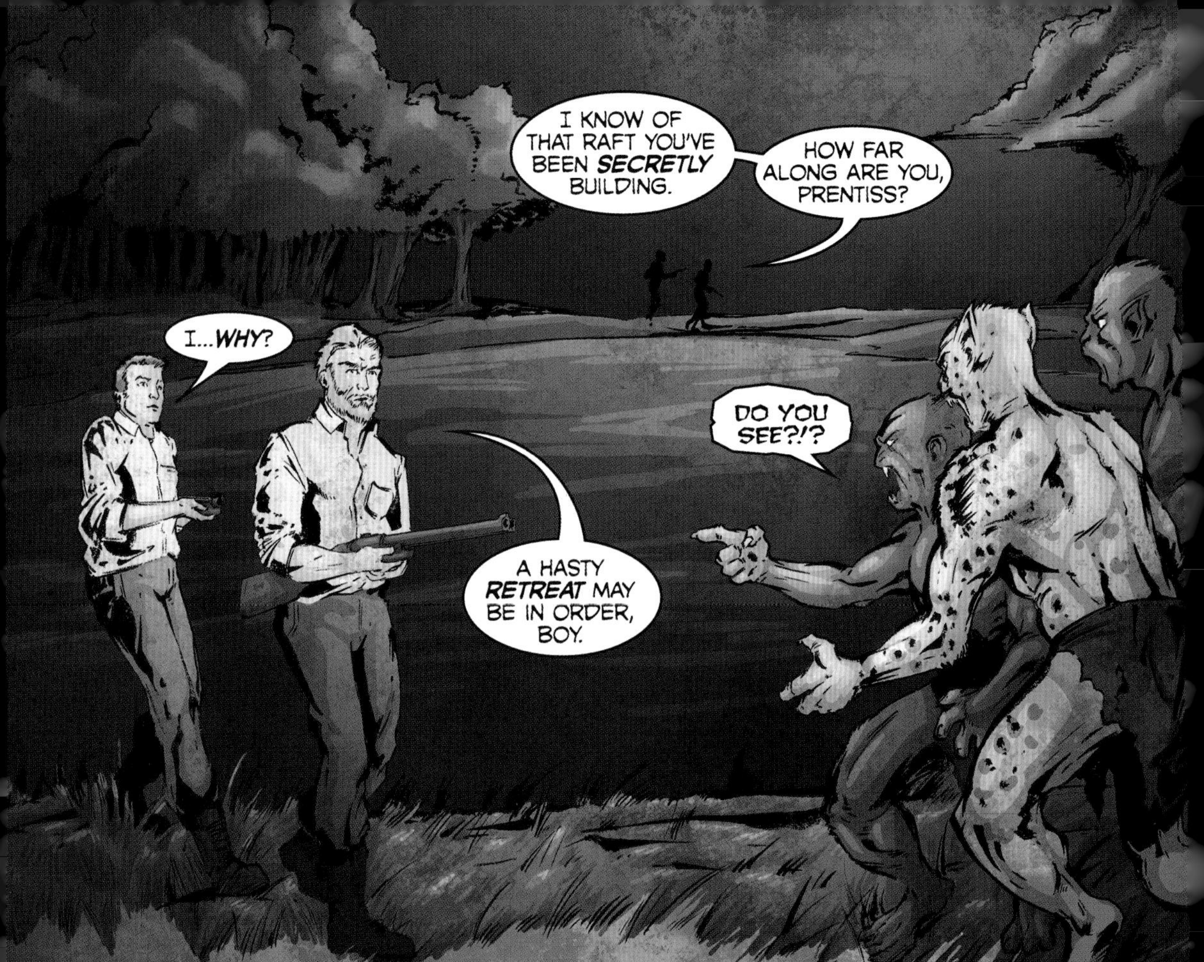
I KNOW OF THAT RAFT YOU'VE BEEN SECRETLY BUILDING.
HOW FAR ALONG ARE YOU, PRENTISS?
I...WHY?
DO YOU SEE?!?
A HASTY RETREAT MAY BE IN ORDER, BOY.

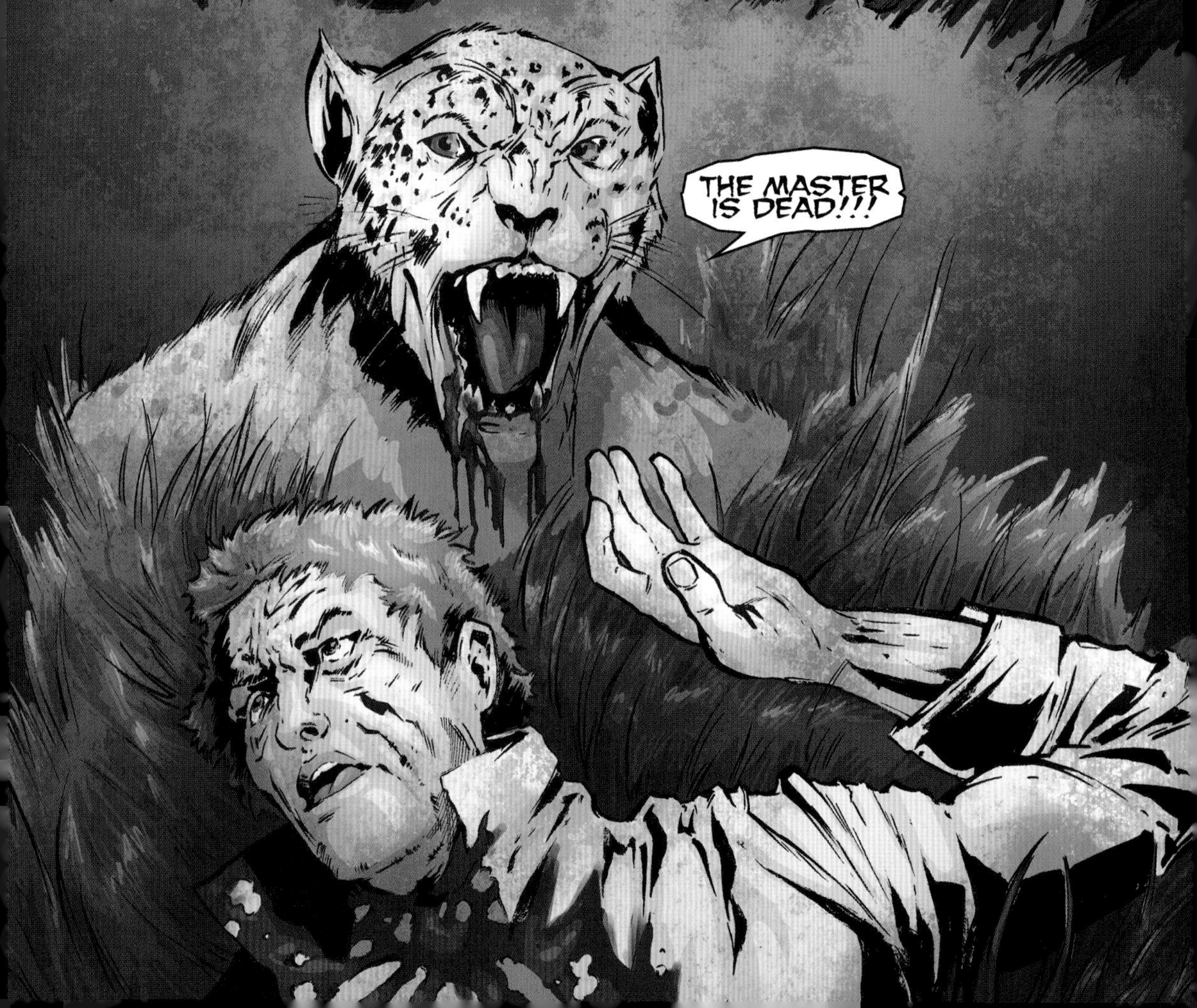
THE MASTER IS DEAD!!!

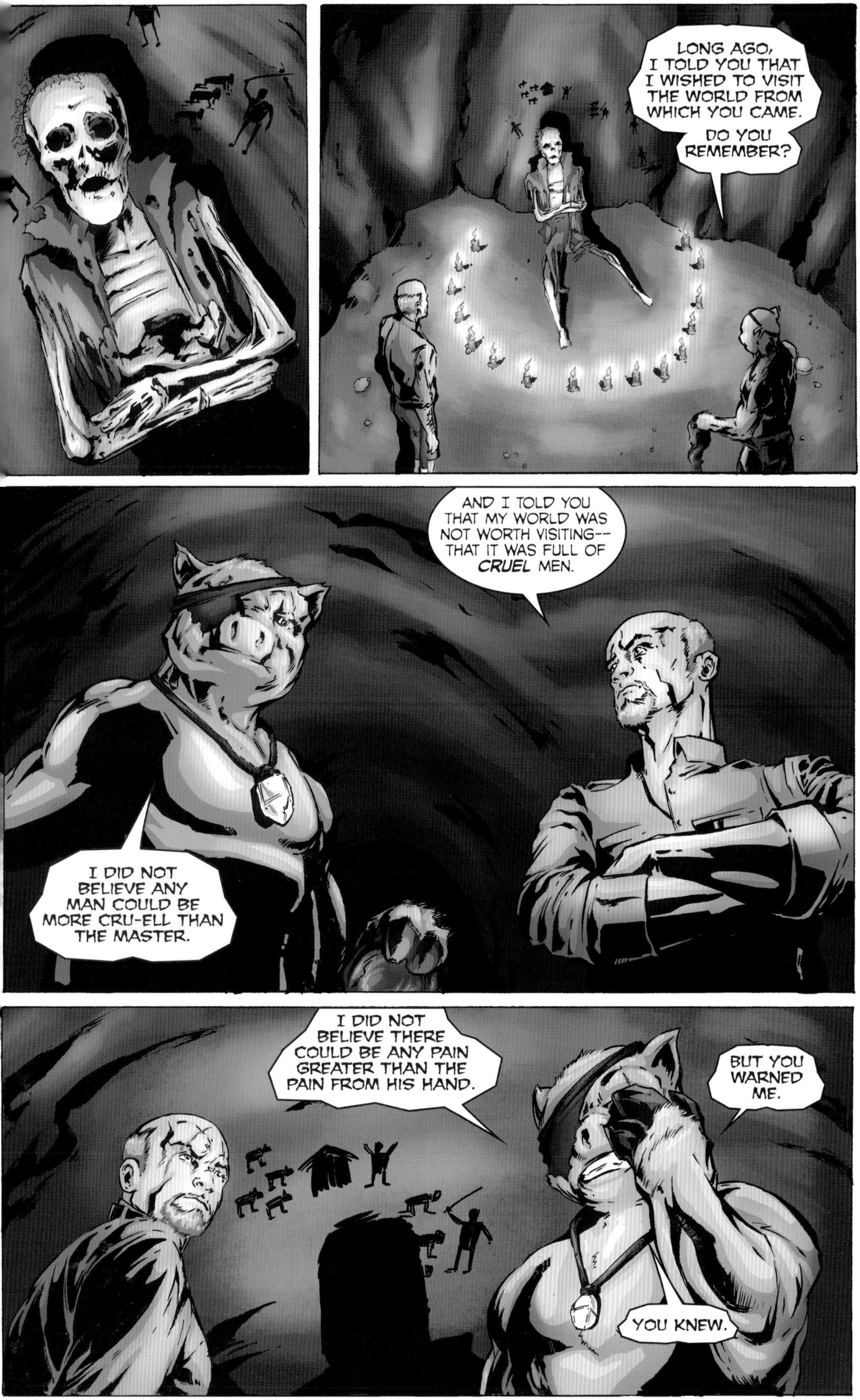

LONG AGO, I TOLD YOU THAT I WISHED TO VISIT THE WORLD FROM WHICH YOU CAME.
DO YOU REMEMBER?
AND I TOLD YOU THAT MY WORLD WAS NOT WORTH VISITING-- THAT IT WAS FULL OF *CRUEL* MEN.
I DID NOT BELIEVE ANY MAN COULD BE MORE CRU-ELL THAN THE MASTER.
I DID NOT BELIEVE THERE COULD BE ANY PAIN GREATER THAN THE PAIN FROM HIS HAND.
BUT YOU WARNED ME.
YOU KNEW.

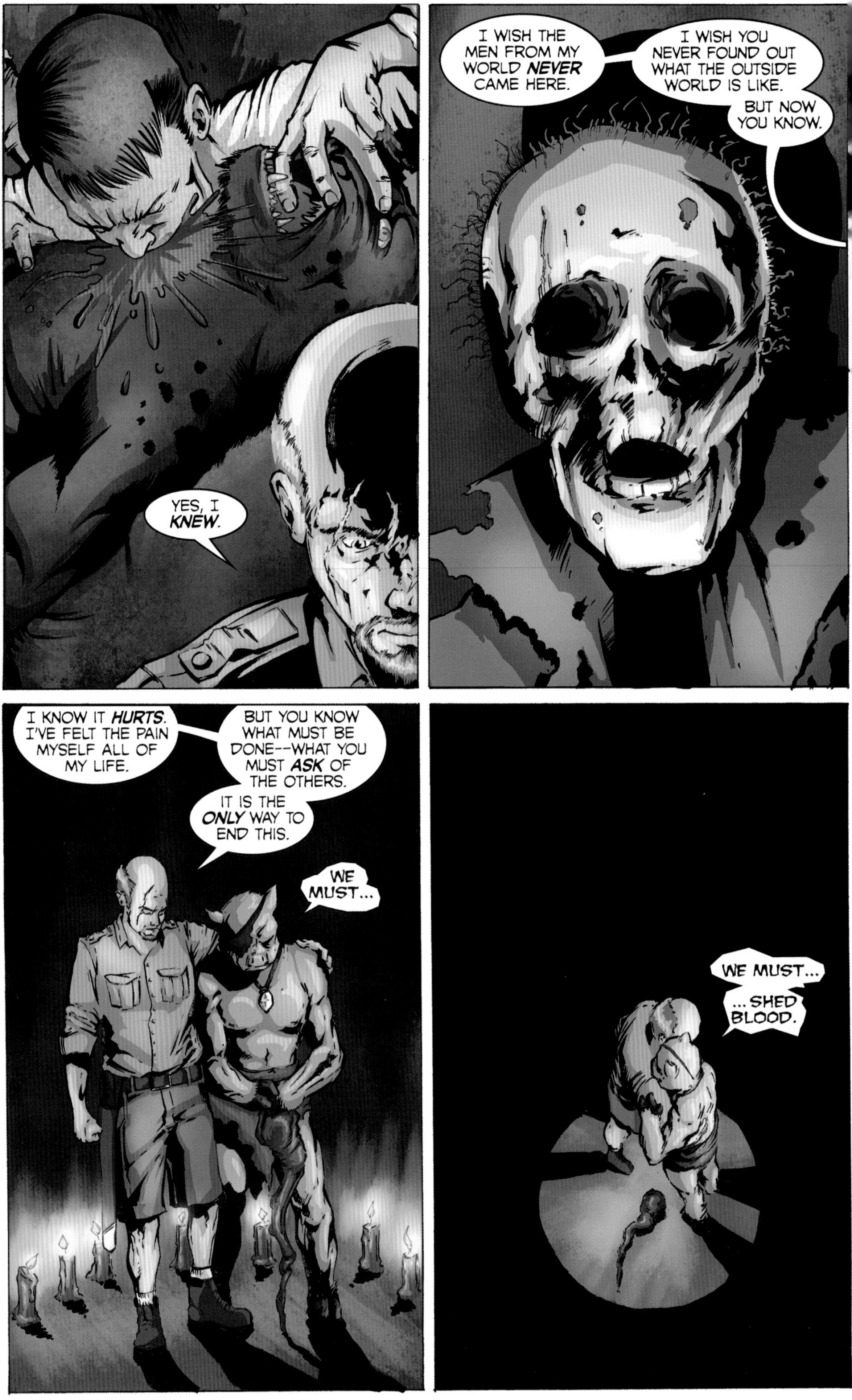
YES, I KNEW.
I WISH THE MEN FROM MY WORLD NEVER CAME HERE.
I WISH YOU NEVER FOUND OUT WHAT THE OUTSIDE WORLD IS LIKE.
BUT NOW YOU KNOW.
I KNOW IT HURTS. I'VE FELT THE PAIN MYSELF ALL OF MY LIFE.
BUT YOU KNOW WHAT MUST BE DONE--WHAT YOU MUST ASK OF THE OTHERS.
IT IS THE ONLY WAY TO END THIS.
WE MUST...
WE MUST...
...SHED BLOOD.

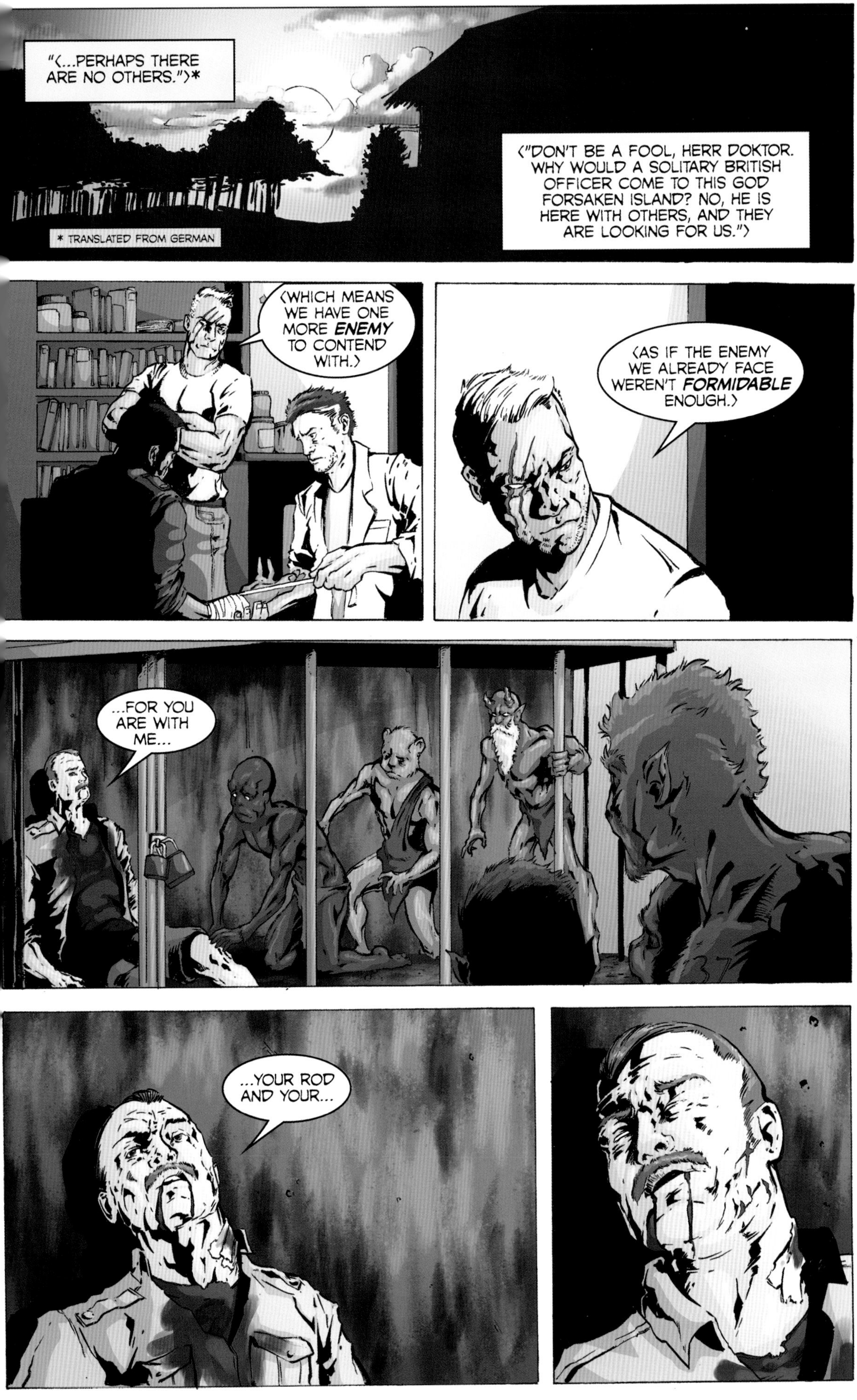
"‹...PERHAPS THERE ARE NO OTHERS."›*
* TRANSLATED FROM GERMAN
‹"DON'T BE A FOOL, HERR DOKTOR. WHY WOULD A SOLITARY BRITISH OFFICER COME TO THIS GOD FORSAKEN ISLAND? NO, HE IS HERE WITH OTHERS, AND THEY ARE LOOKING FOR US."›
‹WHICH MEANS WE HAVE ONE MORE ENEMY TO CONTEND WITH.›
‹AS IF THE ENEMY WE ALREADY FACE WEREN'T FORMIDABLE ENOUGH.›
...FOR YOU ARE WITH ME...
...YOUR ROD AND YOUR...

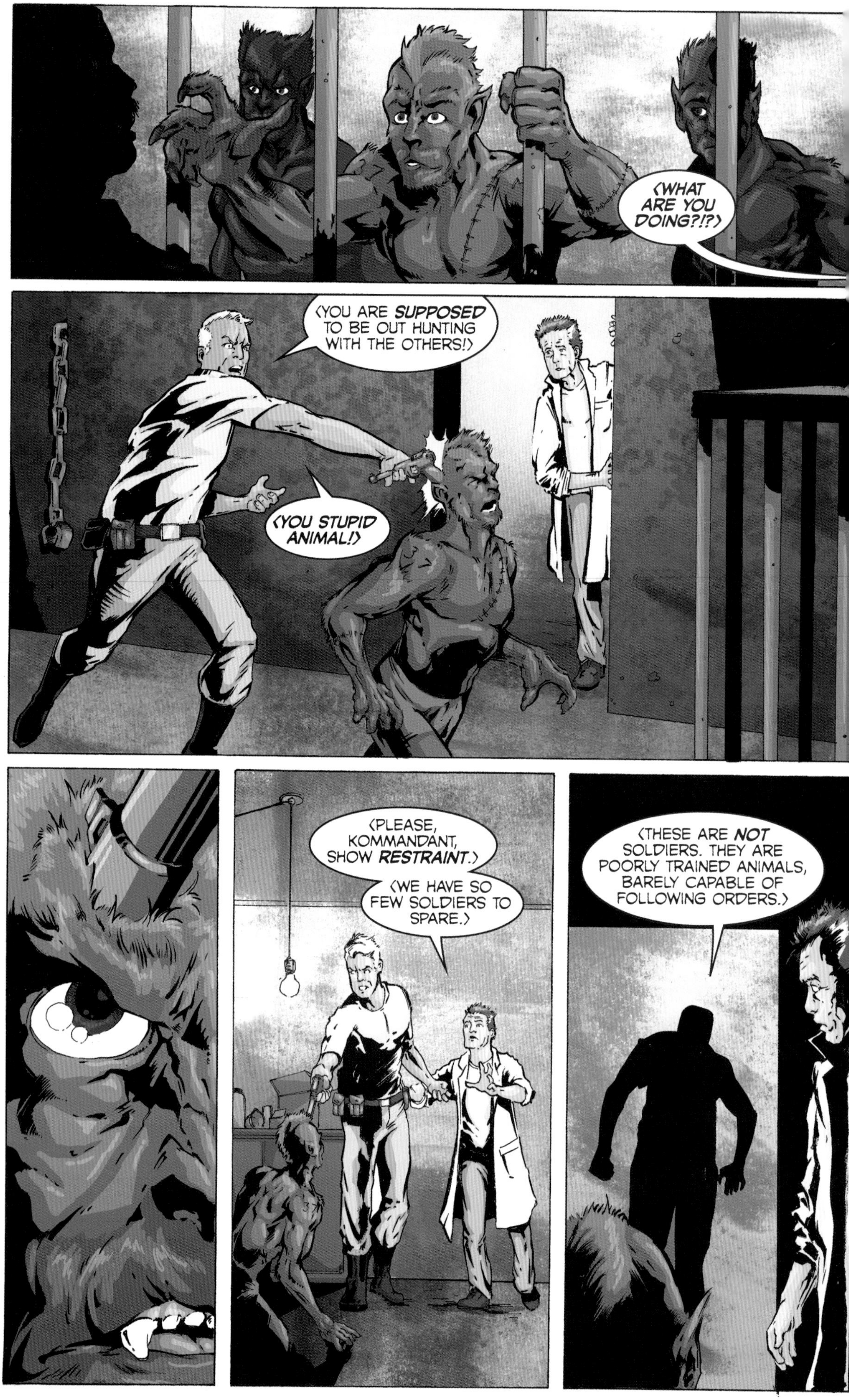

‹WHAT ARE YOU DOING?!?›
‹YOU ARE SUPPOSED TO BE OUT HUNTING WITH THE OTHERS!›
‹YOU STUPID ANIMAL!›
‹PLEASE, KOMMANDANT, SHOW RESTRAINT.›
‹WE HAVE SO FEW SOLDIERS TO SPARE.›
‹THESE ARE NOT SOLDIERS. THEY ARE POORLY TRAINED ANIMALS, BARELY CAPABLE OF FOLLOWING ORDERS.›

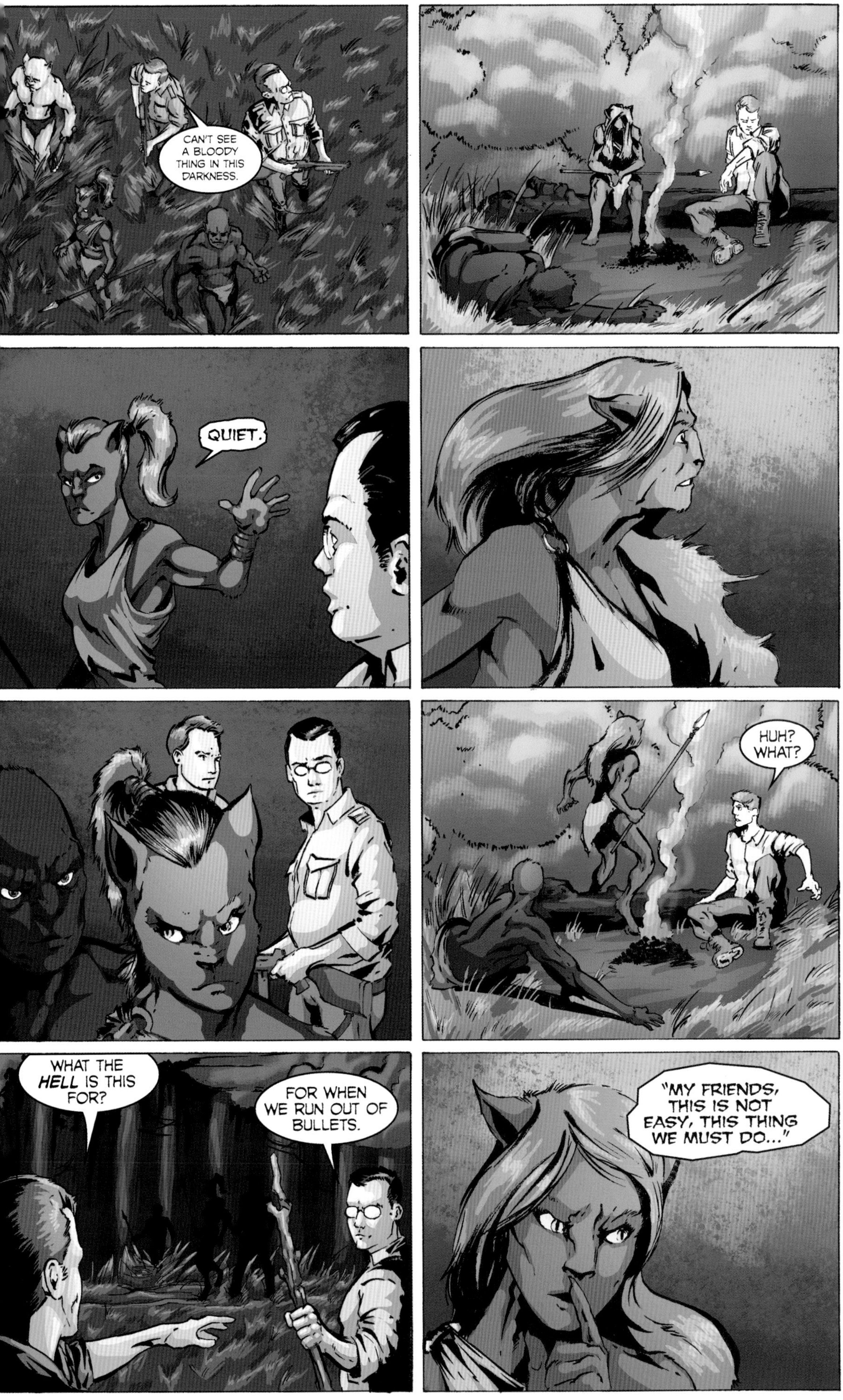
CAN'T SEE A BLOODY THING IN THIS DARKNESS.
QUIET.
HUH? WHAT?
WHAT THE HELL IS THIS FOR?
FOR WHEN WE RUN OUT OF BULLETS.
"MY FRIENDS, THIS IS NOT EASY, THIS THING WE MUST DO..."

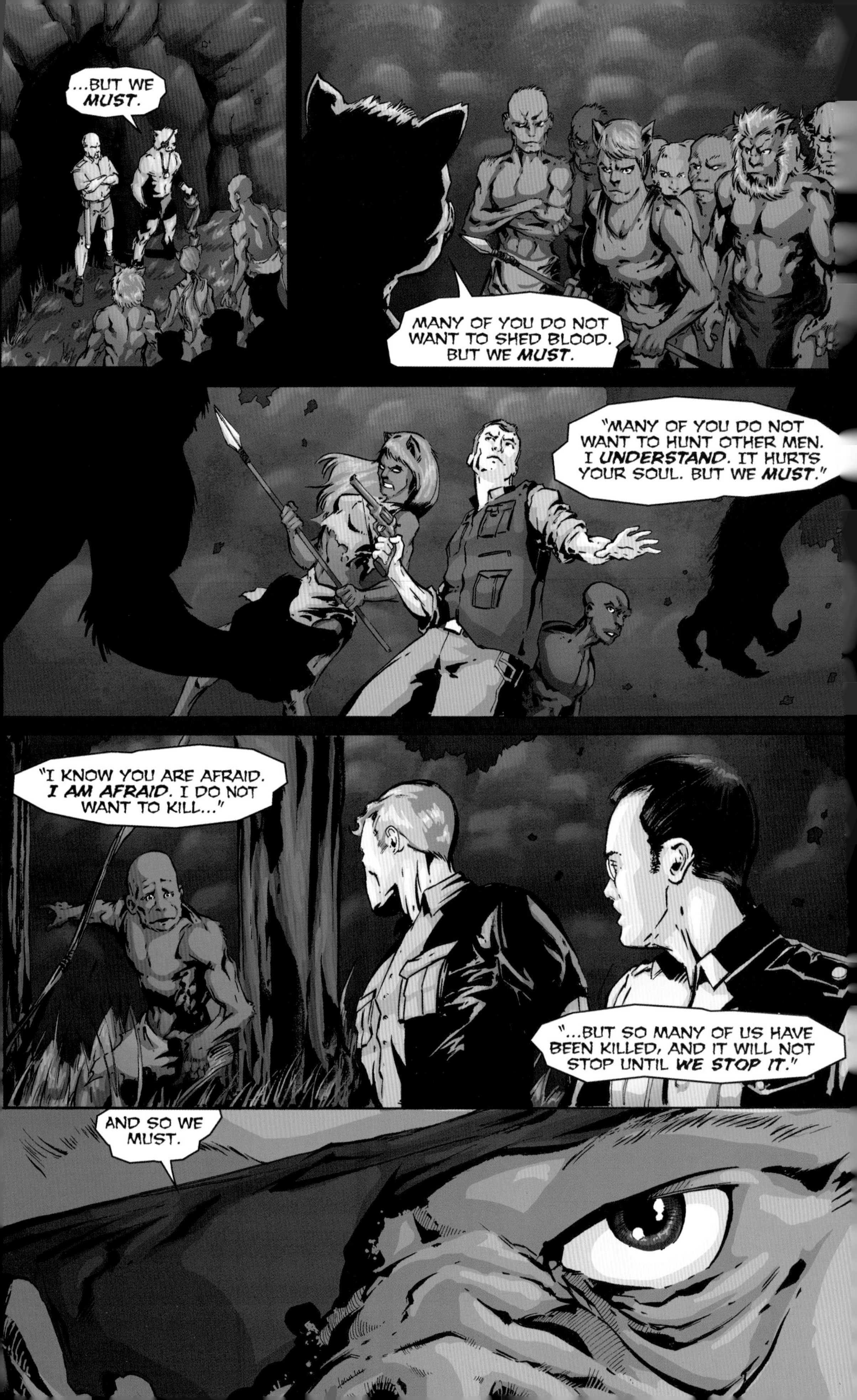
...BUT WE **MUST**.
MANY OF YOU DO NOT WANT TO SHED BLOOD. BUT WE **MUST**.
"MANY OF YOU DO NOT WANT TO HUNT OTHER MEN. I **UNDERSTAND**. IT HURTS YOUR SOUL. BUT WE **MUST**."
"I KNOW YOU ARE AFRAID. **I AM AFRAID**. I DO NOT WANT TO KILL..."
"...BUT SO MANY OF US HAVE BEEN KILLED, AND IT WILL NOT STOP UNTIL **WE STOP IT**."
AND SO WE MUST.

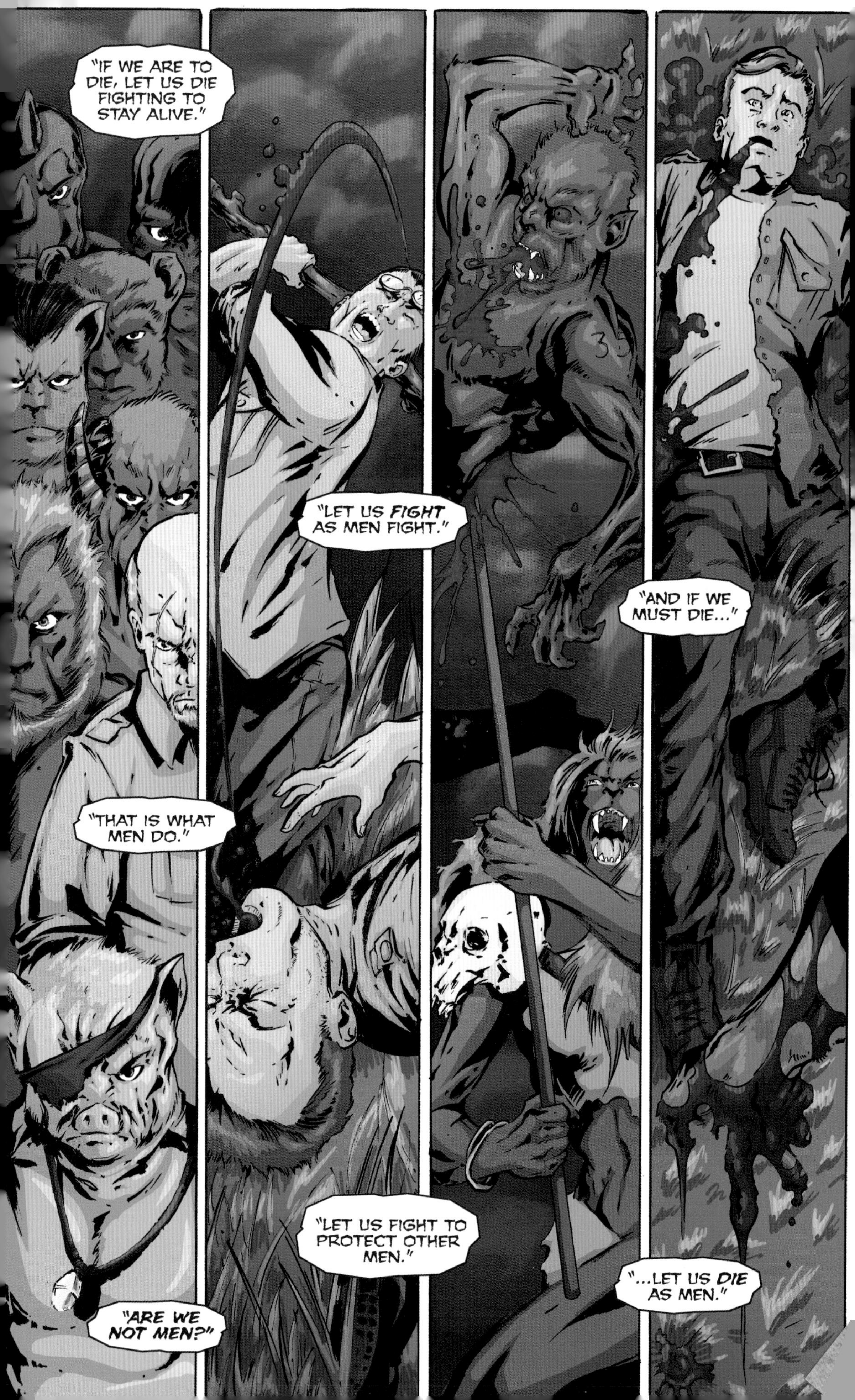
"IF WE ARE TO DIE, LET US DIE FIGHTING TO STAY ALIVE."
"THAT IS WHAT MEN DO."
"ARE WE NOT MEN?"
"LET US FIGHT AS MEN FIGHT."
"LET US FIGHT TO PROTECT OTHER MEN."
"AND IF WE MUST DIE..."
"...LET US DIE AS MEN."

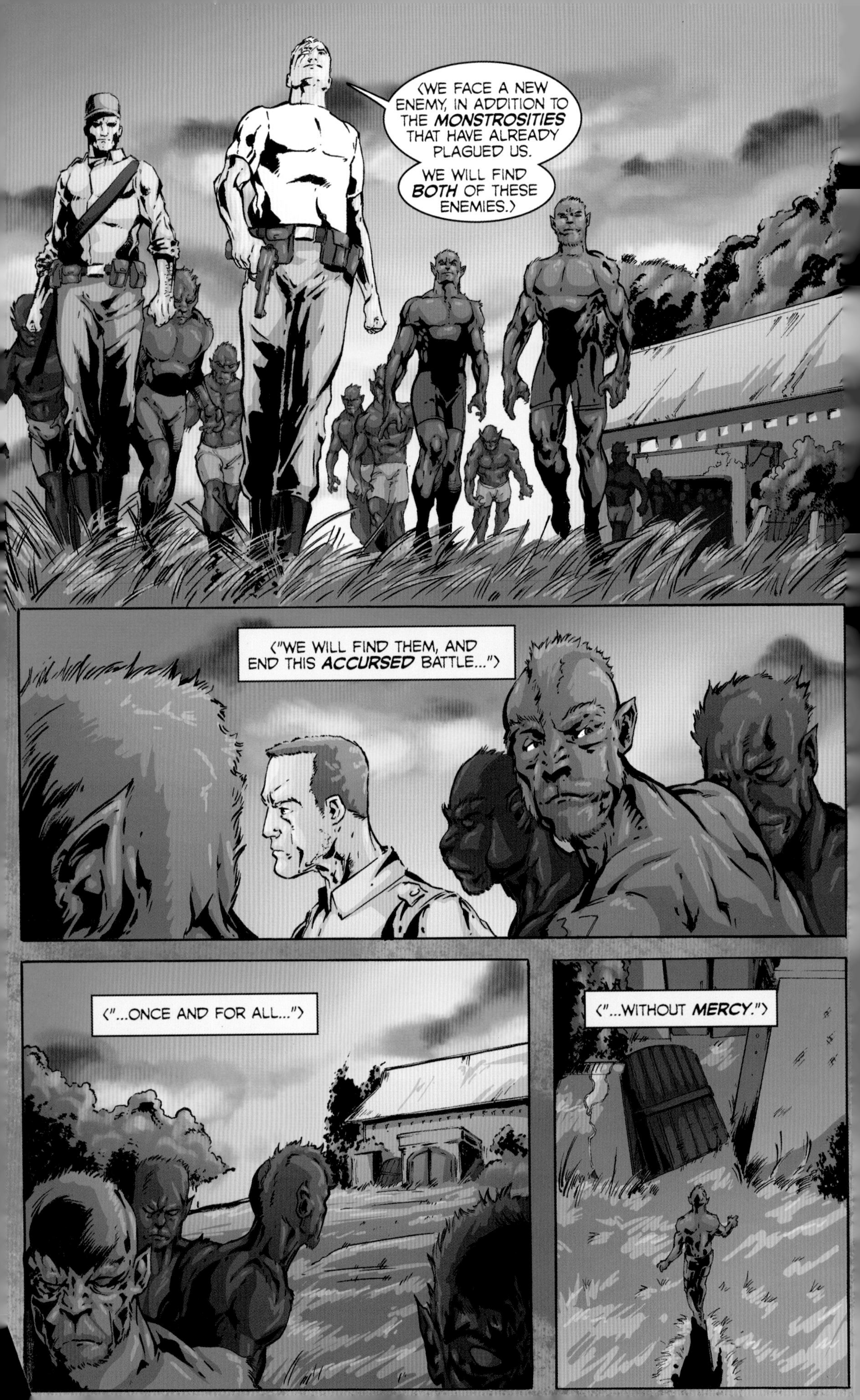

‹WE FACE A NEW ENEMY, IN ADDITION TO THE **MONSTROSITIES** THAT HAVE ALREADY PLAGUED US.
WE WILL FIND **BOTH** OF THESE ENEMIES.›
‹"WE WILL FIND THEM, AND END THIS **ACCURSED** BATTLE..."›
‹"...ONCE AND FOR ALL..."›
‹"...WITHOUT **MERCY**."›

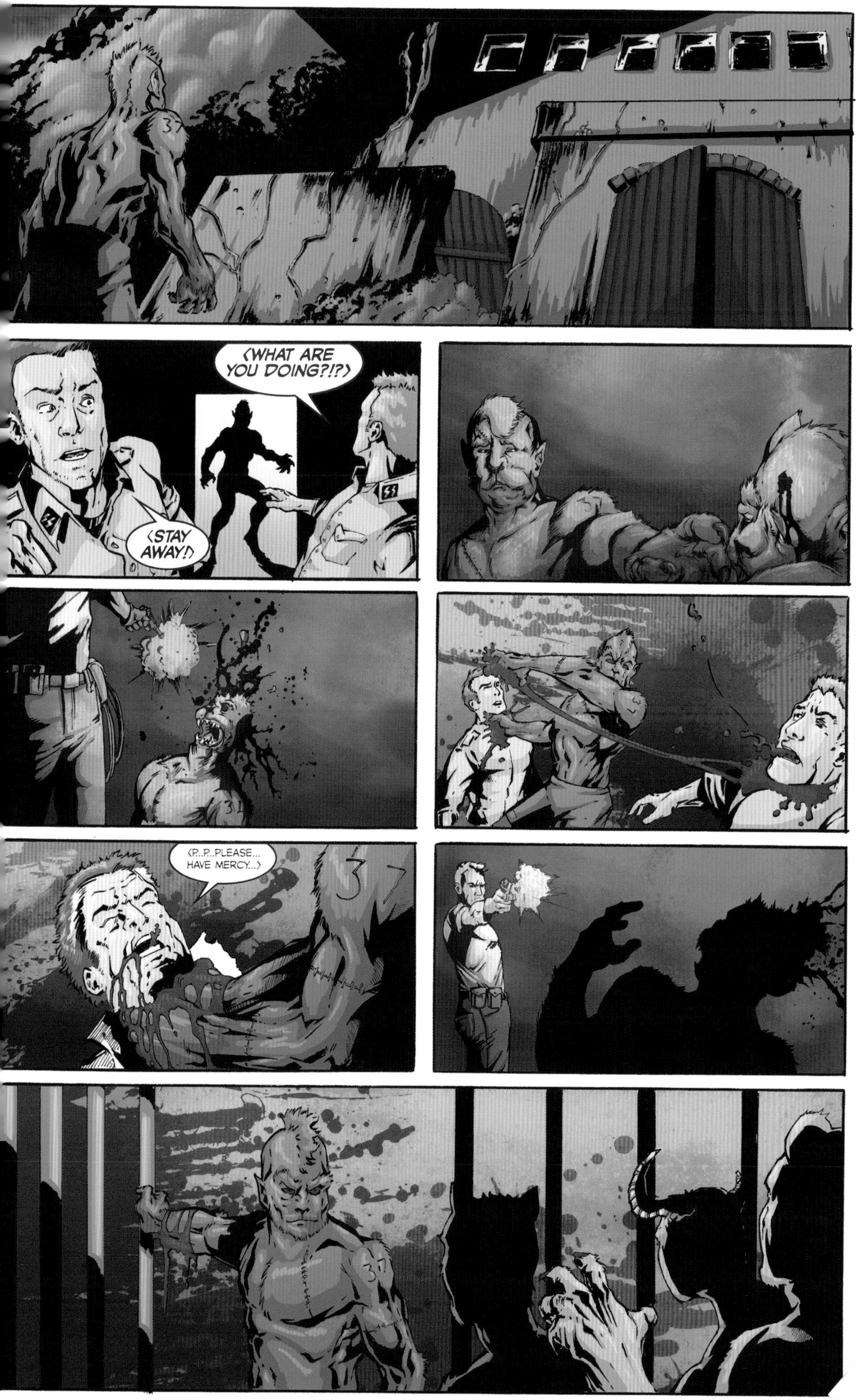

‹WHAT ARE YOU DOING?!?›
‹STAY AWAY!›
‹P...P...PLEASE... HAVE MERCY...›

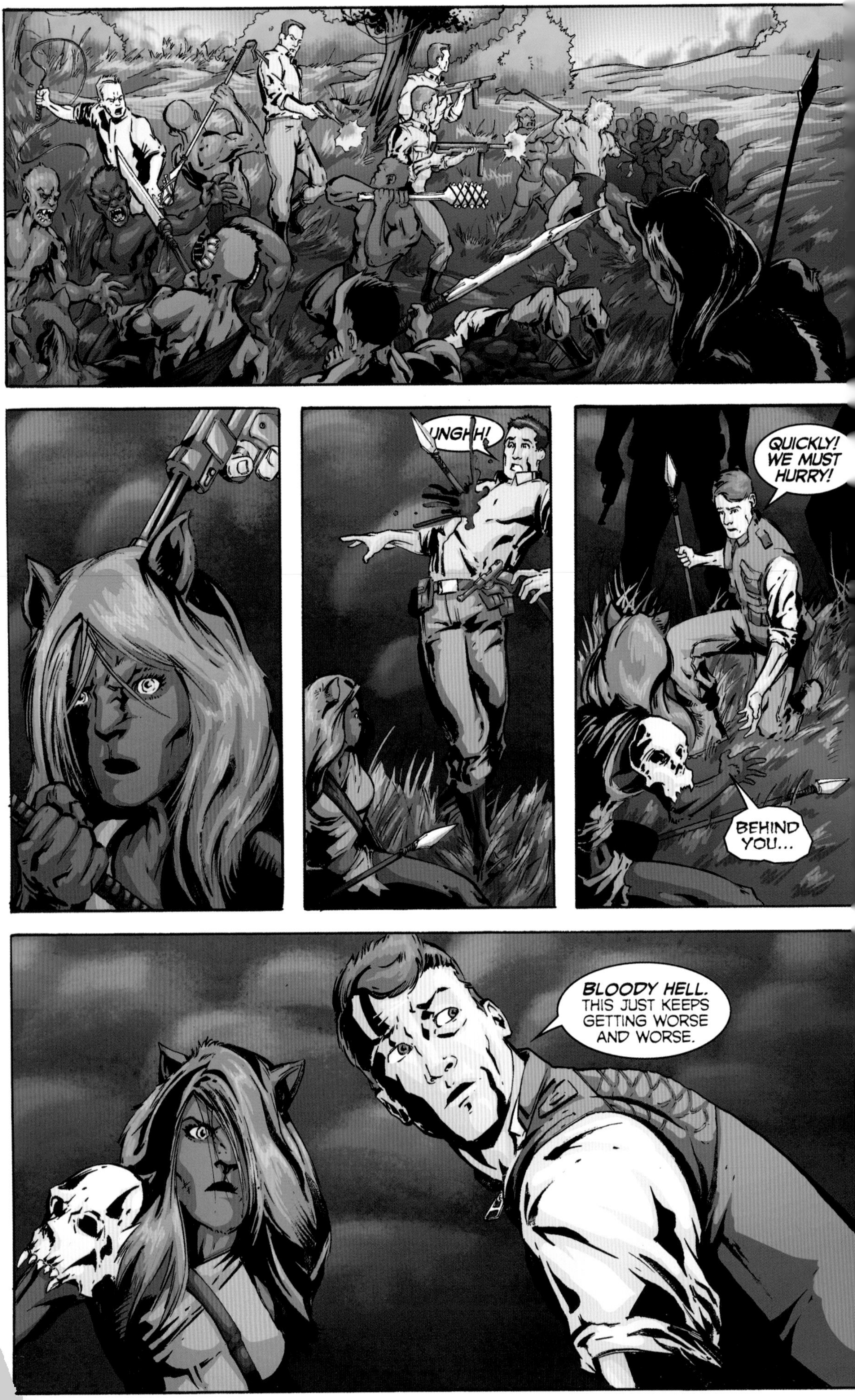
UNGHH!
QUICKLY! WE MUST HURRY!
BEHIND YOU...
BLOODY HELL. THIS JUST KEEPS GETTING WORSE AND WORSE.

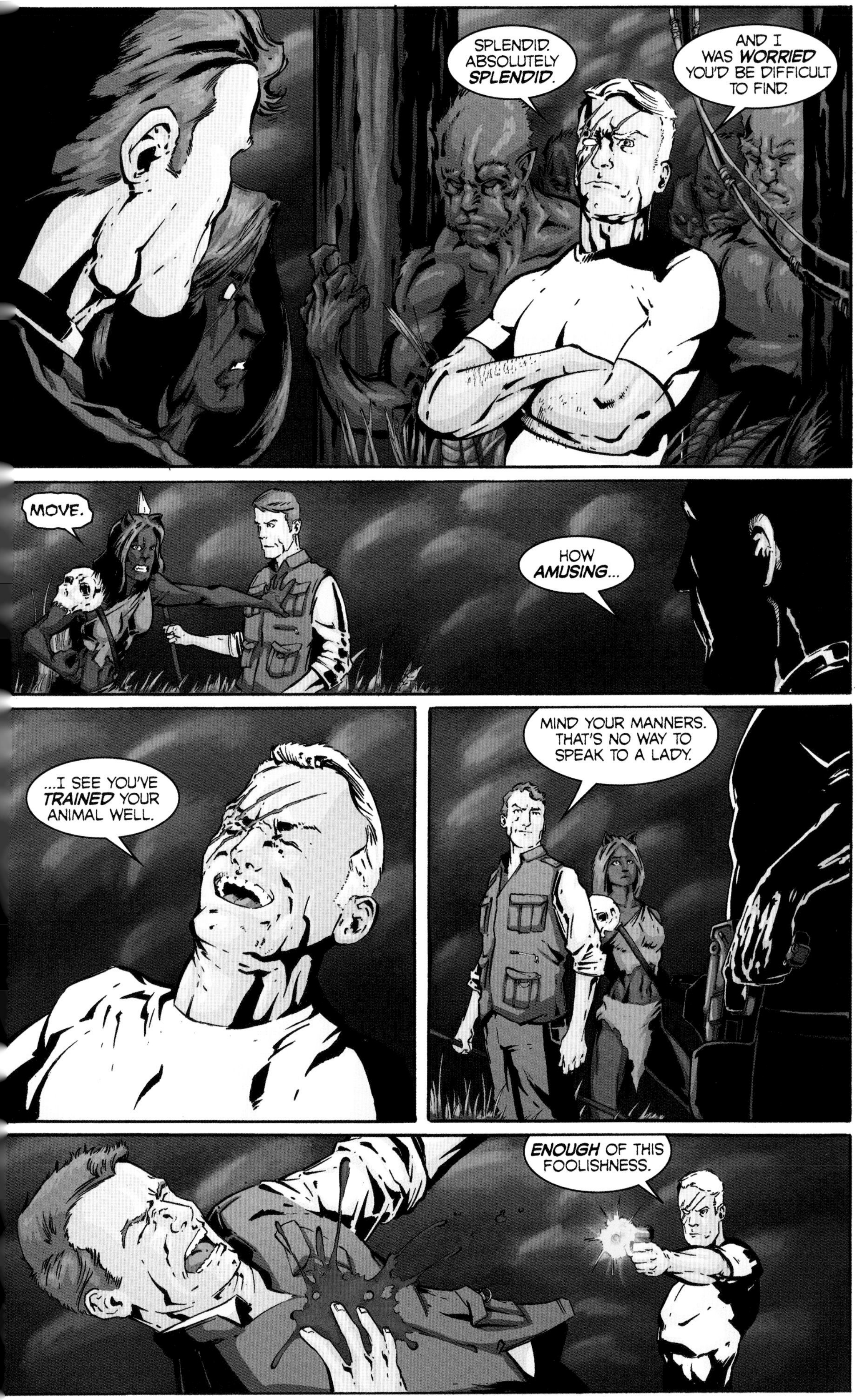
SPLENDID. ABSOLUTELY SPLENDID.
AND I WAS WORRIED YOU'D BE DIFFICULT TO FIND.
MOVE.
HOW AMUSING...
...I SEE YOU'VE TRAINED YOUR ANIMAL WELL.
MIND YOUR MANNERS. THAT'S NO WAY TO SPEAK TO A LADY.
ENOUGH OF THIS FOOLISHNESS.

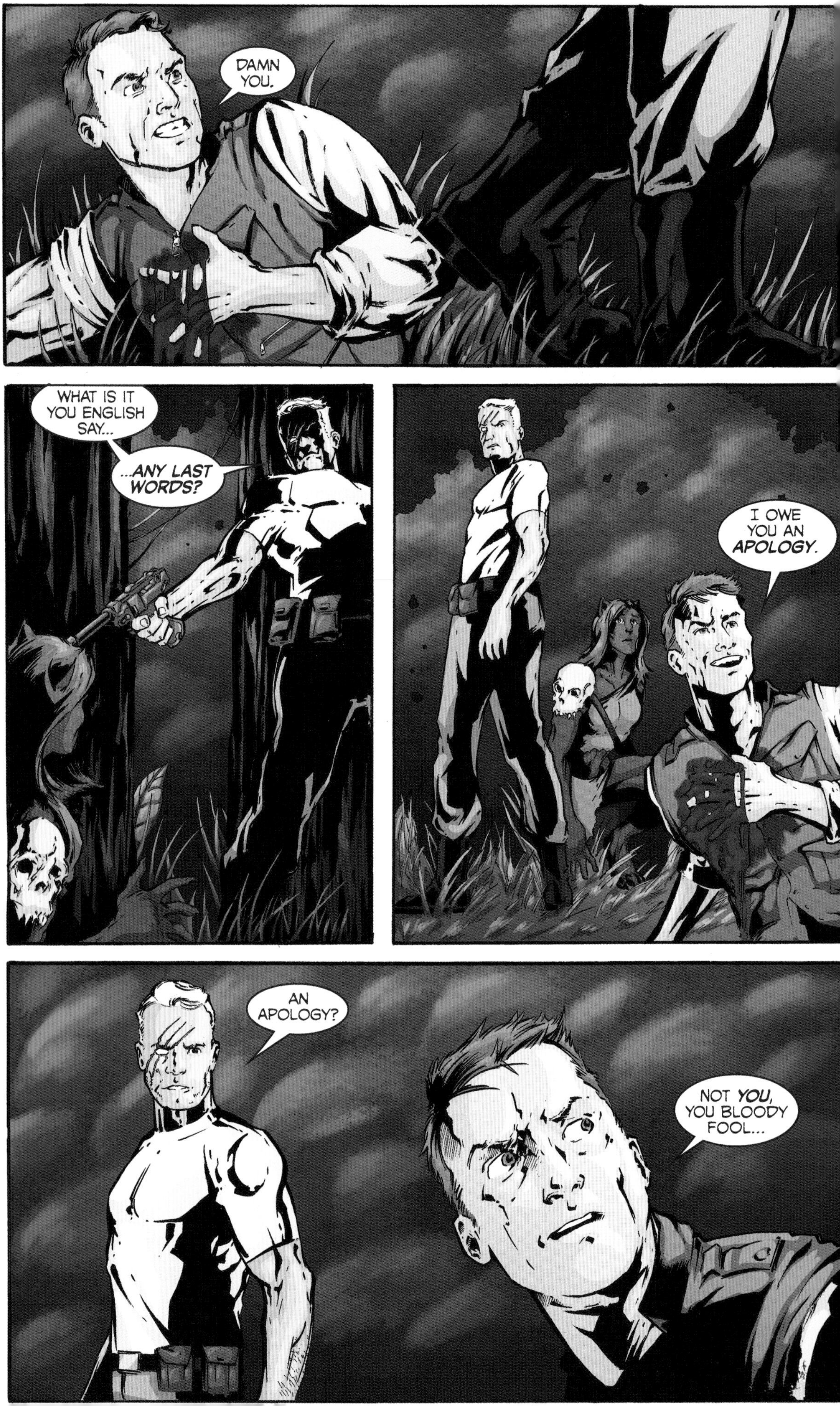
DAMN YOU.
WHAT IS IT YOU ENGLISH SAY...
...ANY LAST WORDS?
I OWE YOU AN APOLOGY.
AN APOLOGY?
NOT YOU, YOU BLOODY FOOL...

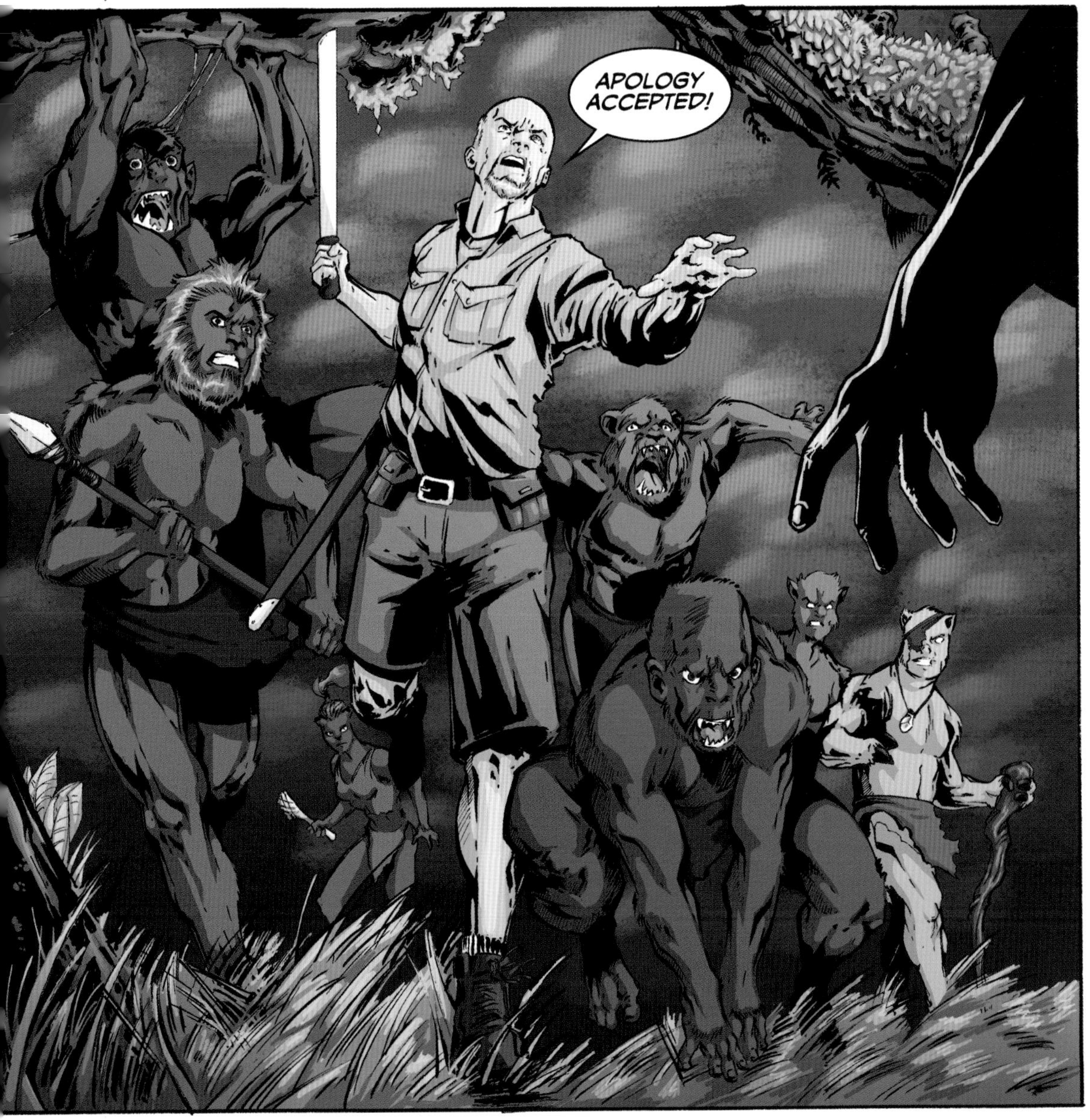
APOLOGY ACCEPTED!

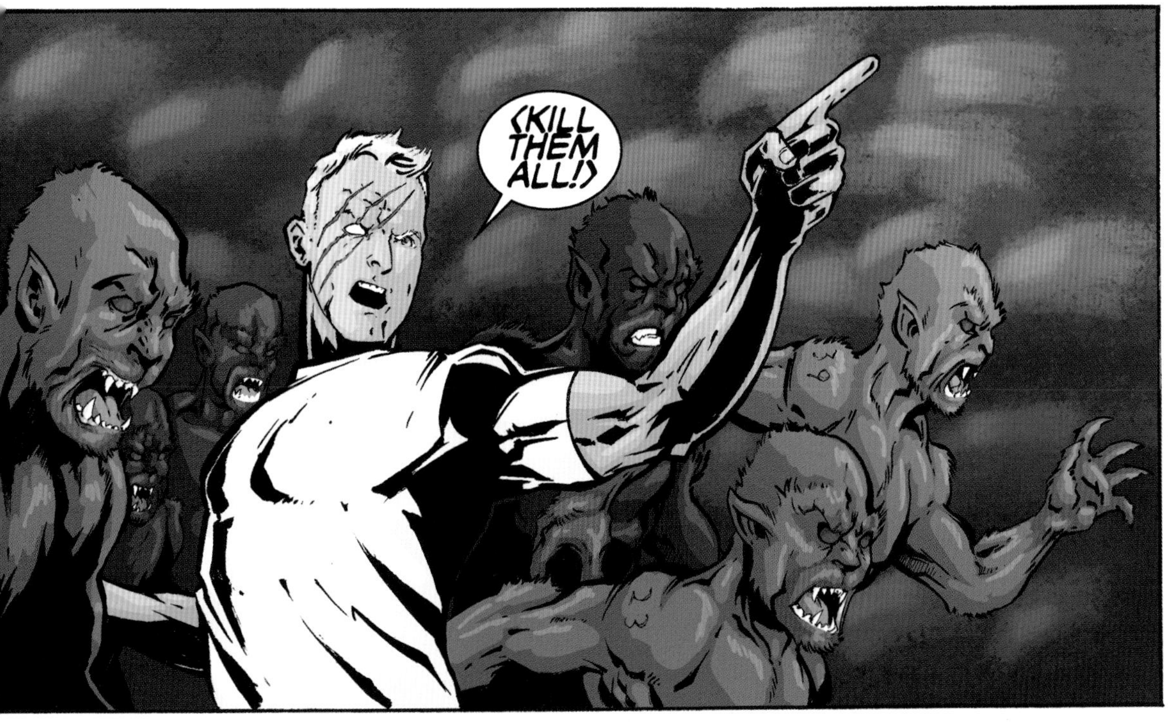
<KILL THEM ALL!>

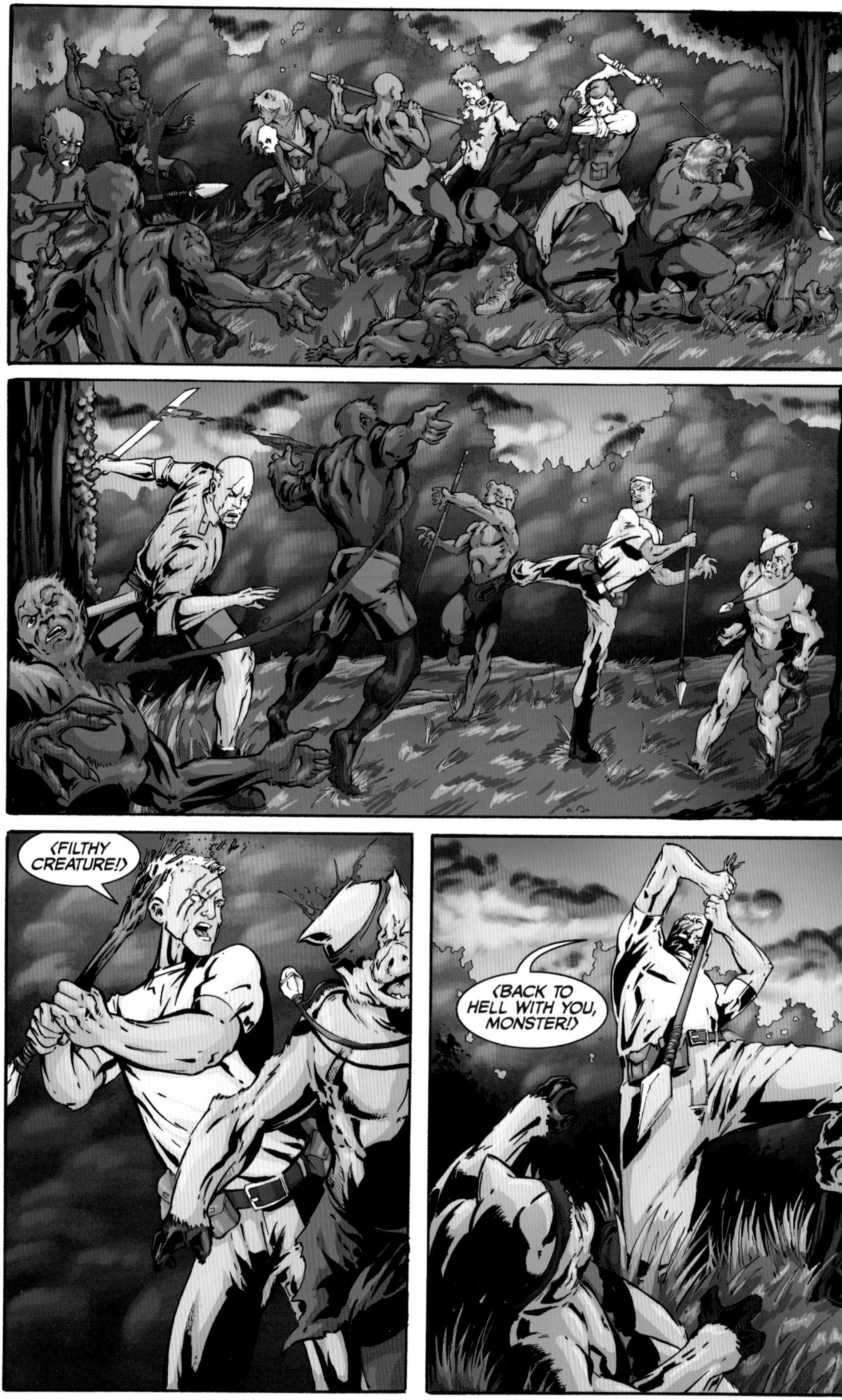
‹FILTHY CREATURE!›
‹BACK TO HELL WITH YOU, MONSTER!›

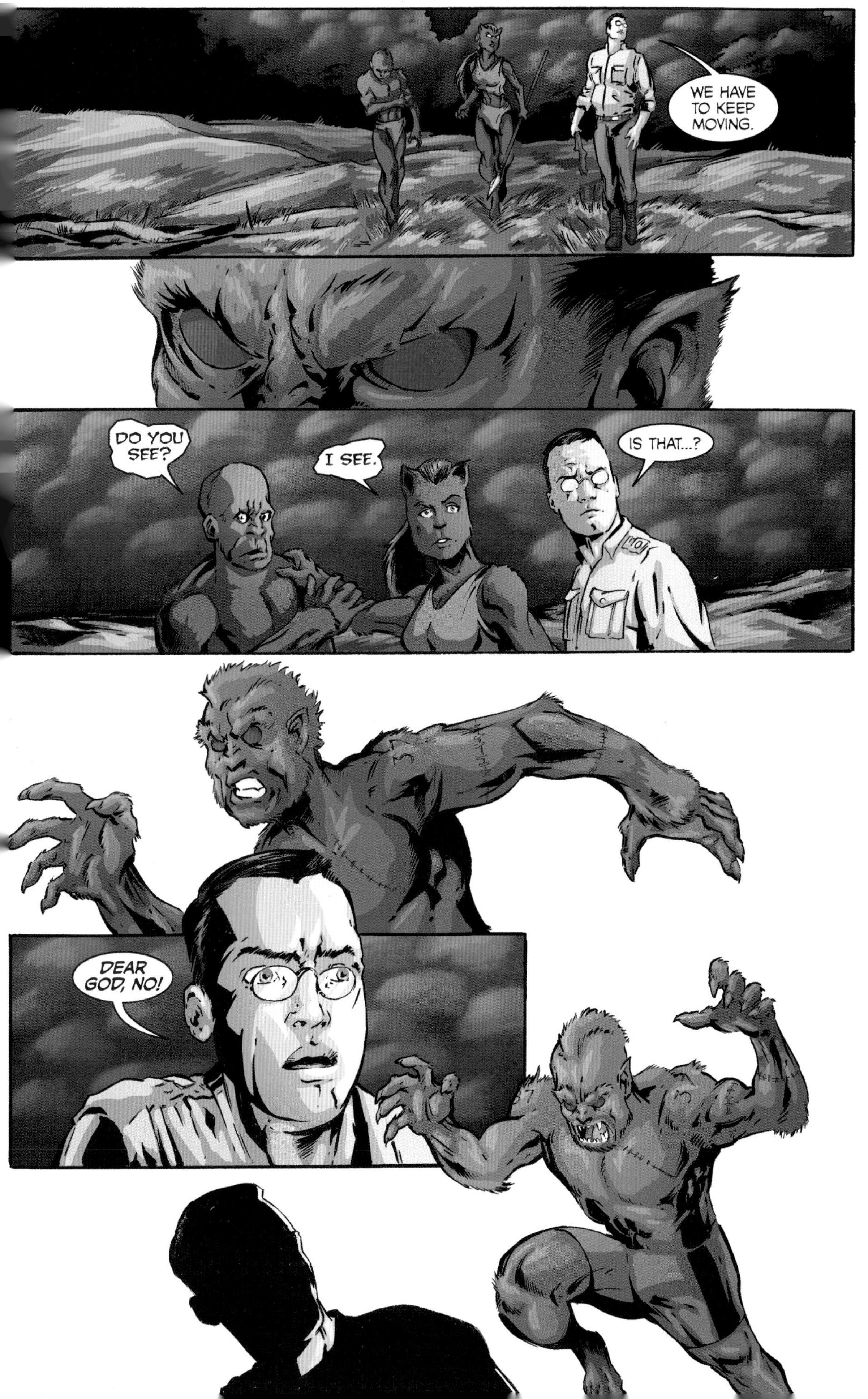

WE HAVE TO KEEP MOVING.
DO YOU SEE?
I SEE.
IS THAT...?
DEAR GOD, NO!

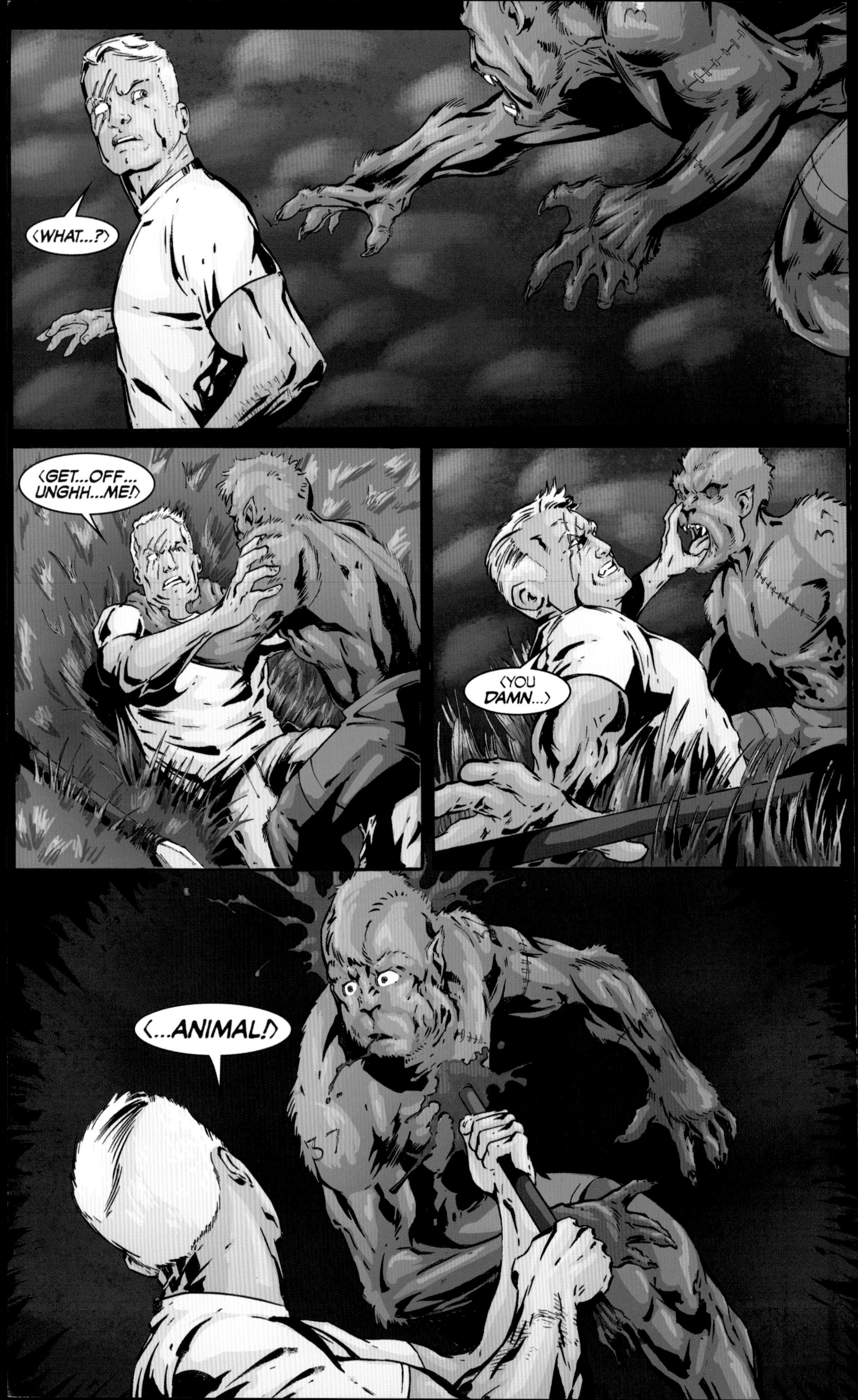

<WHAT...?>
<GET...OFF... UNGHH...ME!>
<YOU DAMN...>
<...ANIMAL!>

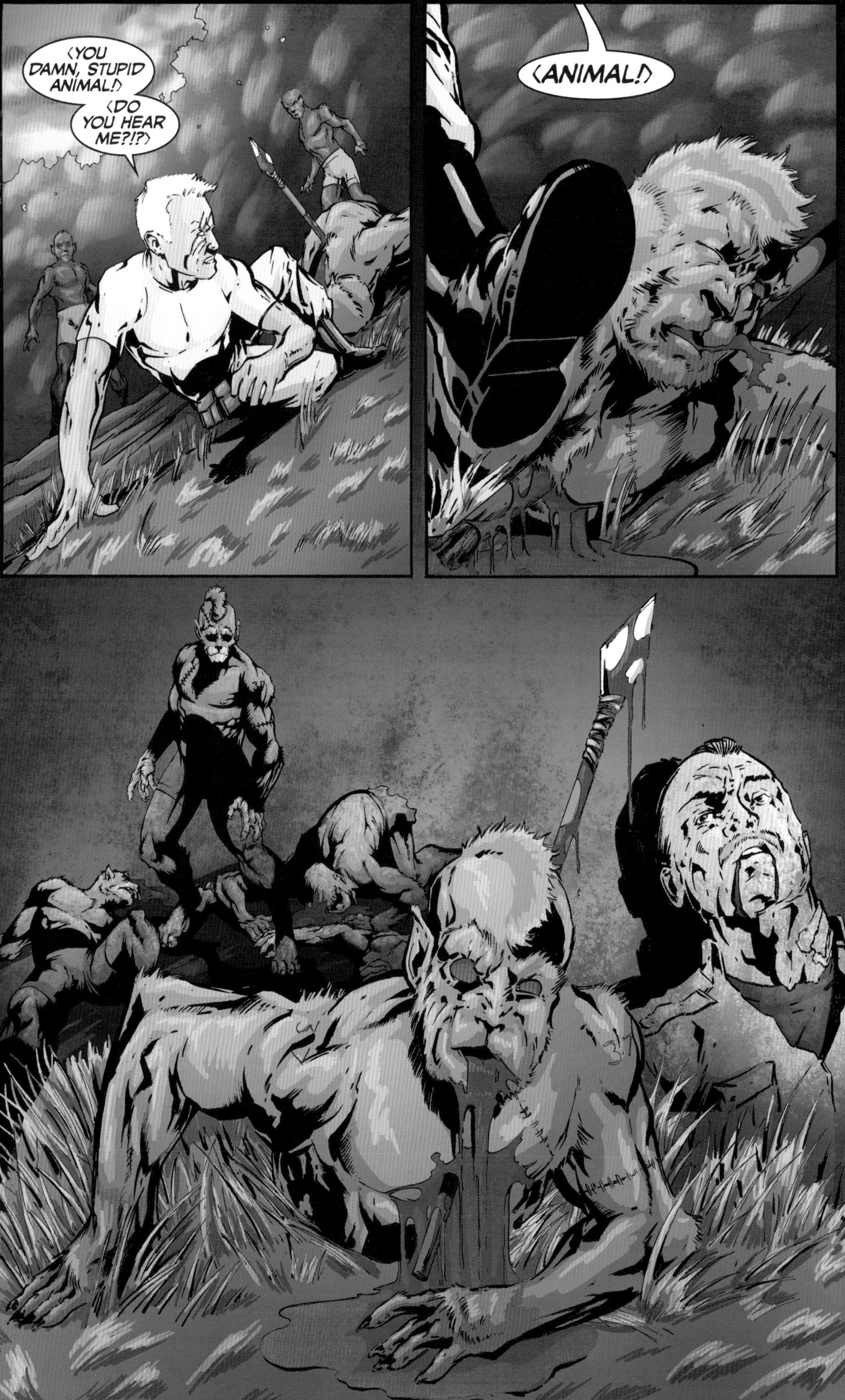

‹YOU DAMN, STUPID ANIMAL!›
‹DO YOU HEAR ME?!?›
‹ANIMAL!›

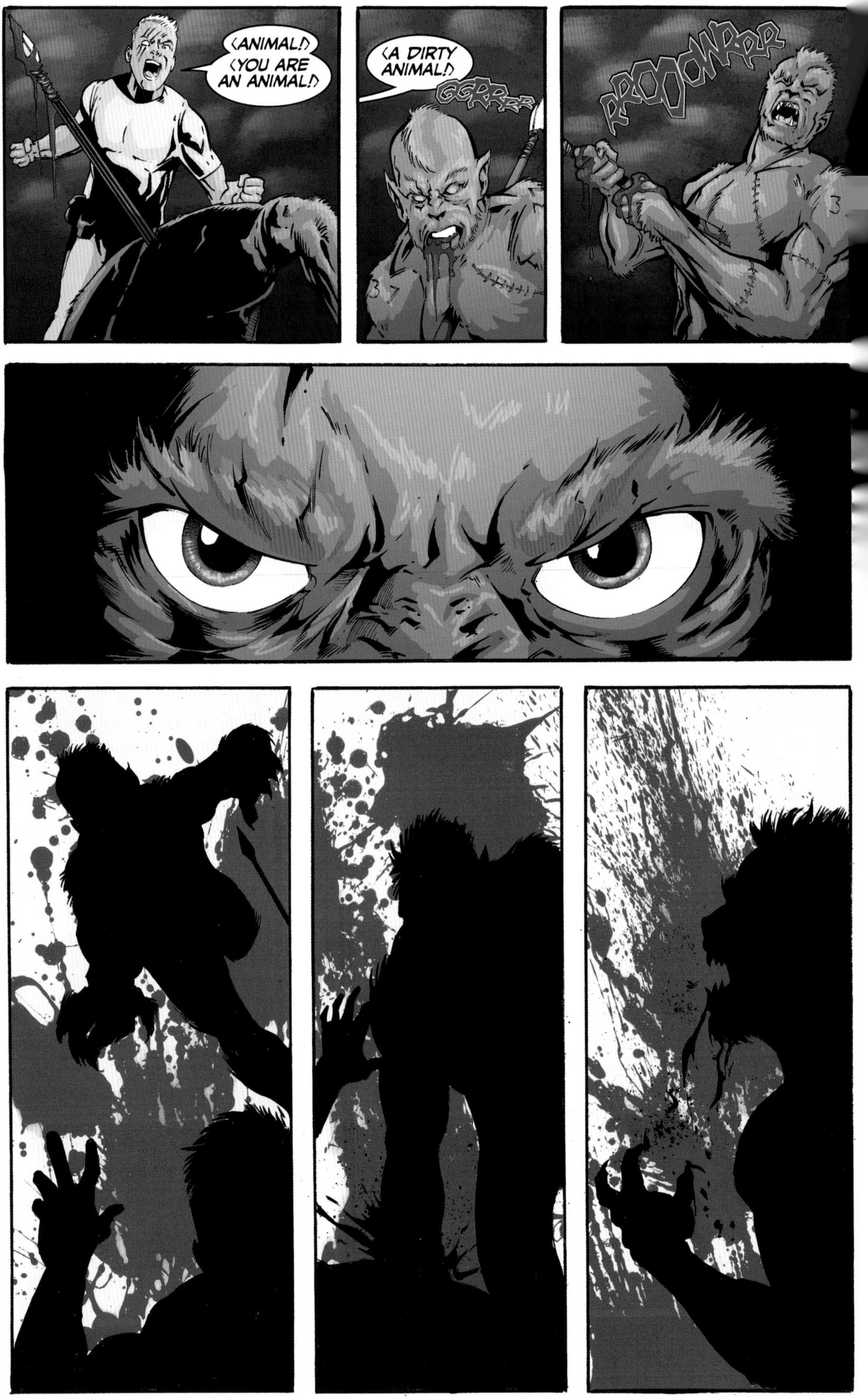

‹ANIMAL!›
‹YOU ARE AN ANIMAL!›
‹A DIRTY ANIMAL!›
GGRRRR
RROOOWRRR

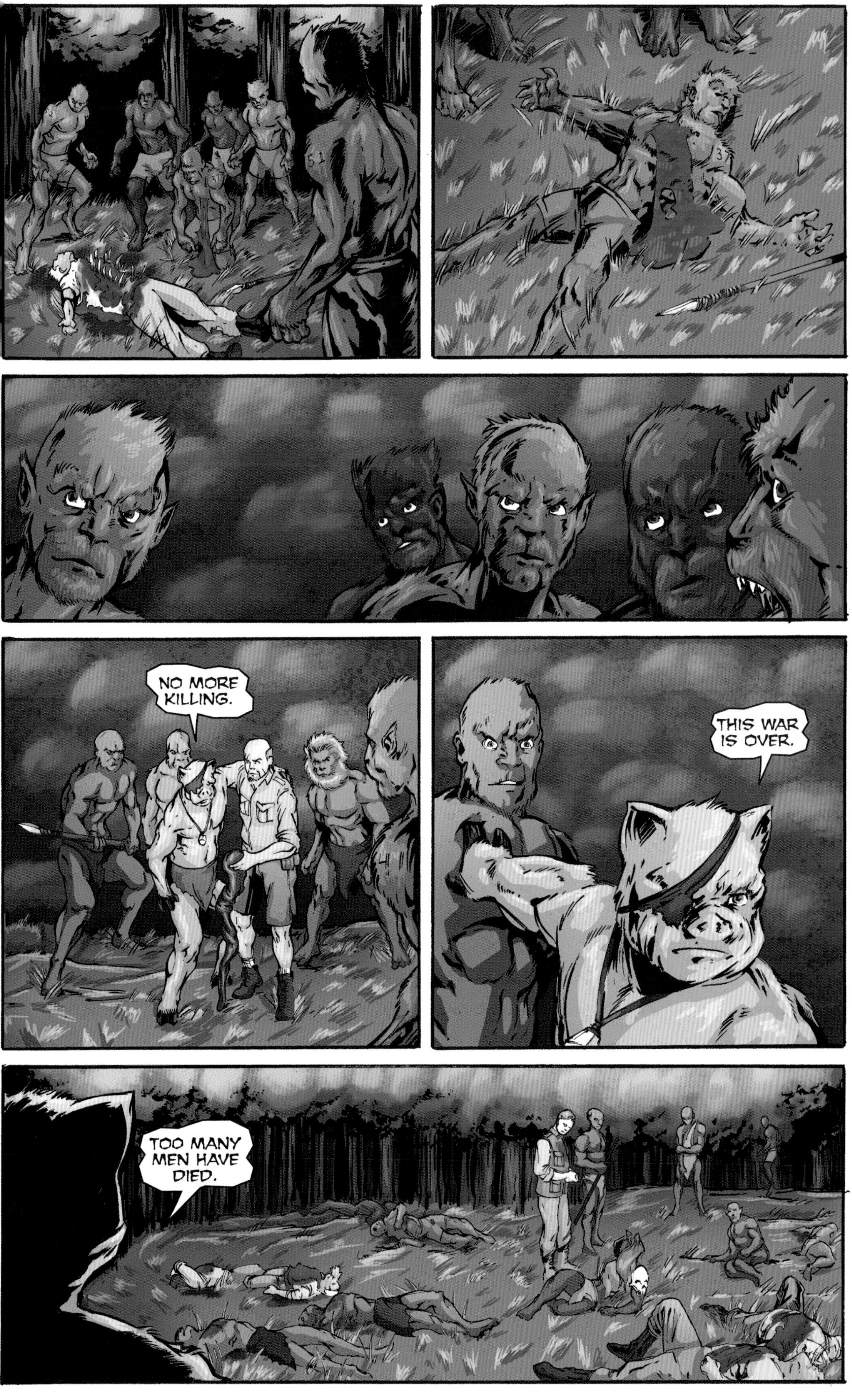
NO MORE KILLING.
THIS WAR IS OVER.
TOO MANY MEN HAVE DIED.

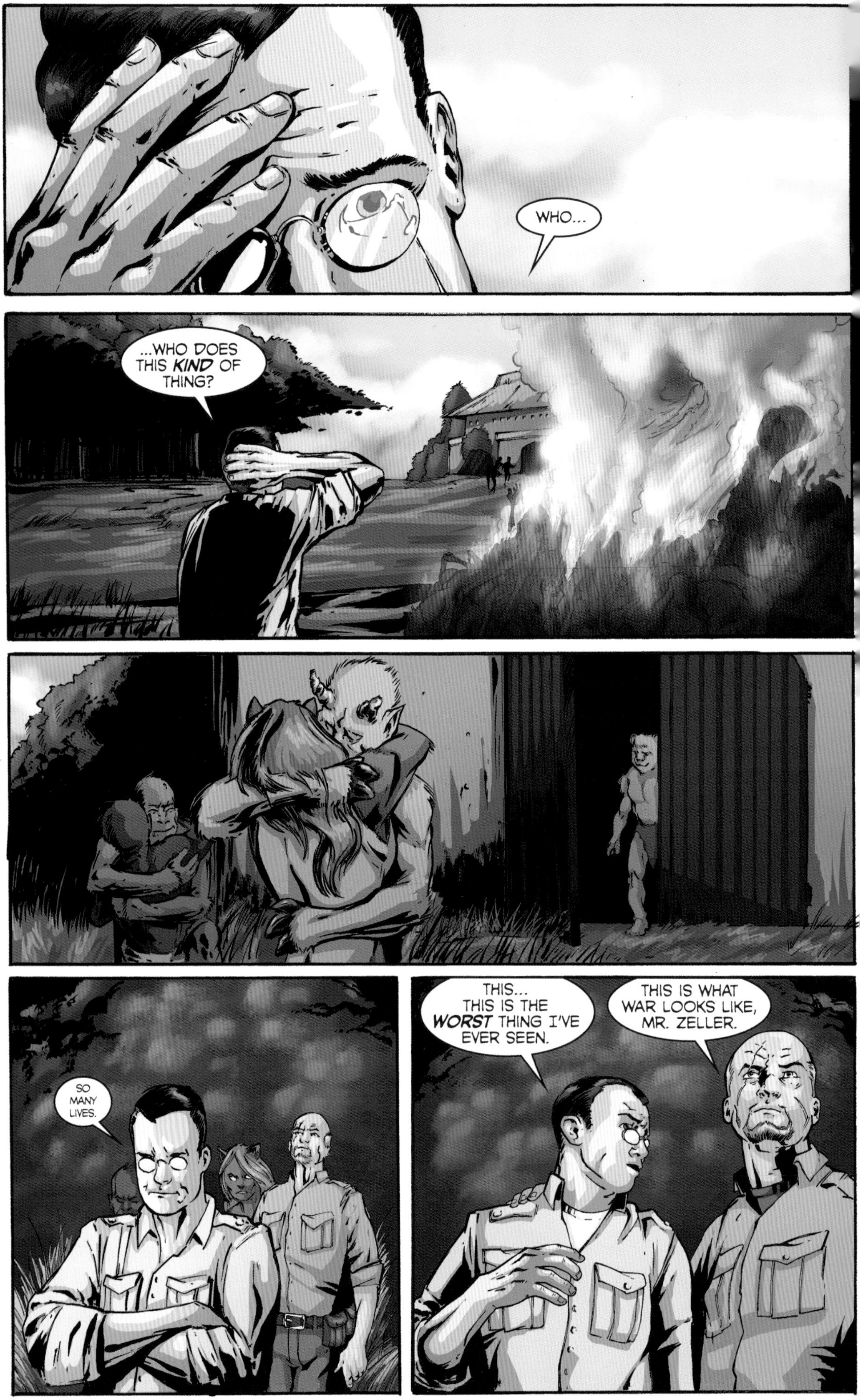
WHO...
...WHO DOES THIS *KIND* OF THING?
SO MANY LIVES.
THIS... THIS IS THE *WORST* THING I'VE EVER SEEN.
THIS IS WHAT WAR LOOKS LIKE, MR. ZELLER.

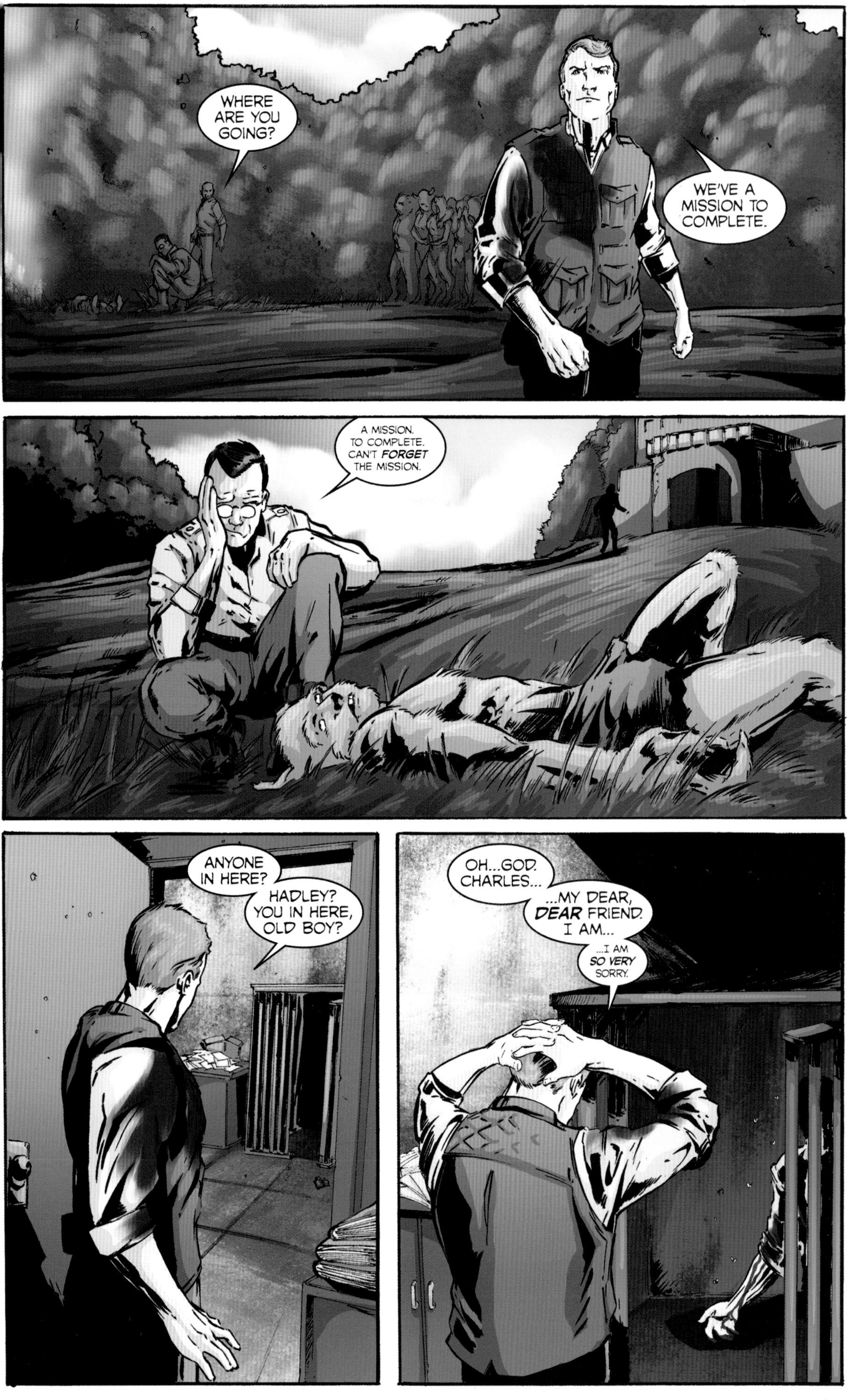
WHERE ARE YOU GOING?
WE'VE A MISSION TO COMPLETE.
A MISSION. TO COMPLETE. CAN'T *FORGET* THE MISSION.
ANYONE IN HERE?
HADLEY? YOU IN HERE, OLD BOY?
OH...GOD. CHARLES...
...MY DEAR, *DEAR* FRIEND. I AM...
...I AM *SO VERY* SORRY.

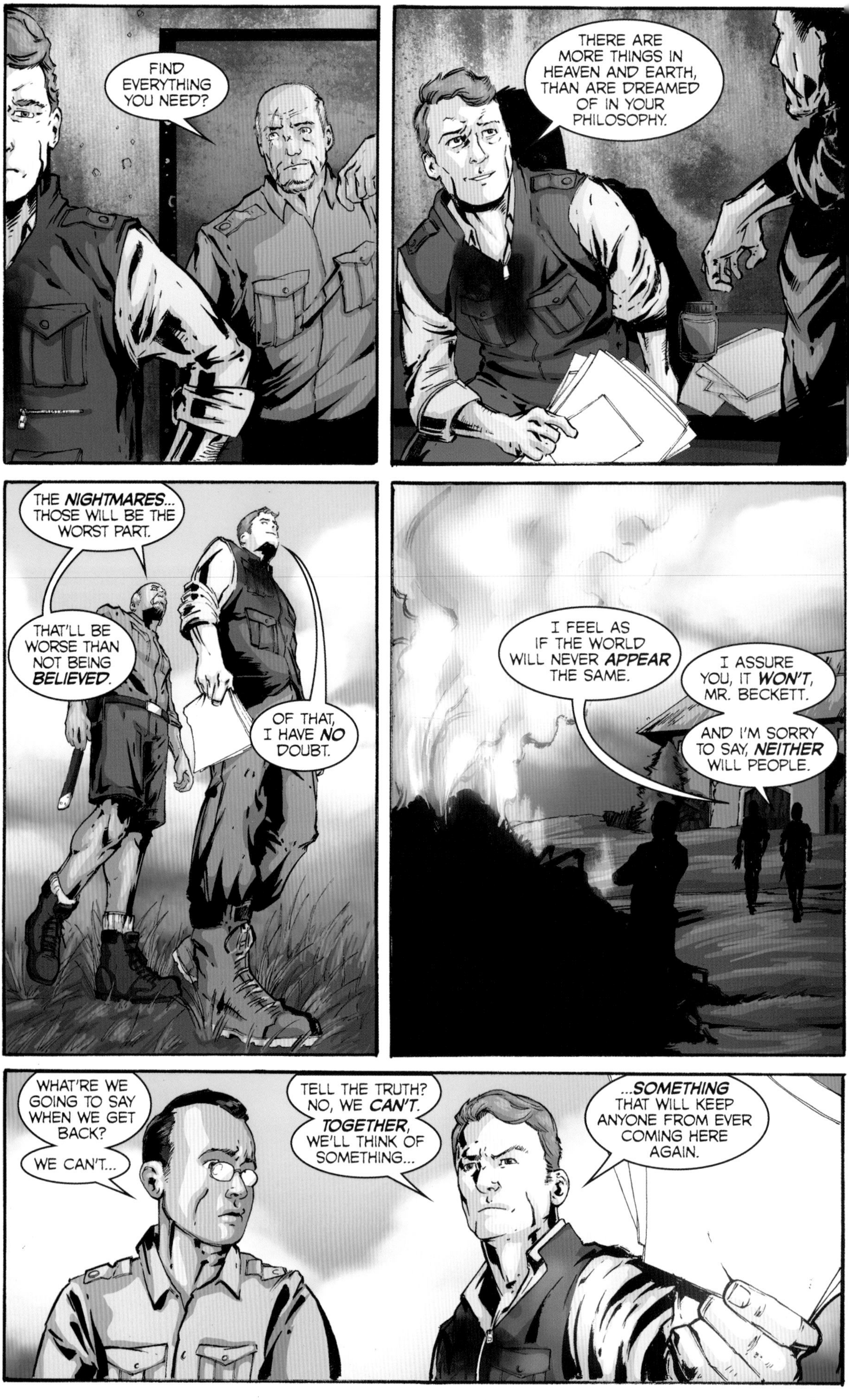
FIND EVERYTHING YOU NEED?
THERE ARE MORE THINGS IN HEAVEN AND EARTH, THAN ARE DREAMED OF IN YOUR PHILOSOPHY.
THE ***NIGHTMARES***... THOSE WILL BE THE WORST PART.
THAT'LL BE WORSE THAN NOT BEING ***BELIEVED***.
OF THAT, I HAVE ***NO*** DOUBT.
I FEEL AS IF THE WORLD WILL NEVER ***APPEAR*** THE SAME.
I ASSURE YOU, IT ***WON'T***, MR. BECKETT.
AND I'M SORRY TO SAY, ***NEITHER*** WILL PEOPLE.
WHAT'RE WE GOING TO SAY WHEN WE GET BACK?
WE CAN'T...
TELL THE TRUTH? NO, WE ***CAN'T***. ***TOGETHER***, WE'LL THINK OF SOMETHING...
...***SOMETHING*** THAT WILL KEEP ANYONE FROM EVER COMING HERE AGAIN.

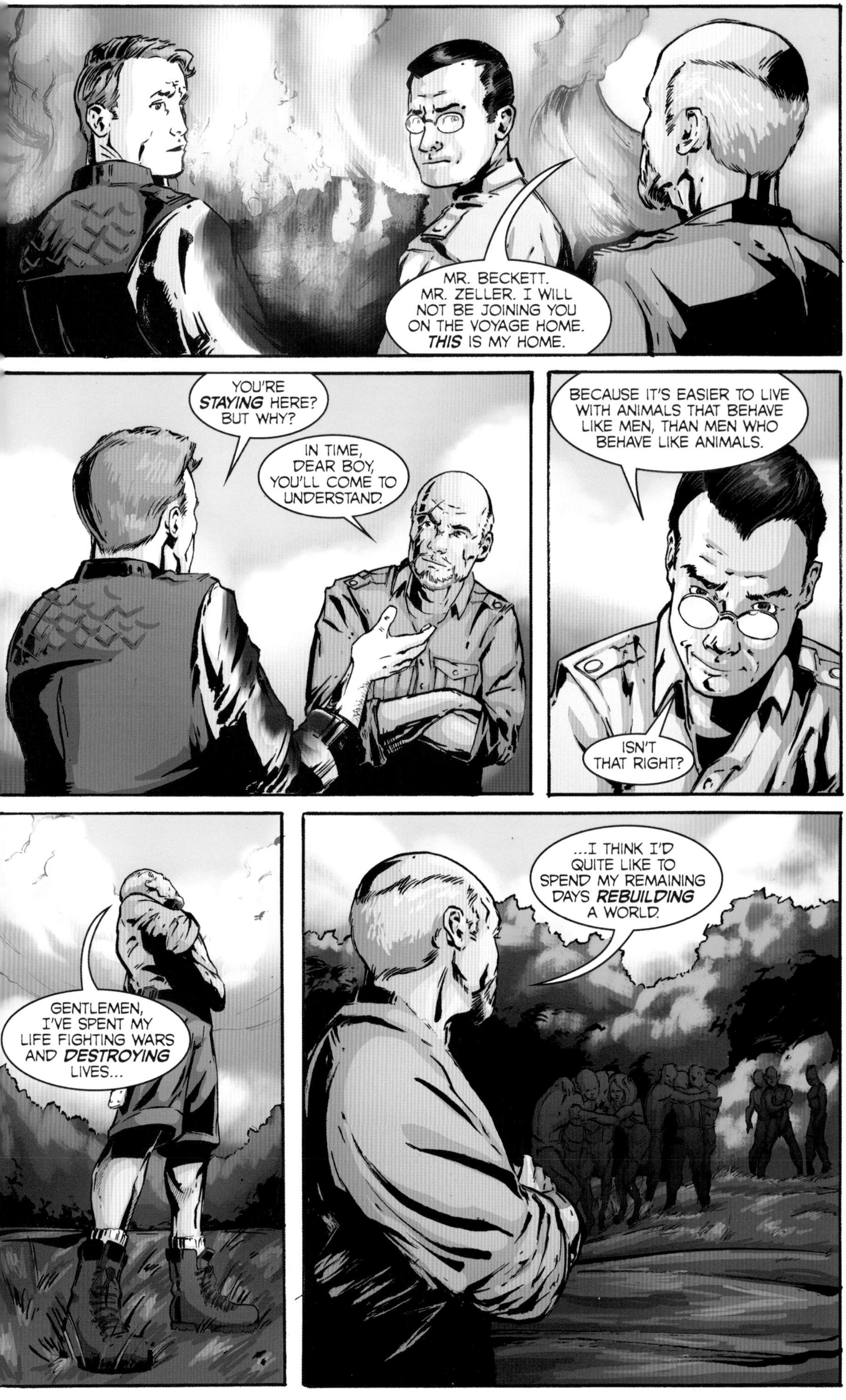

MR. BECKETT. MR. ZELLER. I WILL NOT BE JOINING YOU ON THE VOYAGE HOME. *THIS* IS MY HOME.
YOU'RE *STAYING* HERE? BUT WHY?
IN TIME, DEAR BOY, YOU'LL COME TO UNDERSTAND.
BECAUSE IT'S EASIER TO LIVE WITH ANIMALS THAT BEHAVE LIKE MEN, THAN MEN WHO BEHAVE LIKE ANIMALS.
ISN'T THAT RIGHT?
GENTLEMEN, I'VE SPENT MY LIFE FIGHTING WARS AND *DESTROYING* LIVES...
...I THINK I'D QUITE LIKE TO SPEND MY REMAINING DAYS *REBUILDING* A WORLD.

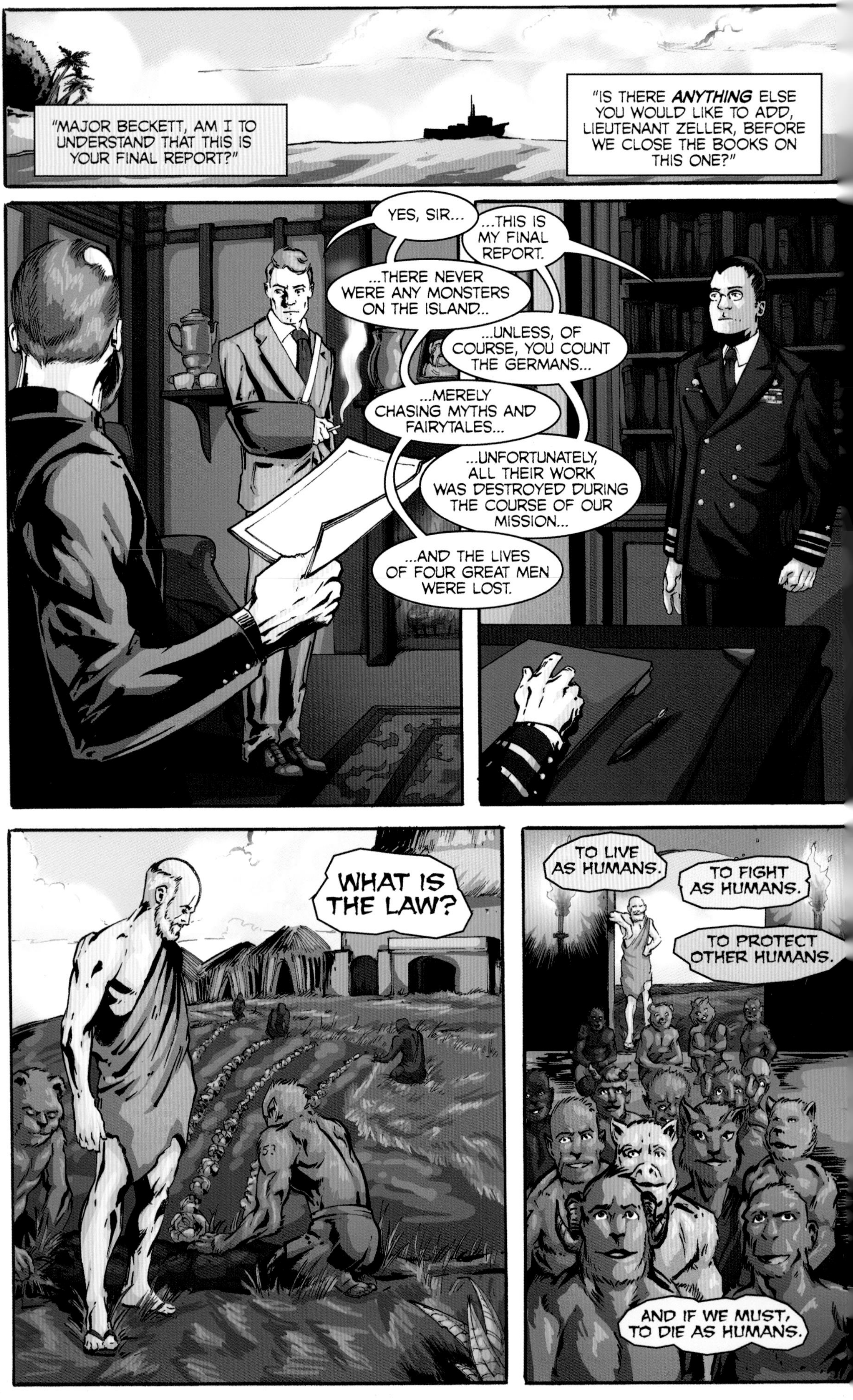
"MAJOR BECKETT, AM I TO UNDERSTAND THAT THIS IS YOUR FINAL REPORT?"
"IS THERE ANYTHING ELSE YOU WOULD LIKE TO ADD, LIEUTENANT ZELLER, BEFORE WE CLOSE THE BOOKS ON THIS ONE?"
YES, SIR...
...THIS IS MY FINAL REPORT.
...THERE NEVER WERE ANY MONSTERS ON THE ISLAND...
...UNLESS, OF COURSE, YOU COUNT THE GERMANS...
...MERELY CHASING MYTHS AND FAIRYTALES...
...UNFORTUNATELY, ALL THEIR WORK WAS DESTROYED DURING THE COURSE OF OUR MISSION...
...AND THE LIVES OF FOUR GREAT MEN WERE LOST.
WHAT IS THE LAW?
53
TO LIVE AS HUMANS.
TO FIGHT AS HUMANS.
TO PROTECT OTHER HUMANS.
AND IF WE MUST, TO DIE AS HUMANS.

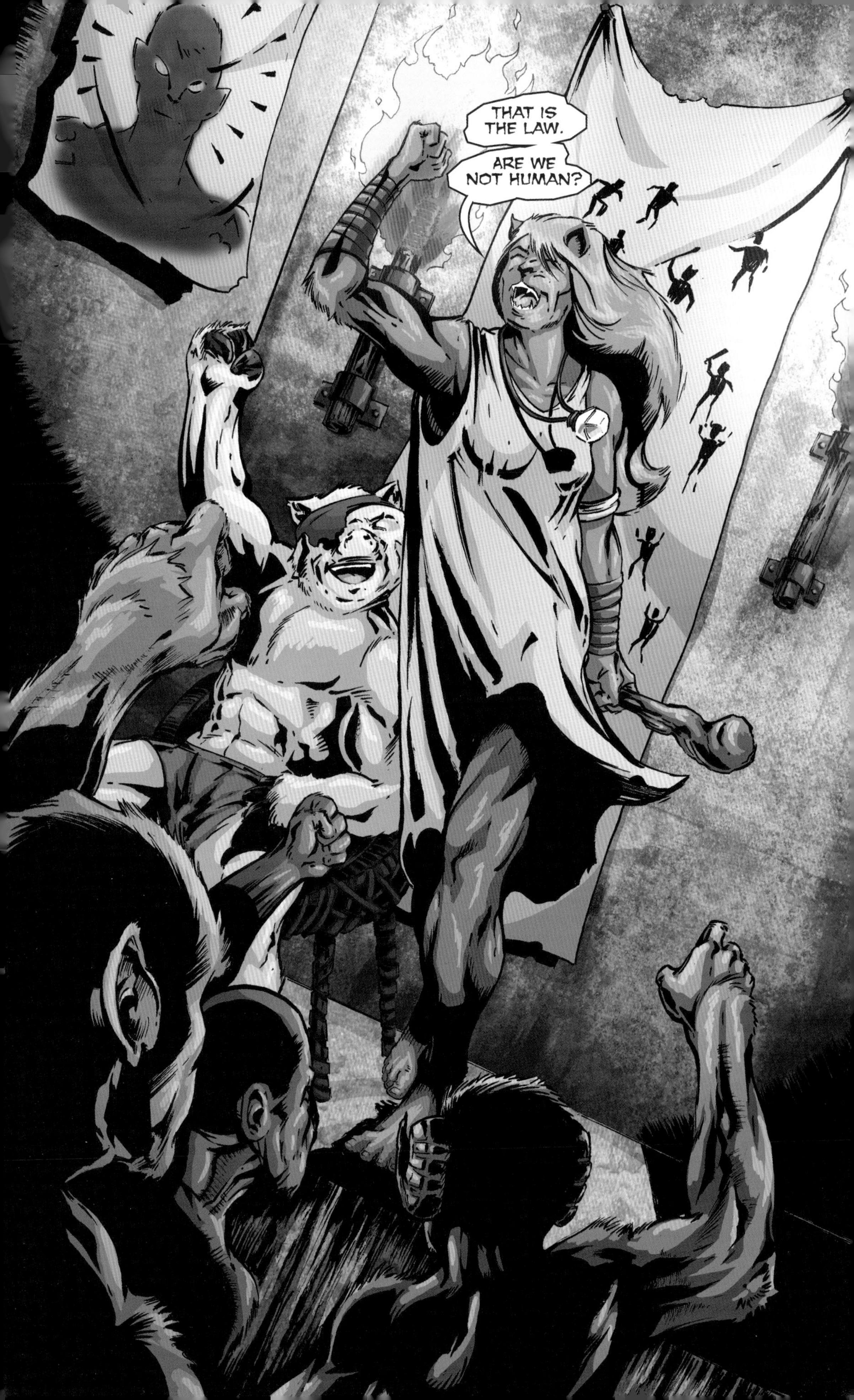
THAT IS THE LAW.
ARE WE NOT HUMAN?

BONUS MATERIAL

THE PROCESS

Hi everyone—it's Carl, and I want to take you through what goes into creating a page for the *Army of Dr. Moreau*. It all starts with David's script. Here's the original draft for Issue One, Page Seven.

PAGE 7

Panel 1 – Day - Wide shot of Prentiss outside, chopping wood. In the background we can see a car approaching (keep in mind this is England in the winter of 1939).

Panel 2 – Beckett and Zeller getting out of the car.

1. BECKETT: Edward Prentiss?

Panel 3 – Prentiss' face in the extreme foreground, Beckett in the background.

2. PRENTISS: Aye.

3. BECKETT: Might we have a word with you, sir?

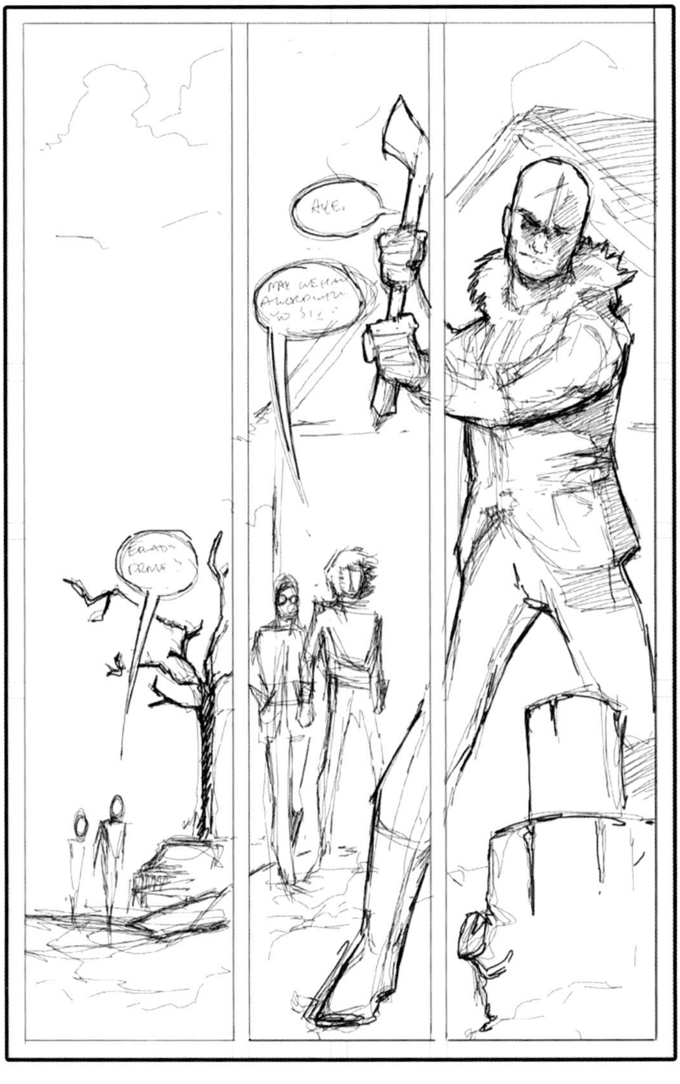
AYE.

After reading the script, I wanted to create a page with three panels, which featured the action progressing across the same background. It required a little shuffling of the action called for in the script, so I sketched that out on my Cintiq, and roughed in word balloons to make sure that there was room for all of the dialogue.

Next I move onto bluelines, which are basically digital pencils done on my Cintiq. I typically use photo reference of myself, particularly when I'm drawing clothes with some complicated folds that I might not have memorized.

Next, I print the bluelines onto bristol board, and then ink them. I mostly use a Winsor & Newton Series 7 brush, with some Microns thrown in for smaller details or ruler work.

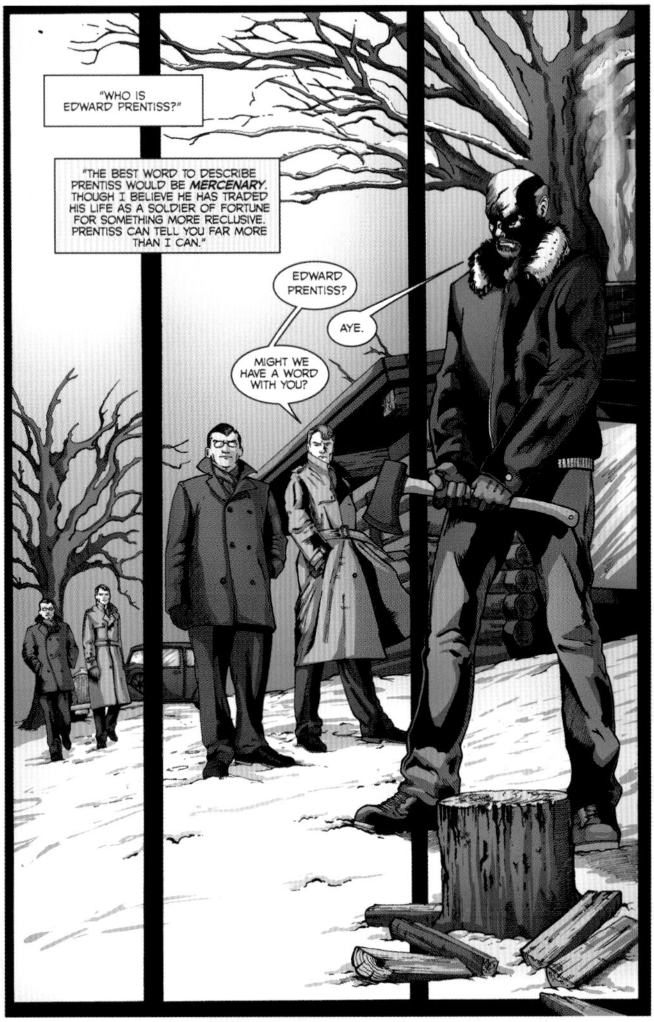
"WHO IS EDWARD PRENTISS?"
"THE BEST WORD TO DESCRIBE PRENTISS WOULD BE MERCENARY. THOUGH I BELIEVE HE HAS TRADED HIS LIFE AS A SOLDIER OF FORTUNE FOR SOMETHING MORE RECLUSIVE. PRENTISS CAN TELL YOU FAR MORE THAN I CAN."
EDWARD PRENTISS?
AYE.
MIGHT WE HAVE A WORD WITH YOU?

Finally, I scan the inked page, and upload it so that Sara can color it (and make my work look decent), and then hand it off to David for lettering (so that it makes sense!). After that, the page is done, and it's off to Monkeybrain.

CONCEPT ART

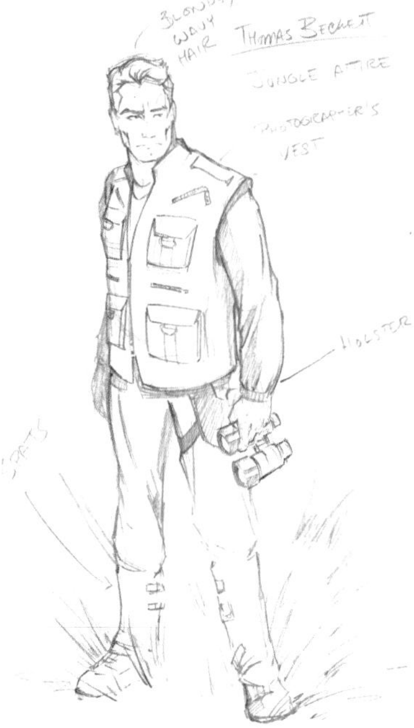
BLONDE, WAVY HAIR
THOMAS BECKETT
JUNGLE ATTIRE
PHOTOGRAPHER'S VEST
HOLSTER
BOOTS

BECKETT

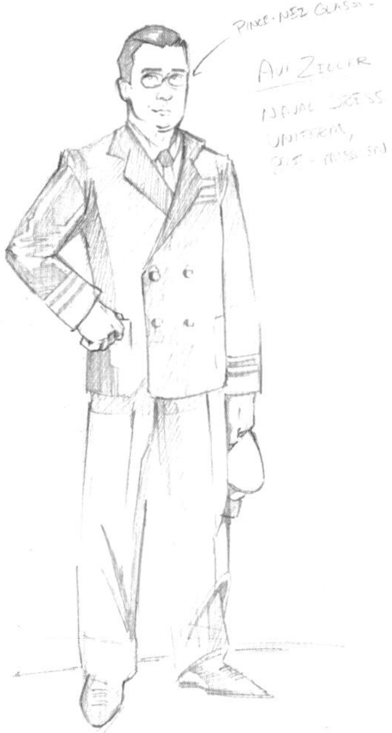
PINCE-NEZ GLASSES
AVI ZELLER

ZELLER

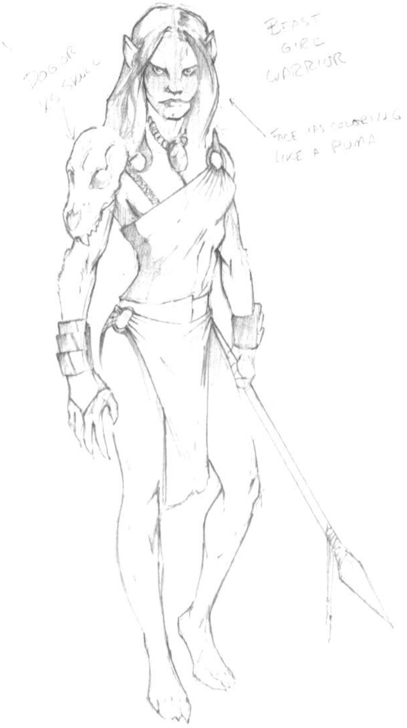
BEAST GIRL WARRIOR
FACE HAS COLORING LIKE A PUMA

BEAST WOMAN

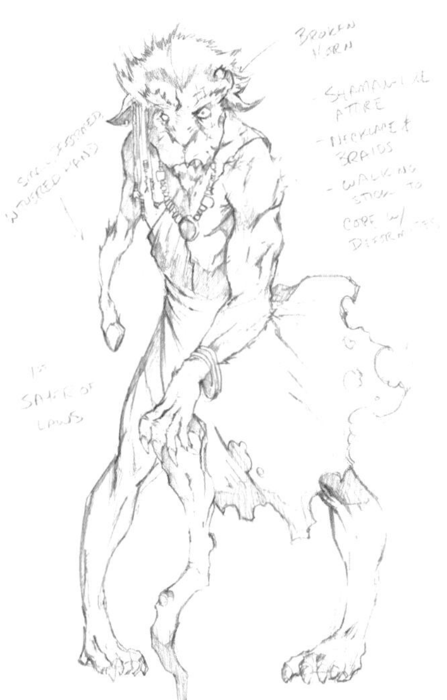
BROKEN HORN
SHAMAN-LIKE ATTIRE
NECKLACE & BRAIDS
WALKING STICK TO COPE W/ DEFORMITIES

SAYER OF THE LAW